HOBBES AND THE LAW OF NATURE

HOBBES AND THE LAW OF NATURE

Perez Zagorin

PRINCETON UNIVERSITY PRESS

Princeton and Oxford

Copyright © 2009 by Princeton University Press

Published by Princeton University Press, 41 William Street, Princeton, New Jersey 08540

In the United Kingdom: Princeton University Press, 6 Oxford Street, Woodstock, Oxfordshire OX20 1TW

press.princeton.edu

All Rights Reserved

Library of Congress Cataloging-in-Publication Data

Zagorin, Perez.
   Hobbes and the law of nature / Perez Zagorin.
      p. cm.
   Includes bibliographical references and index.
   ISBN 978-0-691-13980-7 (hardcover : alk. paper)   1. Hobbes, Thomas, 1588–1679.
2. Natural law.   I. Title.
   JC153.H66Z34 2009
   171'.2—c22   2009010318

British Library Cataloging-in-Publication Data is available

This book has been composed in Minion
Printed on acid-free paper. ∞
Printed in the United States of America
10 9 8 7 6 5 4 3 2 1

To Honoré, undying love

CONTENTS

PREFACE *ix*

ABBREVIATIONS *xi*

CHAPTER 1 Some Basic Hobbesian Concepts *1*

The Law of Nature *5*
Hobbes's Critique of the Natural Law Tradition *11*
Natural Rights *20*

CHAPTER 2 Enter the Law of Nature *30*

Human Nature *32*
The State of Nature or Man's Natural Condition *36*
The Precepts of the Law of Nature *42*
Natural Rights and the Creation of the Commonwealth *54*
Consent, Fear, Obligation, and Populism *60*

CHAPTER 3 The Sovereign and the Law of Nature *66*

The Theory of Sovereignty *66*
The Liberty of Subjects *75*
Hobbes's Very Moral Sovereign *84*

CHAPTER 4 Hobbes, the Moral Philosopher *99*

Self and Others *99*
Obligation *106*
Is and Ought *112*
Religion and Toleration *117*
Conclusion *127*

NOTES *129*

INDEX *171*

PREFACE

Few people today, in the first years of the twenty-first century, have any knowledge or awareness of the concept of the law of nature or natural law in its relation to morality, law, or politics. Even lawyers know little or nothing about it unless their legal education happens to have included some instruction in the history and philosophy of law. If asked today what the law of nature means, most people would be likely to answer that it probably refers to causal order and invariable regularities in the phenomena of physical and biological nature that scientists have established or discovered, such as the laws of gravity, Boyle's law, or the double-helix structure of the DNA molecule. This is not, however, what it signifies in the history of Western thought. Looked at in this long temporal context and described in the very largest sense, the law of nature was an idealistic concept founded on the philosophical and religious assumption that nature and the universe as a divine creation of the eternal God are mindful of mankind and repositories of purpose, norms, and meanings based on right reason that include the principles of morality for human beings. Regarded in this light, the concept of a moral law of nature, which originated in classical Greek philosophy, occupied a dominant position in reflection on law, ethics, and politics for over two thousand years. During this period it was discussed by innumerable theologians, jurists, and philosophers, including some of the greatest minds, and was understood by many thinkers to constitute both a standard of legal justice and a moral standard for human actions. The decline of this concept, which began in the later eighteenth century and continued thereafter, was due to a number of factors: to the development of skepticism, empiricism, and utilitarianism, which questioned or denied the existence of a moral law of nature; to the displacement in legal thought of the abstract rationalism associated with the concept of natural law by a historical jurisprudence that looked upon law as a product of historical evolution and the collective social life of peoples and nations; and finally to the growth of legal positivism, philosophical naturalism, and moral relativism. In the present age, a belief in the law of nature has largely disappeared. While by no means extinct, it has ceased to be a significant influence in legal, political, and moral philosophy and survives mainly among Catholic thinkers and in Catholic philosophy and theology, which continue to uphold it as a moral guide. To some extent, what has taken its place in today's world is the current belief in human rights.

The work that follows is a study in both intellectual history and the history of philosophy, in particular the concept and theory of natural law. It is concerned with the great seventeenth-century philosopher Thomas Hobbes and his conception of the law of nature and also of natural rights, ideas that occupy a supremely important place in his thought. The justification for writing about this subject is explained in the first chapter. In dealing with natural law, Hobbes touched on a considerable number of other topics, and this book therefore includes a discussion of his moral and political philosophy in relation to his understanding of both the law and the right of nature. Hobbes is a fascinating but difficult thinker whom I have been reading closely on and off for more than fifty years. I have written a long chapter in an earlier book and a number of articles about him, and the present book fulfills a longstanding desire to make a fuller statement of what it seems to me Hobbes was about and what his chief importance is in the history of moral and political thought. Like so many other Hobbes scholars to whose work I am so deeply indebted, I have done my best to get Hobbes right, but because his thought is so rich, broad, and complex despite its clarity and rigor, I can hardly be confident that I have succeeded. In any case, however, this work has two main aims. One is to analyze and explain Hobbes's conception of natural law in its historical context. The other is to make clear the considerable originality and large significance of Hobbes as a humane moral philosopher and theorist of natural law.

As on previous occasions, I want to acknowledge my gratitude to the University of Virginia, which in 1995 appointed me a Fellow of its Shannon Center for Advanced Studies without limit of term and extended to me the privileges of a faculty member in this great university. I should like to record that this study of Hobbes is the fourth book I have published since that appointment began. I must also express my warm thanks to the librarians of the Alderman Library at the University of Virginia for their constant help and cooperation in the course of my research. Finally, I wish to thank the friends and colleagues with whom I have discussed Hobbes in the last few years, in particular George Klosko, Henry L. and Grace Doherty Professor in the Department of Politics of the University of Virginia, for his encouraging comments and criticisms, which have been of great value to me even in instances when I have not accepted them. Several of the thoughts expressed in this book were first presented in the Political Theory Seminar offered by the Department of Political Science at the University of Virginia.

July 2008
Charlottesville, Virginia

ABBREVIATIONS

The notes in this book refer to Hobbes's three most important political treatises, as follows:

EL = *The Elements of Law Natural & Politic*, ed. Ferdinand Tönnies (Cambridge: Cambridge University Press, 1928). This work was first circulated in manuscript in 1640 and printed in 1650 in two parts entitled *Humane Nature: Or, The Fundamental Elements of Policie* and *De Corpore Politico: Or The Elements of Law, Moral & Politick*.

DC = *De Cive*, English version, ed. Howard Warrender (Oxford: Clarendon Press, 1998). The original Latin edition, entitled *Elementorum Philosophiae Sectio Tertia De Cive*, was first published in 1642. The first English translation was published in 1651 with the title *Philosophical Rudiments Concerning Government and Society*.

L = *Leviathan, Or The Matter, Forme, & Power of A Commonwealth Ecclesiasticall and Civill*, ed. Edwin Curley (Indianapolis: Hackett, 1994). The first edition of this work appeared in 1651.

I have also sometimes cited other of Hobbes's writings, as follows:

EW = *English Works*, ed. William Molesworth, 10 vols. (London, 1839–45).

LW = *Latin Works*, ed. William Molesworth, 6 vols. (London, 1839–45).

HOBBES AND THE LAW OF NATURE

CHAPTER 1

Some Basic Hobbesian Concepts

The major masterpieces of philosophy are never out of date. They continually stimulate us to fresh questioning, present us with ideas about the world, mankind, and history that can enrich, clarify, and correct our own ideas, and offer us reflections, challenges, and options on living that may be of value to us in our coping with our own human problems and moral difficulties. Thomas Hobbes was a great systematic philosopher and one of the foremost universal minds of the seventeenth century.[1] Although his writings encompassed a wide range of subjects, including various branches of philosophy, the natural sciences, mathematics, psychology, religion, history, and other areas, his largest fame has always been due chiefly to his work as a political philosopher and as the author of *Leviathan*, one of the classics of Western political theory, no less important as a distinctive view of man and government than are *The Republic* of Plato, the *Politics* of Aristotle, and *The Prince* of Machiavelli. As a political philosopher Hobbes has most commonly been identified especially with two ideas. The first is the concept of sovereignty. He has been considered the first thinker to achieve a clear and unambiguous comprehension of the principle of sovereignty in its various attributes as the defining characteristic of the state or commonwealth. The second is the concept of the prepolitical, antisocial state of nature as a condition of endless war and unrestricted natural right and his development of the principle of covenant, contract, and consent as the necessary presupposition and basis of the existence of the political order, sovereign power, and political obligation. Assessments of his significance as a political thinker in light of these ideas typically picture him as essentially a theorist of the unity and comprehensive sovereignty of the state over all its subjects, concerned above all with the preservation of civil peace and obedience and accordingly an uncompromising proponent of governmental absolutism and centralized power. Otto Gierke, a great historian of political theory and natural law, said of Hobbes that by "remorseless logic and arbitrarily assumed premises . . . he created the idea of a single State personality" that overwhelmed the rights of the individual. Carl J. Friedrich, a noted political theorist, described Hobbes as "the philosopher of power par excellence" who held "the most secular view of the all-powerful state as a system of ordering the universe of human life."[2]

While not erroneous or false, these characterizations of Hobbes as a political philosopher are nevertheless one-sided and unbalanced, and hence fail to convey an adequate understanding of his political thought and values. Hobbes was much more than a theorist of sovereignty and political absolutism. He was likewise a great moral philosopher and philosopher of law. Because his moral philosophy and analysis of law were a vital part of his political theory, he belongs as much to the history of ethics and legal philosophy as to the history of political thought. His moral philosophy derived from his theory of natural law, and it also included his theory of natural right. Natural law and natural right were thus the twin foundations on which he built the entire structure of his moral and political theory. No reader of Hobbes can fail to notice the pivotal importance he assigns to the law of nature in his political writings. Few readers understand, however, why he based his moral philosophy on this principle or what its point or purpose is in his political theory. In particular, there is little understanding of the role played by natural law in qualifying his theory of political absolutism.

This book, which can perhaps be termed a historical-philosophical essay, is primarily a discussion of Hobbes as a theorist of natural law and moral philosopher in relation to his political philosophy. The literature on Hobbes has become almost overwhelmingly large and is also very controversial. While every work concerned with his political thought has had to pay some attention to his treatment of the law of nature, the writings dedicated to the exploration of this subject in depth and that attempt to define its historical relationship to the tradition and the wider stream of natural law theory and to explain the particular features that make for its profound originality are comparatively few.[3] As far as I know, there is no modern study by an Anglophone or other scholar that concentrates mainly on Hobbes's interpretation of the law of nature and its implications. While numerous authors have recognized his unorthodoxy as a natural law theorist, persisting disagreements and divergences in the Hobbes literature regarding the meaning of his concept of natural law are the rule rather than the exception and make it difficult to gain a clear grasp of his unique historical position as a natural law theorist and moral philosopher. In an interesting essay on Hobbes's moral philosophy dating from the 1960s, Michael Oakeshott, a leading Hobbes scholar, spoke of "the obscure heart of Hobbes's moral theory" and noted a number of conflicting interpretations of his concept of the law of nature, as well as apparent contradictions in his moral philosophy. This caused him to conclude that "every interpretation" of Hobbes "leaves something that [he] wrote imperfectly accounted for." One of the main questions about Hobbes's thought that Oakeshott believed remained unresolved was whether he held that the law of nature was really law, and therefore obligatory as law upon all mankind.[4]

This situation has not changed much in the intervening years. In a 2001 essay, the distinguished Hobbes scholar David Gauthier points to various inconsistencies in the philosopher's discussion of the law of nature and maintains that he was confused as to whether its precepts should be understood primarily as theorems of reason, commands of God, or commands of the civil sovereign. Gauthier decides in favor of the first alternative as the only choice available to Hobbes, and also holds that he failed to think through the issues connected with the roles the law of nature had to play in his argument.[5] Gauthier's interpretation is in striking contrast to the one proffered by A. P. Martinich in his debatable 1992 study, *The Two Gods of Leviathan*, which contends that Hobbes was an orthodox religious Christian of Calvinist persuasion and that inherent in his concept of natural law was its character as a divine command, which alone made it genuine law.[6]

Among the issues posed by Hobbes's moral and political theory and its thought on law is not only his understanding of the relationship between natural law, divine law, and civil law but whether or not he should be considered a legal positivist. Legal positivism holds that there is no such thing as natural law and that the latter involves a conceptual confusion between law as it is and law as it ought to be. For this reason, legal positivism has always been considered antithetical to natural law. It is a doctrine whose origins are associated with the philosophy of utilitarianism and the jurisprudence of Jeremy Bentham (d. 1832) and John Austin (d. 1859). Both of these thinkers defined law exclusively as a command of the sovereign or a superior addressed to those who are obligated or accustomed to obey (the imperative theory of law). They also denied that the concept or definition of law and the criterion of legal validity had any necessary connection with moral values, whether justice or any other (the separation of law and morals). Austin called the confusion between law and morals a "most prolific source of jargon, darkness, and perplexity." Bentham, besides rejecting the existence of natural law, was no less skeptical of the theory of natural rights, which he dismissed as nonsense. Legal positivism in the form of the thesis of the separation between law and morals is widely prevalent in contemporary Western legal philosophy and has been espoused by such influential thinkers as the Briton H.L.A. Hart and the Austro-German Hans Kelsen.[7] Hobbes's discussion in his political theory of the supremacy and scope of civil law as the will of the sovereign has often caused him to be seen as one of the founders of legal positivism. M. M. Goldsmith describes him as a legal positivist in a recent survey of his concept of law. So likewise do Gregory Kavka, Jean Hampton, and S. A. Lloyd in their studies of Hobbes's moral and political philosophy.[8] On the other hand, Gauthier considers it misleading to regard him as a forerunner of legal positivism, because for Hobbes the obligation to obey the civil law of the sovereign stems ultimately from the consent of subjects and is therefore prior to the existence of civil law and outside the positive legal system itself.[9] The late distinguished Italian political philosopher and legal scholar Norberto Bobbio, while emphasizing Hobbes's importance and distinction as a natural law theorist, has pictured him nevertheless as fundamentally a legal positivist, that is, a thinker in whose system "the laws of nature finally have no other role than that of providing the ground of validity for a state that recognizes only positive law, and who therefore accepts natural law only "in the service of a consistent and coherent theory of positive law."[10] Is it possible that Hobbes could have been both an exponent of natural law and a legal positivist? If the answer is yes, we shall need to explain how he could have combined these two positions, which are historically and intellectually opposed to each other, within the body of his philosophy.

Hobbes never doubted the rigor, logic, or scientific character of his moral and political philosophy and frequently stated that he had proved the truth of the arguments propounded in his political writings. Not hesitating to rank himself with such eminent scientific inaugurators as Copernicus, Galileo, and Dr. William Harvey, he claimed that he had founded the science of civil or political philosophy in his book *De Cive*.[11] He considered that in the latter he had "demonstrated by a most evident connexion . . . the rudiments both of morall and civill prudence." Of *Leviathan* he stated that its "whole doctrine" and the principles he set forth in it "are true and proper, and the ratiocination solid."[12] He was fully aware, nevertheless, of the problem and frequent difficulty of interpretation in determining the true meaning of a text. His penetrating comment in *Leviathan* on the subject of interpretation should always be borne in mind when we read and analyze his own work:

> For it is not the bare words, but the scope of the writer, that giveth the true light by which any writing is to be interpreted; and they that insist upon single texts, without considering the main design, can derive nothing from them clearly, but rather . . . make everything more obscure than it is.[13]

This is very sound advice that instructs us to pay attention not only to particular passages in his work but to its main design, or to what Oakeshott called "the structural principles of Hobbes's view of things."[14] Hobbes had a sweeping intellectual ambition, and he thought so much and wrote so much on such a variety of subjects that he could hardly have failed at times to create puzzles for his readers or to be guilty of slips, inconsistencies, and confusions. These are faults from which no philosopher can be free, and in discussing Hobbes's work I have not been particularly concerned to give them much attention. This is because I believe that Hobbes was a great constructive thinker whose moral and political philosophy sprang from a few fundamental insights that, despite any lapses or inconsistencies we may detect in his development of them, shaped the general character and dominant tendencies of his thought. These insights constitute a large view of life, and it is they, particularly as they are expressed and involved in the Hobbesian concepts of natural law and natural right, that are the main subject of this essay.

The Law of Nature

Natural law or the law of nature is a grand and venerable concept dating back to classical antiquity, one whose importance can hardly be overestimated, exerting as it did a profound influence on Western thought and culture for many centuries. In the sense in which Hobbes and his predecessors employed it, it had nothing to do, needless to say, with the scientific, empirical investigation of the physical world and should not be confused with the belief that physical phenomena are governed by causal necessity or uniform laws of nature. It pertains wholly to the moral, legal, and political domain and is a metaphysical and teleological doctrine that conceives the basic rules of morality as genuine and universal law whose source is not in any human legislator but in Nature, and ultimately in the reason or will of God the creator. But why should ancient philosophers have added the word "Nature" to the word "Law"? "Nature" in Greek (*physis*), Latin (*natura*), and the modern Western languages covers an exceptionally broad semantic field containing a multiplicity of meanings that are by no means invariably consistent with one another. Underlying the idea of natural law as it emerged in Greek philosophy is that of nature as a norm, whose historical background and vocabulary have been traced by Lovejoy and Boas in their exemplary study of primitivism and related ideas in antiquity. This idea is at bottom and in its origins an animistic personification and endowment of nature with an intelligent, rational, purposive, and ethical character. Lovejoy and Boas observe that "one of the strongest, most potent and persistent factors in human thought" has been the use of the term nature to express a standard of value and hence to identify the good with that which is natural or according to nature. By the fifth century BCE, the word *physis* or nature had already acquired, they tell us, "a peculiar sanctity in Greek usage and carried a definitely eulogistic connotation." The difference pointed to by the Sophists, Plato, and other Greek philosophers between nature, on the one hand, and its opposite, *nomos*, or custom, convention, and local law, on the other, signified a constant contrast between that which is normal, permanent, objectively right, and the same everywhere and that which consists of varying, dissimilar, and hence arbitrary human laws and practices. Nature could also mean the original form of something and therefore its right or best condition.[15]

While Aristotle's *Nicomachean Ethics* may be regarded in retrospect as a work of moral philosophy, it is much more concerned with the formation of character, the virtues, human happiness, and the good life for man than it is with moral obligation and imperatives of good and evil. The philosophy of Aristotle did not allude to the moral law of nature, but it is shot through with a teleological view of nature as a purposive agency that does nothing in vain and whose works have a universal validity. He distinguished in his ethics between natural justice and the merely legally and conventionally just, the former being that which has the same force everywhere and does not depend on or vary with people's opinions. His *Politics* famously invokes the idea of nature as an end-directed process to explain that man is by nature a *zoon politikon* or political animal who in order to fulfill his needs is impelled to seek association and cooperation with others. The creation of the *polis*, the city or state, is then shown to be due not to prior convention or deliberate agreement but to an unfolding teleological process in which the natural union of male and female in forming families in order to supply basic human needs, and the natural inclination of families to unite in villages and larger communities, leads eventually in an evolutionary development to the emergence of the state as a natural political order that, originating in the bare necessities of life, continues its existence as a self-sufficient association for the sake of a good life for its human members.[16]

Although some of its elements are traceable to earlier Greek thinkers, the concept of the law of nature as a moral norm or standard was first formulated in the philosophy of Stoicism during the Hellenistic era in the fourth and third centuries BCE. This philosophy, which also dealt with logic and physics but whose most lasting influence was in the field of ethics and politics, looked upon nature and the cosmos as a harmonious order pervaded by divine reason and universal law. Its ethical teaching exalted reason and virtue as necessary to happiness and disparaged the emotions. It conceived natural law as a dictate of reason grounded in nature which prescribes what is right and just to human beings and is knowable to them through the faculty of reason with which nature has endowed them. With Stoicism, the idea of duty or *kathekonta* seems to make its earliest appearance in moral philosophy.[17] In the second and first centuries BCE, Greek Stoic philosophers brought their conviction of a moral world order under the guidance of nature and reason to Rome, where it was absorbed by many Romans of the highest rank. Among the latter was the statesman, orator, and man of letters Cicero (d. 43 BCE), one of the most important thinkers of the ancient world in his influence on posterity, who discussed the law of nature in several of his works.[18] In a famous description in his dialogue *On the Commonwealth*, he defined it as right reason in agreement with nature, universal, unchanging, and everlasting, summoning to duty by its commands and averting from wrongdoing by its prohibitions, valid for all nations and all times, binding on everyone in its obligation, and deriving from God as its author and promulgator.[19] This classic statement would have been known during the succeeding centuries to every writer on natural law in early Christian, medieval, and early modern Europe, including, of course, Hobbes. Through Cicero and other ancient authors the law of nature also left its stamp on Roman law. The eminent jurists of imperial Rome whose opinions were later recorded in the *Digest* as a part of the Emperor Justinian's great legal codification of the earlier sixth century CE, the *Corpus Iuris Civilis* (*Corpus of the Civil Law*), viewed the *ius naturale* or law of nature as belonging to the general structure of law. They related it to justice as a universal law and described it in several different ways. According to one opinion, natural law was not limited to the human species but was an ordinance that nature taught to all living creatures, and from which came such things as the union of the sexes and the procreation and rearing of offspring. Another opinion identified the law of nature with the law of nations or peoples, *ius gentium*, as a common law that natural reason had ordained for all mankind. A third declared that the law of nature was a name applied to that which in all circumstances is good and equitable.[20]

Roman jurists did not place the law of nature above their own civil law, but the normative character of natural law as an implicitly higher moral law applicable to all of humanity was one of its features that became increasingly prominent with the spread of Christianity and the Christianization of the law of nature in the following centuries. St. Paul affirmed the existence of the universal law of nature in a remarkable passage of his letter to the Romans, which stated that although the Gentiles, unlike the Christians, lacked the law of Moses, they nevertheless did by nature the things required by the law, which was written in their hearts and attested by their conscience (Romans 2:14–15). With the decline of Roman civilization, it was in part owing to Christian authors such as the church fathers St. Ambrose, St. Augustine, and St. Isidore of Seville that the classical conception of the immutable natural law and its association with justice and other moral values was transmitted to the Christian Middle Ages to become an essential element in medieval and early modern moral, legal, and political philosophy.[21]

Medieval theologians, church lawyers, and philosophers who discussed the law of nature were in agreement that its origin lay in God and nature and that its principles were identical with the law of God contained in Scripture and the Gospels. An early authoritative expression of this opinion appeared in the canonist Gratian's twelfth-century compilation of the canon law, the *Decretum*. This work began with the dictum that two laws, the law of nature and of custom, rule mankind, and that the first of these is contained in the law and the Gospel in the command that everyone should do to another as they would be done by and forbidding the doing to another of what one does not wish to be done to oneself. Gratian also stated that natural law began with the creation of man as a rational being and is unchangeable. Because he conceived it as an offspring of divine law, he ranked the law of nature above all other laws in its antiquity and dignity. Its superiority was emphasized in his further comment that "whatever has been recognized by custom, or laid down in writing, if it contradicts natural law, it must be considered null and void."[22]

The transcendental foundation of natural law in God and nature, its innateness in human minds and equivalence with reason, and its position above other kinds of law except divine law were among the principles stated by many scholastic philosophers of the later Middle Ages. The works of Aristotle on ethics, politics, metaphysics, and other subjects, which became available in Latin translations in the later twelfth century and the thirteenth century, introduced Aristotelian naturalism to Christian philosophers and made known to them its teleological conception of everything in nature being directed toward an end and its distinction between natural and conventional or local justice. The revival of the study of Roman law in Italy and elsewhere from the eleventh century onward passed on to medieval canonists and lawyers the legacy of Roman jurisprudence and its reflections on the law of nature. The list of medieval thinkers who concerned themselves with natural law is a long one. It includes such distinguished names as Abelard, Alexander of Hales, Bonaventura, Albertus Magnus, Thomas Aquinas, Duns Scotus, William of Ockham, Jean Gerson, and numerous others.[23] The most important of medieval natural law theorists was Aquinas (d. 1274), the harmonizer of Aristotelian naturalism with Christian supernaturalism, who dealt architectonically and comprehensively with the subject of law and envisaged natural law as participating in the eternal law through which God ruled the universe. I return to this great Catholic philosopher of natural law in relationship to Hobbes later in this essay.

Historians of natural law and moral philosophy have noted and stressed the distinction that appeared in the later thirteenth and the fourteenth century among scholastic thinkers and philosophers of natural law between voluntarism and intellectualism. Voluntarism gave primacy to God's sovereign will and divine omnipotence as the source of the dictates of the law of nature and the determination of moral rules and values. According to this view, actions are good not because they are inherently so and rooted in the nature of things but because God's will has chosen to define them as such, and so in this sense, the rules of morality are arbitrary, being based entirely on God's infinite power. The alternative view, intellectualism, gave primacy to God's intellect and held that God ordained the rules of morality because he knew them to be good; these rules were accordingly recognized by God's supreme reason as objectively real and right, and thus could not be other than they were. While Aquinas was an exponent of intellectualism, Duns Scotus (d. 1308) and William of Ockham (d. c.1349) were among the foremost exponents of voluntarism. The differences between these two positions, which philosophers discussed in a very sophisticated way, were connected with additional questions concerning God's freedom and human free will and determinism.[24] We should not exaggerate their opposition, however, since philosophers usually seem to have tried to make allowance for both God's will and his reason in dealing with the basis of natural law.[25] Hobbes has often been considered to be a voluntarist in his treatment of natural law, and voluntarism has sometimes been seen as the forerunner of legal positivism.[26]

The law of nature remained an essential concept in the moral and political philosophy of early modern Europe, discussed in various contexts by many authors, most of whom are now very obscure, between the sixteenth century and the late eighteenth century. During the Middle Ages the doctrine of natural law was assimilated into the moral theology of the Catholic Church and used in Catholic casuistry in the guidance and direction of the moral conscience in matters of conduct. Aristotle's *Nicomachean Ethics* was the most widely studied work of moral philosophy in the early modern universities, and Aristotelian logic, metaphysics, science, and teleology based on the philosopher's doctrine of final causes dominated the university curriculum in both Catholic and Protestant countries after the Reformation. In Protestant Germany, the eminent scholar, humanist, and teacher Philipp Melanchthon, a close associate of the reformer Martin Luther, equated moral philosophy with explication of the law of nature by the use of reason in order to establish rules to govern behavior. Some of the foremost Protestant theologians of the sixteenth century, despite their belief in the sinfulness and corruption of human nature, appropriated the doctrine of natural law as a guide to human conduct implanted in man by God. Neostoicism, an intellectual movement originating in the later sixteenth century, was based on the ethics of Stoicism as a model for living and enlisted the allegiance of a number of noted European thinkers and statesmen. In

England the principal sixteenth-century writer who discussed the different kinds of law and the law of nature was the Elizabethan theologian and political philosopher Richard Hooker, author of *The Laws of Ecclesiastical Polity*. In Catholic Spain in this period, a line of Dominican and Jesuit theologians and jurists belonging to the scholastic tradition, such as Francisco Vitoria, Domingo Soto, Gabriel Vazquez, Gregory of Valencia, and Francisco Suárez, were among the noted figures who dealt with the law of nature in treatises on law and justice and commentaries on the work of St. Thomas Aquinas.[27] As Gierke pointed out, the belief was very general among early modern theorists of law and politics that natural law was unalterable by any human power, that all positive law was derived from it, and that an enactment contrary to the law of nature was null and void.[28]

In 1625 the Dutch Protestant jurist Hugo Grotius published his celebrated work, *The Law of War and Peace* (*De Iure Belli ac Pacis*), one of the founding texts of international law, which was also concerned with the law of nature. Grotius (d. 1645) and Suárez (d. 1617) were Hobbes's most important immediate predecessors as natural law theorists. In 1641 the English lawyer John Selden, a great scholar, antiquarian, and Orientalist renowned for his Hebraic learning, brought out his treatise, *De Iure Naturali et Gentium juxta Disciplinam Ebraeorum* (*The Law of Nature and Nations According to the Teaching of the Hebrews*), which discussed natural law in light of the Jewish tradition and the commands God gave to Noah and his sons and descendants after the flood. After the appearance of Hobbes's main political works, the Anglican cleric Richard Cumberland and the philosopher John Locke were the chief English writers on the law of nature in the later seventeenth century. On the continent in the same period the foremost theorist of natural law was the German jurist and philosopher Samuel Pufendorf. The literature of natural law continued to increase in Germany and other countries during the eighteenth century until the time of the philosopher Kant.[29] Hobbes was widely recognized in his own time and later as a great thinker and exerted a large influence on his contemporaries and successors as a political and natural law theorist, though mainly more negatively than positively, through the critical reaction his work provoked.

When we survey the idea of the law of nature over its long history prior to its gradual decline and widespread rejection in the course of the nineteenth and twentieth centuries, there is one observation to be made about it that I find rarely, if ever, mentioned in the historical literature on the subject and that is also very germane to Hobbes. This is that the concept of natural law is a very comforting and consoling one that suits our human desire for cosmic meaning. It is linked to the kind of theism that affirms a beneficent nature and God's providential government of the world. Historically, however, it belongs to a prescientific outlook based on a belief in final causes, one that assumes a teleologically directed cosmic order and tends to exalt mankind above all other created beings as the possessor of a divinely ordained and naturally implanted reason that makes known to human beings the universal principles of the moral law of nature. This fact is of great importance when we recall that the scientific revolution of the seventeenth century, of which Hobbes was part, undermined the traditional Christian, value-graded picture of the universe and its hierarchically structured levels of being, demoting man and the earth from their central position in the pre-Copernican universe and giving gradual rise to a nonanthropomorphic, mechanistic, frequently materialist, and nonteleological view of nature. This transition is what the historian of science Alexander Koyré aptly summed up in the phrase, "from the closed world to the infinite universe."[30] In a recent comment by the British moral philosopher John McDowell, published in a *Festschrift* dedicated to another distinguished moral philosopher, Philippa Foot, the author remarked that "modern science has given us a disenchanted conception of the natural world. A proper appreciation of science makes it impossible to retain the common medieval conception of nature as filled with meaning.... The tendency of the scientific outlook is to purge the world of meaning."[31] The idea of natural law, however, which continued to flourish in the seventeenth and eighteenth centuries, is an exception to this development. What this idea precisely helped to do in the same century that witnessed the eventual victory of Copernicanism, the growth of empiricism and experimentalism, and the unprecedented development of science, mathematics, cosmology, and various forms of scientific philosophy in the work of Bacon, Kepler, Gilbert, Telesio, Bruno, Harvey, Galileo, Descartes, Hobbes, Spinoza, Boyle, Hooke, Leibnitz, Newton, and many others, was to preserve meaning in the world by positing the existence of universal, immutable moral principles that derived from nature and the will and reason of God and existed as law on a rational foundation as part of human knowledge. Hobbes, however, although an exponent of scientific philosophy, occupies a unique position within the historical development of European thought in the era of the scientific revolution, for while he retained the concept of natural law as a rational construct, he was also to subvert and transform it.

Hobbes's Critique of the Natural Law Tradition

In his distinguished and still valuable history of Western political theory, G. H. Sabine commented that "it would have undoubtedly been easier for Hobbes if he could have abandoned the law of nature altogether, as his more empirical successors, Hume and Bentham, did."[32] Such a move, however, would probably have been impossible for him, for at least two reasons. First, natural law was a doctrine he could hardly have avoided or ignored, because it occupied such a dominant position in the classical and Christian philosophical tradition of reflection on morality and law and their transcendental or cosmic grounding in nature, the order of the universe, and the reason and will of God. Second, from the later sixteenth century onward, natural law constituted one of the strands in the development in Europe of a revolutionary political theory sanctioning a right of resistance to kings and unjust governments. During these years the law of nature was among the doctrines French Protestant writers invoked to justify and legitimize the Huguenot rebellion in the religious civil war against the French Catholic monarchy, and it was likewise advanced in the next century by radical English political publicists during the civil war of the 1640s to justify resistance to and the overthrow of the monarchy of Charles I.[33] Hobbes, who lived through the English civil war as an exile in France, condemned this revolutionary theory as a false moral doctrine and political philosophy and lamented its destructive consequences. "How many kings," he asked,

> . . . hath this one errour, That a Tyrant King might lawfully be put to death, been the slaughter of? How many throats has this false position cut, That a Prince for some causes may by some certain men be deposed? And what blood-shed hath not this erroneous doctrine caused, That Kings are not superiour to, but administrators for the multitude?[34]

Since his chief aim as a political philosopher was to demonstrate the necessity of the absolute obedience of subjects to their sovereigns and the error of any pretended claim to a right of resistance, he had to take the theory of natural law into account in framing his argument.

Not only did Hobbes need the concept of natural law, it is impossible to overestimate the importance he attributed to it. Although natural right was an equally essential concept for him and one I shall come to presently, he devoted much less space to its explication than he did to the law of nature. As its title indicates, his first political work, *The Elements of Law Natural & Politic*, was intended in part as a treatise on natural law. In *De Cive* he told the reader that the whole book consisted of his endeavor to "unfold" the law of nature.[35] He regarded moral philosophy and natural law as one and the same, and in defining moral philosophy as "the science of virtue and vice," he also affirmed that "the true doctrine of the laws of nature is the true moral philosophy."[36] Yet within the long and venerable tradition of natural law, he seems to have been the first thinker of any stature who ventured to criticize and fault this tradition for its persisting intellectual deficiencies and failure to advance. He expressed a low estimate of the way previous moral philosophers had dealt with natural law and disparaged them for their erroneous opinions on the nature of right and wrong and for their endless disputes on moral questions in which they contradicted both one another and themselves. Complaining that moral philosophers had built the foundations of natural law in the air, he claimed that knowledge of this law had not made the slightest progress since the time of antiquity and that it had "become of all laws the most obscure."[37] These negative comments on his predecessors leave no doubt that the moral philosopher Hobbes envisaged himself as a reformer or renovator of natural law and was particularly conscious of the necessity of repairing its foundations and providing it with a firm and irrefutable grounding.

It is possible that Hobbes first discussed the law of nature in "A Discourse of Laws," one of three discourses published in 1620 as part of an anonymous publication entitled *Horae Subsecivae* (*Leisure Hours*). Until a few years ago, the author of this work was usually thought to be Hobbes's pupil and employer William Cavendish, second Earl of Devonshire, but more recently a stylometric analysis by Noel B. Reynolds and Arlene W. Saxonhouse led them to attribute the three discourses to Hobbes himself.[38] Since the publication of their work, however, Andrew Huxley has shown that a part of "A Discourse of Laws" consists of an English translation of Francis Bacon's unpublished *Aphorismi de Jure Gentium Maiore sive de Fontibus Justiciae et Juris* (*Aphorisms on the Law of Nations or the Sources of Justice and Law*). Huxley has also speculated that Bacon may have written the entire discourse or that William Cavendish wrote it for Bacon.[39] "A Discourse," which is a eulogy of law, is quite conventional in its brief remarks on the law of nature, which are unlike Hobbes's later views. It describes the law of nature as common to human beings and all other living creatures and responsible for such actions as "the commixture of the several sexes which we call Marriage, generation, education, and the like." It also distinguishes natural law from the law of nations, which is "the rules reason has prescribed to all men in general, and such as all Nations one with another do allow and . . . observe for just." Although it has not been previously noticed, these passages derive directly from the well-known statements by the Roman jurists Ulpian and Gaius on the law of nature and nations dating from the second century and earlier third century CE, which, as I have pointed out above, were later incorporated into the *Digest* as part of the law code authorized by the Emperor Justinian.[40] Despite the claims of the editors of *Three Discourses*, it seems to me doubtful that any part of "A Discourse of Laws" was written by Hobbes or casts any light on his understanding of natural law.

We might wonder about Hobbes's knowledge of the literature of natural law. In 1640, when he wrote his first political treatise, *The Elements of Law*, in which he discussed the law of nature at length, he was already fifty-two years old and a mature philosopher. By then it is probable that he possessed a wide acquaintance with writings on the law of nature as well as with those in the related area of ethics or moral philosophy. Save for Aristotle, whose opinions on ethics, politics, and metaphysics he often criticized as mistaken, absurd, and ignorant,[41] he was usually very sparing in mentioning or citing other authors and their books by name in his published works. We have little direct evidence, therefore, to indicate what he may have read pertaining to natural law.

During his long life, however, he had available to him the substantial library of the second and third Earls of Devonshire, his employers, patrons, and friends, at their country mansions of Chatsworth and Hardwick Hall. Among the Hobbes manuscripts at Chatsworth is a catalogue of the Hardwick Hall library dating mainly from the 1620s, with some additions in the 1630s apparently compiled by the philosopher himself. It includes more than fourteen hundred titles in various languages by classical, medieval, modern, and contemporary writers dealing with theology, religion, philosophy, civil and ecclesiastical history, Roman law and English common law, politics, science, mathematics, geography, travel, and other subjects. Although it does not reveal which of the books in the Hardwick library Hobbes actually read, the catalogue lists numerous works that might have been of use to him in the formation of his moral and political theory and his critical conception of natural law.[42] His classical education, early humanistic interests, and proficiency as a classical scholar, as shown by his English translation of Thucydides' *History* in 1629, would have made available to him the main sources of ethical reflection and natural law in ancient philosophy and Roman law and jurisprudence. He would likely also have known some of the patristic and medieval scholastic writers on the law of nature, foremost among them Thomas Aquinas, and possibly even including William of Ockham and Marsilio of Padua.[43] He could also have looked into the works on law and natural law by some of the sixteenth-century Spanish school of philosophers and theologians, who were mainly Thomists, in particular the Jesuit Francisco Suárez. In *Leviathan* he quoted from a book on theology by Suárez, whom he criticized by name along with other scholastic thinkers for what he called their abuse of language and insignificant speech.[44] He might therefore have been acquainted as well with Suárez's discussion of the law of nature in his *Tractatus de Legibus ac Deo Legislatore* (1612) (*On Laws and God the Lawgiver*), which, like other treatises of this kind, contained a great many references to a host of authors. He had certainly read widely in the works of the Italian Jesuit philosopher and theologian Cardinal Robert Bellarmine (d. 1621), to whom *Leviathan* devotes more space than to any other modern author in attacking him for his erroneous opinions in favor of the power and independence of the papacy.[45] In *The Elements of Law* Hobbes refers to the concept of sovereignty in Jean Bodin's *De Republica* (1576), a famous political treatise that also discusses the law of nature as a rule sovereigns are obliged to observe.[46] He had probably also read Machiavelli's *Discourses on the First Ten Books of Livy*, which, however, like Machiavelli's other political writings, totally ignores the subject of natural law.[47] Although he never refers to Hooker, he would probably have been aware of the discussion of natural law among the several kinds of law in the first book of Hooker's *The Laws of Ecclesiastical Polity* (1593). He might have also read the well-known work on common law, *Dialogue Between a Doctor of Divinity and a Student of the Laws of England* (1530), by the eminent English lawyer Christopher St. German, which includes a discussion of the law of nature and conscience.[48]

Except for Suárez, all of these authors who preceded Hobbes are included in the Hardwick library catalogue, as is likewise Grotius's *The Law of War and Peace*. Subsequent Protestant authors on natural law in the seventeenth and eighteenth centuries tended to regard this treatise by Grotius, despite the faults they may have found in it, as marking a new era in the philosophy of natural law. In the preface to his own famous work, *De Iure Naturae et Gentium* (1672) (*On The Law of Nature and Nations*), Pufendorf praised Grotius's pioneer achievement and described him as the man who first taught his age to value the study of natural law. Elsewhere he commended him as the first thinker to distinguish correctly the laws of nature from human positive law and to put them in the proper order. As a critic of Grotius, however, Pufendorf also observed that the former had omitted many subjects, treated others too lightly, and made errors that proved he too was only human.[49] Jean Barbeyrac (d. 1744), a French Protestant natural law theorist, disciple of John Locke, and erudite editor and commentator on the treatises of Grotius and Pufendorf, which he translated from Latin into French, was another of Grotius's admirers. His perspective on natural law was heavily influenced by Pufendorf. In a brief critical survey of the history of moral philosophy and natural law first published in 1706, he disparaged ancient and especially medieval moral philosophy while picturing his own time as an enlightened age that had "shaken off the Yoke of ill grounded authority" and raised "the Science of Morality ... from the Dead." It was Grotius, he believed, who, inspired by Francis Bacon's earlier reform of philosophy, "first ... broke the Ice" and effected the revival of the philosophy of natural law by his renowned work, *The Law of War and Peace*. But though he praised Grotius, Barbeyrac also noted some of his flaws, such as his lack of mastery in the art of reasoning and methodizing his thoughts, his passing over some important subjects, his false and confused ideas in various matters, and the inadequacy of his treatment of law and natural law. On these grounds he concluded that as a thinker, Grotius was much inferior to Pufendorf, for whom he expressed the greatest esteem.[50]

Two other recent natural law theorists to whom Barbeyrac gave some attention were Selden and Hobbes. He did not assign a high rank to Selden's treatise on natural law. Although remarking on its vast erudition, he placed it well below the work of Grotius and called it obscure and poorly organized. He observed that Selden did not derive the principles of the law of nature from "the pure Dictates of Reason" but from the seven precepts given by God to Noah, which were founded on a doubtful tradition.[51] Referring to Hobbes, Barbeyrac called him "one of the most penetrating Genius's of his age," but pointed to his "dangerous errors," such as basing the origin of civil society on self-preservation and self-interest and giving an unlimited authority to kings even in matters of religion. He also noted that Hobbes had a reputation as an atheist because of his belief that everything was corporeal, and conjectured that certain "seeming Contradictions" in Hobbes's work were due to the fact that the philosopher "durst not speak all he thought." Barbeyrac nevertheless endorsed Pierre Bayle's judgment that "no one had ever yet so far discover'd the Foundations of Civil Policy" as Hobbes did.[52] Pufendorf, who was both much influenced by Hobbes and had various disagreements with him, similarly spoke very highly of him, praising his deep understanding of human and civil society and crediting him with applying to moral philosophy the type of precise demonstration used by mathematicians.[53]

Grotius's *Law of War and Peace* was not primarily a treatise on the theory of natural law or political and moral philosophy but a work of jurisprudence dealing mainly with the law of nations or international law. Witnessing the widespread wars of his time, which involved large parts of Germany and the Holy Roman Empire and all the greater states of Western Europe, Grotius was deeply troubled by what he called the Christian world's "lack of restraint" in the prosecution of war. Aiming to moderate the conduct of war, he sought principally in *The Law of War and Peace* to present a systematic treatment of "the body of law . . . concerned with the mutual relation among states," to show how this law applied even in war, and to explain the conditions of a just war.[54]

Pufendorf's and Barbeyrac's view of Grotius as a major innovator in the domain of natural law has been followed by a line of recent historians who regard him as the founder of the "modern" theory or school of natural law. Richard Tuck, for example, echoing Barbeyrac, states that "Grotius made the breakthrough into a modern science of natural law."[55] It has remained a matter of debate, however, in precisely what way the Grotian theory of natural law was either modern or a science. Sabine associated the "modernized" idea of natural law with secularism, rationalism, and a detachment from theology, and other scholars have mentioned its introduction of the concepts of the state of nature and natural rights.[56] Grotius's *Law of War and Peace* certainly differed from its medieval predecessors in its style of presentation. Unlike the work of scholastic thinkers, it was not structured in a logical order of questions, replies, arguments, and objections and was far more the creation of a classically educated humanist lawyer than of a rigorous systematic philosopher. Yet it has been recognized by numerous scholars that Grotius was by no means a revolutionary and that the content of his natural law theory was continuous with that of medieval scholasticism. As historians of natural law, Rommen and d'Entrèves have stressed the element of rationalism as a new feature of the law of nature in the seventeenth century, but have nevertheless also emphasized Grotius's indebtedness to medieval natural law and scholasticism.[57] Haakonssen too has commented that Grotius's theory of natural law "conveyed to Protestant Europe large parts of natural law material utilized by the great scholastic thinkers, especially those of sixteenth-century Spain."[58] Reviewing the question of Grotius's modernity, the medievalist Brian Tierney observed that despite the belief that he inaugurated a new era of modern natural law, there is little agreement about what was distinctively modern in his work, and on the whole affirmed his continuity with the medieval tradition.[59]

One of the grounds for the claim that Grotius initiated a new and modernized interpretation of the law of nature is the famous sentence, often referred to with the shorthand *etiamsi daremus*, that is included in the Prolegomena of *The Law of War and Peace*. In this passage Grotius declared that the law of nature would possess "a certain validity even if we should concede [*etiamsi daremus*] what cannot be conceded without the utmost wickedness, that there is no God, or that the affairs of men are of no concern to Him."[60] But far from inaugurating a new era in the theory of natural law by severing it from its theistic roots, as some scholars have mistakenly imagined, Grotius's statement, which was not original with him, merely reiterated a well-known speculative notion familiar to natural law theorists since at least the fourteenth century. The possibility that natural law might be binding even if God did not exist was entertained as a hypothesis by Gregory of Rimini (d. 1358) and Gabriel Biel (d. 1495), and was also discussed by some of their Catholic successors in the sixteenth century.[61] As far back as 1880 the German historian Gierke remarked on the fact that "already medieval Schoolmen had hazarded the saying, usually referred to

Grotius, that there would be a Law of Nature discoverable by human reason and absolutely binding, even if there were no God, or the Deity were unreasonable or unrighteous."[62] It could well be the case that Grotius first learned of this hypothesis from Suárez's treatise *On Laws and God the Lawgiver*, who mentioned it and previous authors on the subject in his discussion of natural law. Among the points he touched on was the possibility that natural law does not have the character of a command that depends on the will of God but merely indicates what ought and ought not to be done, and is therefore licit even if there is no God.[63] Needless to say, however, Grotius never accepted for a moment the possibility of God's nonexistence and expressly stated that the acts of moral baseness or moral necessity prohibited or required by the laws of nature are also "either forbidden or enjoined by the author of nature, God."[64] Since both he and other theorists who cited this hypothesis totally rejected it as not only false and wicked but contrary to reason, they continued to assume that God was the ultimate source and sanction of natural law. At times, however, Grotius appears to suggest that the dictates of reason could in themselves create obligation. As between intellectualism and voluntarism, he was an intellectualist and therefore contended that not even God, though infinite in power, could change the law of nature, because this would be a contradiction in his godhood. Just as God could not cause two times two to be more or less than four, so likewise he could not cause what is intrinsically evil not to be evil.[65] Suárez, however, held that law and obligation could not be created simply as an effect of reason but required the will and command of a superior or legislator.[66] This was later also the position of Hobbes, who consistently defined law as a command and an expression of the sovereign's will.

Although the reform of method in philosophy and science was a question of profound importance to many seventeenth-century thinkers and was discussed by such outstanding minds as Francis Bacon, Galileo, and Descartes, as well as by Hobbes, Grotius seems to have given it little attention.[67] Richard Tuck, who has written extensively about Grotius, has contended that he broke with humanism by making mathematics his methodological model in the moral sciences, but there is scarcely anything in Grotius's writings to substantiate this dubious thesis.[68] If we look particularly at his major work, *The Law of War and Peace*, Grotius said in the Prolegomena that he had tried to avoid the controversies of his time, and that "just as mathematicians treat their figures as abstracted from bodies, so in treating law I have withdrawn my mind from every particular fact."[69] Actually, this statement was less than accurate, since Grotius mentioned a great many particular facts in his treatise, but it is also almost the only thing he says in it that has any relation to mathematics. In a later part of the work he specifically denied that mathematics could be applied to moral philosophy and expressed his agreement with Aristotle's well-known opinion that unlike mathematics, moral questions are not capable of certainty. The reason he gives is that mathematical science separates form from substance and considers only the former, whereas in moral questions even trifling circumstances alter the substance and forms that are the subject of inquiry.[70] It is worth noticing that Jean Barbeyrac, in praising Grotius, never said anything to suggest that he used mathematics as a model. Instead, Barbeyrac named Hobbes, whom he called a "great Mathematician," and Pufendorf as the thinkers who deserved the credit for introducing the "Geometrical Method" into the study of political philosophy and law.[71] Grotius's main comment in *The Law of War and Peace* about his method was his admirable short remark that he had aimed in his work at three things above all: to make the reasons for his conclusions as evident as possible, to expound in a definite order the matters needing to be treated, and to distinguish clearly between things that seemed the same but were different.[72]

To my mind, Grotius was hardly more reliant on reason than Thomas Aquinas and other major scholastic thinkers, and, as will be pointed out presently, he failed to formulate a well-developed theory of natural rights. While it is possible (but not likely) that he wished to propound a theory of natural law on rational foundations independent of theology, his concept of the law of nature was certainly not independent of theism, since he needed the Christian God as a source of natural law just as much as his medieval predecessors did.[73]

There can be little doubt that Hobbes had read Grotius and would have been aware of his reputation as a celebrated European thinker, Protestant opponent of Calvinism, and a prominent figure in the early seventeenth-century religious and political controversies of the Dutch Republic, which forced him into a lifelong exile from his country. Grotius was well-known in England, which he had visited during the reign of James I. In 1604–5 he wrote *De Iure Praedae Commentarius* (*Commentary on the Law of Prize*), a youthful work that remained in manuscript and unread for more than three hundred years until its publication in 1868. This treatise, which touched on the law of nature, was a legal and theoretical defense and justification of the incursions and privateering activities of the United Dutch East India Company in the East Indies in regions that were claimed as a monopoly by the Portuguese and Spanish crowns, which were then united in the king of Spain. A single chapter from it was printed in 1609 with the title *Mare Liberum* (*The Freedom of the Sea*), prompted partly by the growing Anglo-Dutch commercial rivalry.[74] In 1636 Hobbes reported from Paris that he was reading John Selden's recently published book *Mare Clausum* (*The Closed Sea*), written in reply to Grotius's earlier *Mare Liberum* to uphold the English monarchy's claim to the dominion or ownership of the sea surrounding Britain. In one of its chapters Selden mentioned Grotius's *Law of War and Peace* as an excellent work, and this reference would have brought it to Hobbes's attention if, as is most improbable, he had not seen it previously.[75]

Despite the total absence of Grotius's name from Hobbes's political writings, he made several indirect allusions to the Dutch thinker that indicate he did not think much of him as a philosopher of natural law. Indeed, G. Croom Robertson declared in his 1886 monograph on Hobbes, which is still worth reading, that Grotius was the author "plainly pointed at by Hobbes throughout as an opponent."[76] In *The Law of War and Peace*, Grotius wrote that to prove the existence of the law of nature, he had availed himself of the testimony of philosophers, historians, poets, and orators, and that when many people at different times and places affirmed the same thing as certain, it should be considered a universal cause and accepted as a correct conclusion drawn from the principles of nature or common consent.[77] It was this argument Hobbes obviously had in mind when he stated in *Leviathan* that he avoided quoting ancient poets, orators, and philosophers "contrary to the custom of late time," partly because in matters not of fact but of right there was no place for the testimony of witnesses, and also because all of those old writers sometimes contradicted themselves and each other.[78] In claiming to prove the existence of the law of nature from common consent, Grotius had also said that what all or the most civilized nations believe accords with natural law.[79] In *The Elements of Law* and again in *De Cive*, Hobbes specifically rejected this opinion affirmed by "certain writers," noting that there was no agreement about who shall judge which nations were the wisest, and denying that the consent of all mankind could determine what was contrary to the law of nature, because in that case, no man could offend against the law of nature.[80] Aside from these allusions, we must also suppose that Hobbes would have included Grotius in his blanket critique of the failure of the doctrine of natural law to make any progress since the days of antiquity. Hobbes was much more of an innovator in the theory of natural law than Grotius ever was, and compared with his originality in this area, the influence on him of his predecessors was relatively small.

Natural Rights

Natural right or the right of nature originated centuries later than the concept of natural law, but like the latter, it occupies a vital place in Hobbes's thought. Together with natural law, it constitutes, as I have said earlier, the foundation of the entire structure of his moral and political philosophy. The language of natural rights, which affected a good deal of political theory in the Anglophone world during the later seventeenth and the eighteenth centuries, is familiar to us today as an essential part of the Western liberal and democratic political tradition as expressed in certain of its most renowned emancipatory proclamations, in particular the American Declaration of Independence of 1776 and the French Declaration of the Rights of Man and the Citizen of 1789, the products respectively of the American and the French revolutions. Invoking in its first sentence "the laws of nature and nature's God," the American declaration announces as a "self-evident truth" that "all men are created equal and endowed by their Creator with certain inalienable rights," including "life, liberty, and the pursuit of happiness." It then goes on to affirm that governments are instituted "to secure these rights" and derive "their just powers from the consent of the governed." The French declaration states that "men are born and remain free and equal in rights" and that "the aim of every political association is the preservation of the natural and inalienable rights of man," which are "liberty, property, security, and resistance to oppression." Natural rights were thus pronounced to be the inborn and inalienable possession of every human being and to be rooted in a natural or original condition of personal freedom. As a matter of historical evolution, it is of the utmost consequence to observe that natural rights are also the direct and immediate forbear of the present concept of human rights, which emerged during the twentieth century to be enshrined after the Second World War in the United Nations' Universal Declaration of Human Rights of 1948 and later international covenants. In our own time, human rights, the offspring of natural rights, have become a global shibboleth, a supreme moral demand, and a worldwide rallying cry in the opposition to totalitarian, authoritarian, and theocratic regimes.[81]

The concepts of natural and human rights have been exhaustively discussed in recent decades in countless books and articles by moral and legal philosophers, political theorists, and historians, who have attempted to explain their origin, their meaning, and their foundation. Although throughout today's world there is a profound and passionate belief shared by many ordinary people, political activists, intellectuals of different stripes, and various philosophers that every human being possesses innate rights that all persons, authorities, and governments are morally bound to respect, a very noticeable feature of the literature on this subject is its failure to offer any convincing ground or proof for the claim that such rights actually exist.[82] The 1948 United Nations' Universal Declaration of Human Rights gave no reason to justify its assumption that the large number of human rights it mentioned were real or universal. The declaration simply asserted their existence as a recognized fact, and insofar as it tried to explain how mankind came by these rights, it attributed them to the dignity of the human person, another moral proposition that, however admirable and appealing, was itself in need of proof and does not refer self-evidently to anything that exists.

The utilitarian Jeremy Bentham, who disbelieved in natural rights as strongly as he did in natural law, stated that "right is with me the child of law.... A natural right is a son who never had a father."[83] Put another way, rights that derive from positive law, whether statutory or constitutional, are unproblematic in origin and their existence is not a mystery or puzzle. Rights of this kind also usually impose or imply a legal obligation on persons and governmental institutions either to refrain from hindering their exercise or to assist in giving them effect. By contrast, rights universally imputed to mankind as an innate possession based on nature or the dignity of the human person have not been known or recognized until very recent times. Unless they acquire legal standing as part of international treaties or are enacted by the legislatures of particular countries, these rights do not in themselves impose legal obligations on anybody and can only be regarded as the wishful creation of philosophers, political writers, and activists in social and political causes. During the seventeenth and eighteenth centuries, however, when the concept of natural rights flourished, skepticism about their existence was hardly typical, because nature was still widely conceived as a normative moral force imbued with intelligent purpose and the agency of God the creator. We need have no doubt that Hobbes would have given serious thought to the difficult question of how the natural rights he posited could be grounded.

Natural rights are personal rights that pertain to every individual, and the theory of natural rights is therefore highly individualistic. A natural right is an assertion on the part of individuals of a normative or moral claim, entitlement, or power to act or refrain that belongs to them simply in virtue of their rational human nature. It is based on the abstract conviction that members of the human race are born with rights imparted to them by nature that entitle them to personal freedom and civil equality. As the legal philosopher H.L.A. Hart has argued in his classic paper, "Are There Any Natural Rights?," if there are any such rights, then at least one of them is the equal right of all human beings to be free.[84] In any political conception of natural rights, and for Hobbes too, as we shall see, the natural right to be free is the primary or original right, and with this right, in the case of Hobbes, is also closely associated the right of self-defense of one's life and body. Historically, to give effect to this principle, one of the political claims most natural rights theorists have made is that governments are legitimate only if they derive from or are based in some way on the consent of the governed and are accountable to the governed for their actions.

The theory of natural rights was unknown in Greco-Roman antiquity and the early Middle Ages.[85] Although the absence of a word in a particular language does not necessarily mean that the speakers of this language also lacked the corresponding concept, it is significant that in neither Greek nor Latin was there any term for rights in the sense of a claim, entitlement, or power to act inhering in an individual as an expression of a natural freedom. The Greeks could speak of *to dikaion*, a term related to *dike* or justice, as that which is objectively just or right, but they lacked a conception of individual rights.[86] It is a striking and often overlooked fact that the original and for many centuries the predominant meaning of right, or in Latin the word *ius*, was not something attributed to individuals as a claim or entitlement but an objective property of rightness pertaining to various actions that made them just or right. *Ius* was accordingly closely akin in its meaning to such terms as *iustitia* and *iustum*, "justice" and the "just." Although the Roman legal system included provision for the rights of persons with respect to the ownership and inheritance of property and a variety of other matters, such rights were the creation of Roman civil law, not nature.[87] The closest that Roman jurists came to the idea of a rightful natural freedom was their supposition that men were born free in the earliest times according to natural law, and that the subsequent existence of slavery, an institution found throughout the world, was due to the *ius gentium* or law of nations, even though contrary to nature.[88] The fact that human slavery was contrary to nature never caused them to question its existence or call for its abolition.

Natural rights were historically an outgrowth of what present-day scholars and theorists have termed subjective rights in the sense that they are thought to be inherent in each individual person by nature. Natural rights are also closely related in their historical development to the doctrine of natural law, which was commonly thought of as a law of reason that conferred certain basic rights on human beings. The emergence of the subjective sense of a right signified a shift or extension from the primary and original meaning of right as the objectively just or right thing to do to that of a moral power, claim, entitlement, or liberty with which God and nature had endowed the individual. Although this liberty could be termed a right partly because it was considered just and right, the concept of natural rights added a subjective side to this meaning that was valid because it was derived from nature.

The concept of subjective and natural rights took shape between the twelfth and sixteenth centuries, as the most recent research has shown.[89]

It first appeared in the writings of some of the twelfth- and thirteenth-century legal commentators and canonists on Gratian's *Decretum* and papal legislation. It underwent further development in the thought of William of Ockham, Jean Gerson, and other medieval philosophers, and from thence was transmitted in the sixteenth century to the philosophers of natural law in Catholic Spain and other countries. In the course of this evolution, the Latin word *ius*, which primarily signified law, including the idea of justice, was coupled with the term *naturale* to acquire the meaning in various contexts of natural right, or *ius naturale*. Brian Tierney has cited examples from twelfth-century canonistic texts in which *ius naturale* was defined as a faculty, power, or force. He suggests that William of Ockham's fourteenth-century antipapal polemic *Breviloquium* may have been the first rights-based treatise on political theory, and quotes it as stating that the abuse of papal power was "opposed to the rights and liberties granted by God and Nature." He also quotes Gerson's subjective definition of *ius* as "an immediate faculty or power pertaining to anyone according to the dictate of right reason" or "according to the dictate of primal justice."[90] More than two centuries later Suárez equated *ius* with a right and said that it meant a faculty or moral power that every man has over his own property or with respect to that which is due to him.[91] Although subjective rights were not necessarily called natural rights, it is easy to see how the idea of a natural right might be introduced when the claim, entitlement, faculty, or power referred to something as fundamental as freedom, which God or nature and natural law were thought to have granted mankind.

The Latin phrase *ius naturale* has been called a semantic minefield, since it had the dual meaning of both natural law and natural right and could shift from the one meaning to the other.[92] The Latin *lex* means law and was often used interchangeably with *ius*, as Aquinas sometimes did, who referred to both *ius naturale* and *lex naturalis* in affirming that right is the object of justice.[93] Suárez pointed out that the word *lex* could be synonymous with *ius*, and that justice was a requirement of each.[94] Natural law and natural rights were accordingly closely related and could even be considered identical, since natural rights were generally regarded as a dictate and product of the law of nature.

Grotius has been seen as a strong and original theorist of natural rights who influenced Hobbes, but I can find no justification for this view.[95] Grotius was far more concerned with the law of nature, which he applied in various contexts, than with natural rights. When he comes to the discussion of rights in the first book of *The Law of War and Peace*, these are subjective rights that he treats under the heading of law. There is a meaning of law, he says, in which it can be regarded as rights that refer to the person, and in this sense, "right is a moral quality of a person, which makes him competent to have or do something lawfully" ("Quo senso jus est, qualitas moralis personae, competens ad aliquid juste habendum vel agendum"); when this moral quality is perfect, it is called a faculty, and when not perfect, an aptitude; a faculty corresponds to an act, an aptitude to a potency. He then goes on to explain that a faculty or legal right is what jurists call a right to one's own, and that he will henceforth regard this as signifying a right or *ius* properly and strictly so called. Included in legal right is a power over oneself, which is called liberty, or over others, such as that of a father or a master of slaves. Also included in it are the right of ownership of property, whether more or less absolute, and contractual rights, to which there are corresponding obligations.[96]

Grotius's discussion of *ius* as a faculty seems to be based entirely on Roman law, as is indicated by the marginal annotation in which he says that "the Roman jurists very properly define liberty as a *facultas* or legal right."[97] I have pointed out in a previous note the close connection in Roman law between the meanings of *facultas, potestas,* and *ius* as a legal right.[98] One of the best accounts of subjective rights in Grotius has been provided by the French Grotian scholar Peter Haggenmacher, who has traced their development in the Dutch jurist's writings and noted the clear differences between him and Hobbes.[99] As treated by Grotius, subjective rights have no affiliation with natural rights but are the creation of law, a part of the juridical order, as Haggenmacher says,[100] and ultimately traceable to natural law. Unlike Hobbes, Grotius never mentions a prepolitical state of nature in which human beings possess natural rights grounded in their desire for self-preservation and the conveniences of life. It is also evident that rights in the sense of the liberty of individuals are not an important theme in *The Law of War and Peace* and that Grotius never achieved a well-defined and fully articulated conception of natural rights.[101] In occasional passing remarks he explained how civil society originated when men in isolated households joined together to resist attack, and thus gave rise to civil power. From those who associated themselves to form civil society, he said, "derives the right which passes into the hands of those who govern." He therefore envisaged that some kind of agreement or consent and a conveyance of rights were necessary to the establishment of government.[102] But he nevertheless rejected as erroneous the opinion that sovereignty always resides in the people and maintained that just as any man may enslave himself if he wishes, so a people may by their own choice legally transfer their right to govern in such a way that they no longer to retain any right in themselves.[103]

He specifically denied the existence of an individual's right to freedom and included among the unjust causes of war the desire of freedom by a subject people.[104]

Hobbes was the first political philosopher to criticize the conflation of right and law as an error and to unpack the difference between the two and hence also between natural right and natural law. In *Leviathan* he pointed out in a manner highly relevant to Grotius that "even the most learned Authors" that speak of the subject

> confound *ius* and *lex*, right and law, yet they ought to be distinguished, because Right consisteth in liberty to do or forbear, whereas Law determineth and bindeth to one of them; so that law and right differ as much as obligation and liberty, which in one and the same matter are inconsistent.[105]

De Cive explained that "Law is a Fetter, Right is freedome, and they differ like contraries."[106] In other formulations, Hobbes identified right or *ius* with "a blameless liberty of using our own natural power and ability" and defined it as "that liberty which every man hath to make use of his naturall faculties according to right reason."[107] For him, therefore, a right, generally speaking, "is that liberty which the civil law leaves us;"[108] it is the freedom to do what we wish in any and all matters in which we are not subject to the obligation of law to do or forbear. "Naturall liberty" is thus "a Right not constituted but allowed by the Lawes; For the Lawes being removed, our liberty is absolute" and "where Liberty ceaseth, there beginneth Obligation."[109] Hobbes's conception is generally one of subjective right, but it also retains some of the older meaning of right as an objective rightness when the acts resulting from the freedom to do or forbear accord with right reason.

It is of great interest that some years later, in the second of his *Two Treatises of Government* (1689), the philosopher Locke took issue with Hobbes's conception of law as a restriction on liberty. While not naming him, it was surely against Hobbes that Locke aimed his comment that

> Law, in its true Notion, is not so much the Limitation as the direction of a free and intelligent Agent to his proper Interest, and prescribes no farther than is for the general Good of those under that Law. Could they be happier without it, the Law, as a useless thing would of it self vanish; and that ill deserves the Name of Confinement which hedges us in only from Bogs and Precipices. . . . [T]he end of Law is not to abolish or restrain, but to preserve and enlarge Freedom . . . where there is no Law, there is no Freedom. . . . But Freedom is not, as we are

told, A Liberty for every Man to do what he lists: (For who could be free when every other Man's Humour might domineer over him?) But a Liberty to dispose, and order, as he lists, his Person, Actions, Possessions, and his whole Property within the Allowance of those Laws under which he is; and therein not to be subject to the arbitrary Will of another, but freely follow his own.[110]

Locke's position as here expressed is actually close to Hobbes's, for it implicitly recognizes the benefits of exchanging unlimited freedom for the rule of law. Hobbes said almost the same thing in language from which Locke may even have borrowed, when he observed that

the use of laws (which are but rules authorized) is not to bind the people from all voluntary actions, but to direct and keep them in such a motion as not to hurt themselves by their own impetuous desires, rashness, or indiscretion, as hedges are set, not to stop travelers, but to keep them in the way.[111]

What, then, is the right of nature or a natural right, as Hobbes understood it? For him, this is the fundamental human right, rooted in what he believes is empirically observable as the most elemental feature of human nature, namely, its instinct and desire for self-preservation and fear of and aversion to death, especially violent death, as the greatest of natural evils. He therefore defines the right of nature, "which writers commonly call *jus naturale*," as "the liberty each man hath to use his own power, as he will himself, for the preservation of his own nature, that is to say, of his own life, and consequently of doing anything which, in his own judgment and reason, he shall conceive to be the aptest means thereunto." Hobbes can justifiably call this a "natural right" because it is in the highest degree natural in the human being, arising, he says, from "a certain impulsion of nature, no lesse then that whereby a Stone moves downward." Hence he concludes concerning this right that

it is neither absurd, nor reprehensible, neither against the dictates of true reason for a man to use all his endeavours to preserve and defend his Body, and the Members thereof from death and sorrowes; but that which is not contrary to right reason, that all men account to be done justly, and with right; Neither by the word Right is any thing else signified, then that liberty every man hath to make use of his naturall faculties according to right reason. Therefore the first foundation of naturall Right is this, That every man as much as in him lies endeavour to protect his life and members.[112]

Elsewhere he states the conclusion of this reasoning as follows: "It is therefore a right of nature: that every man may preserve his own life and limbs, with all the power he hath."[113]

The clarity and logic of Hobbes's analysis of the distinction between right and law and the relationship between the two was unrivaled in the natural law tradition up to his time. Within this tradition as it evolved in the later Middle Ages and the early modern era, the law of nature was generally thought to be the source of rights and natural rights. Without natural law there could be no natural rights. Because it preceded and authorized certain rights, the law of nature occupied a more significant place in legal, moral, and political philosophy than rights did. Indeed, Hobbes's view of natural rights differed radically from that of his predecessors. The law of nature and the right of nature are correlative concepts in his moral, legal, and political theory. The most distinctive feature of Hobbesian natural right is its character as an original prepolitical freedom inherent in human beings and sanctioned by right reason. For Hobbes, natural rights are not the creation of natural law but a primordial entitlement grounded in the most basic instinct and reasonable desire of human nature, the passion and wish to go on living. Hobbes could have argued that the right of nature was not a philosopher's thought imputed to mankind but a rational claim immanent in human nature, since the wish and freedom of individuals to preserve their lives was the ever-present condition of all their other activities and aims.

A half-century ago Leo Strauss's book *Natural Right and History* distinguished between two categories or types of rights, which he designated "classic natural right" and "modern natural right."[114] A celebrated conservative thinker, learned scholar, and inspiring teacher, Strauss is well-known for his critical opposition to the relativism of modern political philosophy and for his belief in the superiority of ancient philosophy, which is reflected in its concern with such profound questions as the highest type of life for man and the best regime. He created some confusion for the readers of his book by referring to classic natural right when he really meant natural law and by speaking at times as though natural law and natural right were synonymous terms. The essential point he makes, however, is that whereas classic natural right as developed in the philosophy of the ancient world and the Middle Ages affirmed the primacy of duties, modern natural right affirmed the primacy of rights. "The premodern natural law doctrines," he observes, "taught the duties of man; if they paid any attention at all to his rights, they conceived of them as essentially derivative of his duties." In the seventeenth and eighteenth centuries, he also noted, rights were given a far greater importance than ever before, so that natural rights tended to displace natural duties. Strauss regarded Hobbes as the seminal thinker who was most responsible for effecting the shift in moral and political theory from duty to rights and thus for the creation of a new political doctrine that was the begetter of liberalism. He deplored this change and associated Hobbes very questionably with the amoral political theory of Machiavelli, despite the fact that the latter lacked any conception of natural rights. He also described Hobbes as the creator of political hedonism, whatever that may mean. He ignored altogether the moral significance of modern natural rights in their contribution to the progress of political freedom, constitutional government, and civil equality in Western society.[115]

The valid core in Strauss's thesis is the fact that Hobbes did propound an original concept of natural rights by making them one of the foundations of the political order. Hobbesian natural right and a certain idea of freedom are interwoven. The right of nature entails an indefinitely wide freedom of each person to decide and act with respect to what conduces to his self-preservation. Hobbes conceived this right, however, as greatest and most absolute in the prepolitical condition he called the state of nature, in which there existed neither government nor law. In the following chapter I discuss his understanding of this condition and the further development of his moral and political philosophy, including the role of the law of nature in curtailing the absolute liberty conferred by the right of nature. During Hobbes's lifetime the principle of natural rights often assumed a revolutionary character when it was invoked in the name of freedom by rebels and radical political movements to justify resistance to divinely ordained kings and to demand far-reaching political reforms. Hobbes, who was a believer in authoritarian government, never intended the doctrine of natural right to be used for revolutionary purposes and took care in his philosophy, as we shall see, to strip it of its revolutionary import.

CHAPTER 2

Enter the Law of Nature

In 1629 Hobbes published an English translation of the Greek historian Thucydides' *History of the Peloponnesian War*. This was the first English-language version of the entire text, which Hobbes augmented with annotations and a map of Greece he made himself. An admirer of Thucydides' keen historical insight and disdain for Athenian democracy, Hobbes called him "the most politic historiographer that ever writ."[1] It is quite possible that Thucydides was one of the strongest influences in inculcating in Hobbes's mind a dislike of popular government and democratic politics and a concern for political order. His translation was an outstanding literary achievement that marked the culmination of his intellectual career as a classically educated humanist scholar. While he never lost interest in history, he concentrated thereafter for a number of years mostly on philosophy, mathematics, and sciences such as physics, optics, and cosmology. During the 1630s he developed into a mature philosopher and an advanced systematic thinker profoundly influenced by the scientific movement of the seventeenth century. Galileo was one of his heroes, and through his personal studies and relationships with men of science and philosophers in both England and France he was immersed in the philosophical and scientific culture of his time. In this period he came to regard large parts of the metaphysics and philosophy of Aristotle as mistaken. He became a corporealist or materialist, a monist, a mechanist, and a strict determinist who denied freedom of the will and believed in universal physical causation. He was among the earliest European philosophers to advance the novel thesis of the subjectivity of secondary qualities, or in other words, to argue that the phenomena of sense perception such as color, sound, and taste were not real properties of the objects we encounter in the external world but "accidents or qualities" of the senses and therefore phantasms or "seemings and apparitions only" in the mind of the perceiving subject. One of the first works in which he stated this thesis was the account of human nature in his earliest political treatise, *The Elements of Law*, where he pointed out that "the things that really are in the world without us, are those motions by which these seemings are caused."[2] Reality for him was defined by two elemental facts, body or matter, of which all entities consisted, and motion, the cause and explanation of all phenomena, including human thought and sensory experience. As he later wrote in

Leviathan, "every part of the universe is body, and that which is not body is no part of the universe. And because the universe is all, that which is no part of it is nothing (and consequently, nowhere)."[3] Hobbes resembled twentieth-century logical positivists and analytical philosophers in ruling out many of the metaphysical concepts of previous scholastic philosophy as simply a misuse of language and lacking in sense. For instance, among various examples cited in *Leviathan* he ridiculed the idea of incorporeal substance, pointing out that substance and body signified the same thing, so that the words "incorporeal" and "substance" destroy each other when joined together, as if one should say "incorporeal body."[4] He conceived of philosophy itself as a science composed of three main parts, body, man, and citizen, all of which were concerned with the investigation of different kinds of body. The first part dealt with body in its most general and fundamental features and with the foundations of knowledge, the second part with natural bodies, in particular human individuals, their passions, actions, and the characteristics of human nature, and the third part with the artificial bodies made by human beings, especially the body politic or commonwealth, its members and sovereign power, and the consequences of its creation.[5]

In light of the vital importance of science in his philosophical outlook, Hobbes could not have contemplated the idea of natural law except in what he deemed to be a scientific spirit. When commenting in *De Cive* on the failure of previous moral philosophers to make any progress in the understanding of natural law, he maintained that moral philosophy must become a rigorous deductive science akin to geometry in its method of reasoning.[6] The model of geometry, which he once called "the only science that it hath pleased God hitherto to bestow on mankind," exerted a powerful influence on his thinking.[7] He was apparently the first European thinker to conceive of moral and political or civil philosophy as sciences. He devoted considerable reflection to the nature of science, of which he gave a number of accounts.[8] All three of his major treatises on politics were intended as contributions to the sciences of moral and political philosophy. He said of *The Elements of Law* that it contained "the true and only foundation" of the science of the law of nature and justice.[9] He claimed of *De Cive*, as I have already quoted in the previous chapter, that with this book he had founded the science of civil (i.e., political) philosophy. *Leviathan* includes discussions of science in the fifth chapter on reason and science and the ninth chapter on the classification of the sciences, the latter of which describes the scientific character of moral and political philosophy and leaves no doubt that this treatise was intended largely as a work of science.

Grotius began his *Law of War and Peace* with a Prolegomena of sixty-one articles setting forth the principles of the work. Among his very first propositions were the dicta that justice and law truly exist and are rooted in nature, that the law of nature also exists, and that man is an animal innately sociable by nature and not motivated solely by his own interest.[10] Hobbes did not begin any of his political works in this way, and his approach to the subject of natural law was very different. In conformity with his conception of moral and political philosophy as sciences, he starts with an analysis of man and human nature as the material of these sciences, followed immediately by an account of the state of nature, a condition in which human beings as he has described them are pictured as existing without institutions, government, or law. Despite the centrality of natural law in his moral and political thought, he considered it essential to complete these preliminaries as part of his method of science before introducing the concept of natural law to the reader.[11]

Human Nature

The natural law tradition from the Stoics onward had commonly assumed that human beings were naturally sociable and inclined to cooperative association with others.[12] Hobbes departed radically from this tradition in his explication of human nature, of which he presented a much fuller, more vivid and detailed account than any previous theorist of natural law had done. The picture he gives focuses principally on what we might call typical human nature in its fundamental characteristics, leaving aside for the most part the variations between individuals. He summarily rejects the famous claim in Aristotle's *Politics* that man is by nature a political creature born fit for society, which he says has been endorsed by "the greatest part of those men who have written ought concerning commonwealths."[13] Instead, he portrays mankind as naturally self-centered, competitive, and aspiring to domination, needing to be made fit for society by education, and driven by a multiplicity of emotions, desires, aversions, fears, and passions. His view of human motives is notoriously unflattering, and he stresses that men do not seek society for its own sake or love of their fellows but for honor or profit and love of themselves.[14] It was in the nature of human beings, he held, that whatever they desired they called good, and whatever they hated or feared they called evil.[15] Of all their desires and passions the most basic was self-preservation and the avoidance of death. "[N]ecessity of nature," he said, makes men "to will and desire... that which is good for themselves, and to avoid that which is hurtful; but most of all that terrible enemy of nature, death, from whom we expect both the loss of all power, and also the greatest of bodily pains in the losing."[16] In maintaining that the human desire for self-preservation was universally compelling, he was not simplistically arguing that human beings always and invariably considered death the worst of evils. He understood very well that men will sometimes prefer death to a life of pain and suffering, or risk death because of pride, and went so far as to say that "most men would rather lose their lives . . . than suffer slander."[17] Such considerations, however, did not invalidate the claim that the desire or motive of self-preservation was most deeply rooted in human beings, and that "the greatest of goods for each [person] is his own preservation."[18]

Hobbes named reason and passion as the "two principal parts" of human nature.[19] His attitude toward the second of the two is quite distinctive and of prime importance in his subsequent treatment of natural law. While sharing the traditional understanding that the passions were a source of partiality and bias that obstructed and deranged the operation of reason and could incite men to bad actions, his view of them was nevertheless broadly naturalistic. He neither attacked nor condemned them, considering them rather as necessary manifestations of human vitality in the ongoing movement of life and the cause of the continual succession of appetites, desires, and aversions inevitable in human beings from birth to death. The old moral philosophers were wrong, he believed, to suppose there could be a highest good or final goal for men, because a person whose desires were at an end could no more live than one could live if one's senses and imagination were at an end. Human felicity did not consist of permanent repose or tranquility of mind, which were an impossibility, but of a continual progression of desires from one object to the next, the attaining of one being merely the way to the attaining of another.[20] This had to be the case, "because life itself is but motion and can never be without desire, nor without fear, no more than without sense."[21] He denied that the passions are inherently wicked or prove that men are evil by nature.[22] As he put it in *Leviathan*, he refused to accuse human nature, and "the desires and other passions of man are in themselves no sin,"[23] a thought suggesting that he probably did not believe in the Christian doctrine of original sin.[24] As he also stressed, it was from the passions of the mind that both just and unjust actions proceeded.[25] Contrary to the Stoic view, therefore, which held that the task of reason was to subdue and overcome the passions, Hobbes thought it necessary to use them, or certain of them, in achieving the moral order of civil society. To reduce the doctrine of justice and policy "to the rules and infallibility of reason," he averred, "there is no way, but first to put such principles down for a foundation, *as passion not mistrusting, may not seek to displace* [italics mine]; and afterward to build thereon the truth of cases in the law of nature."[26]

The high point of Hobbes's description of human nature is the anatomy and definition of the passions as set forth in the early chapters of *The*

Elements of Law and *Leviathan*. Both accounts, however controversial, are masterpieces of naturalistic philosophical psychology.[27] His analysis of certain simple passions or emotional states of mind generally brings out their self-interested character in relation to individuals' success or lack of success in achieving their ends in the competition of life. "Glory," for example, "or internal gloriation of the mind, is that passion which proceedeth from the imagination or conception of our own power, above the power of him that contendeth with us." Its contrary passion, "proceeding from an apprehension of our own infirmity, is called Humility by those by whom it is approved, by the rest, Dejection and poorness."[28] *Leviathan*'s sixth chapter, concerning the passions and their expressions, includes lapidary definitions. Thus, "Hope" is "appetite with an opinion of attaining," "Despair" is "the same without such opinion." "Confidence" is the "constant hope . . . of ourselves," "Diffidence" is the "constant despair . . . of ourselves." "Magnanimity" is the "contempt of little helps and hindrances," and "Valour" or "Fortitude" is "Magnanimity in danger of death or wounds." Hobbes's definition of "Benevolence" is "desire of good to another . . . Good Will, Charity. If to man generally, Good Nature."[29] This statement, one of a number that include his subsequent discussion of the virtues in relation to the law of nature, places it beyond doubt that notwithstanding his emphasis on the self-interested motives of human beings, Hobbes's psychology and moral philosophy also allow for the possibility of unselfish and altruistic actions aimed at the good of others. I return to this subject at a later point.

In *The Elements of Law*, Hobbes compared human life to a race with "no other goal or garland, but being foremost." Based on this image, which he said did not hold perfectly but applied well enough, he briefly defined a number of passions and mental states with respect to their role in the race. The concluding three definitions seem an effective summary of his analogy between life and a race: "Continually to be out-gone, is misery. Continually to out-go the next before, is felicity. And to forsake the course, is to die."[30] Elsewhere Hobbes expressed his conception of the competitive character of human nature and human existence in the following comment, which has often been misunderstood:

> So that in the first place I put for a general inclination of all mankind, a perpetual and restless desire of power after power, that ceaseth only in death. And the cause of this is not always that a man hopes for a more intensive delight than he has already attained to, or that he cannot be content with a moderate power, but because he cannot assure the power and the means to live well which he hath present, without the acquisition of more.[31]

This statement was not a reference to political power and an omnipresent struggle for its possession. Hobbes had previously defined "the power of a man" as "his present means to obtain some apparent future good."[32] The power in question thus referred simply to the resources and ability of individuals to gain their successive ends in the incessant competition of life and the need to acquire further power in order to retain with a bit of security the things already achieved.

Hobbes's examination of human nature led him to conclude that all people were basically equal, even though some were stronger in mind or body than others, because even the weakest of individuals could find a way to kill the strongest. It was characteristic of his conception of human existence in its natural condition in the absence of government that he chose the ability of one person to kill another as a sign of their natural equality. From this he drew the moral corollary that "the difference between man and man is not so considerable as that one man can thereupon claim to himself any benefit to which another may not pretend."[33] The natural equality of human beings, though a common theme in the natural law tradition, was for the most part hardly taken literally as a regulatory principle of social or political life. Although rejected by Plato and Aristotle, it was asserted by the Stoics, by Cicero, Seneca, and a number of other thinkers in the Roman world. It was based on the view that all men were alike in being endowed by nature with reason and the potential to attain a life of virtue, according to the moral standards derived from nature. The Christian New Testament also taught the equality of mankind founded on the common fatherhood of God and the doctrine enunciated by the apostle Paul that in Christ all are one, without any difference between Jew and Greek, freeman and slave, male and female (Gal. 3.28).[34] These Stoic and early Christian statements of human equality must be understood, however, in a purely ideal, abstract, or spiritual sense. They had scarcely any effect on the position or treatment of human beings in ancient society and never brought into question the institution of slavery as the most egregious and exploitive incarnation of the principle of human inequality. Hobbes's moral and political philosophy attributed much more importance to the idea of natural human equality than did any of his predecessors'. Equality plays a crucial part in his subsequent argument because it lends support to the moral principle of reciprocity in human relationships, which he treated as an essential criterion of the law of nature as he presently came to explain it.

The American philosopher William James made a famous distinction among philosophical temperaments between tough-minded and tender-minded thinkers.[35] Hobbes obviously belonged with the tough-minded, as is evident from his materialism, his determinism, his skepticism toward many received beliefs, and his view of human nature. James included pessimism as one of the characteristics of the tough-minded. Despite his view of the predominance of self-interest and self-partiality in human nature, however, Hobbes was not a pessimist. He strove to understand human beings as they really were and as their nature caused them to act, but he did not despair of mankind or condemn individuals for their self-interested passions. The entire purpose of his moral and political philosophy, as his work goes on to reveal, and of the account of human nature with which he begins, was to teach men the necessity and value of peace, the means to achieve and preserve it through the use of reason and the cultivation of various virtues, and the relationship between peace, the goods of civilization, and the flourishing of human life. In the dedication of his first political treatise, *The Elements of Law*, addressed to his friend and patron the Earl of Newcastle and dated May 1640, amidst the growing political crisis between the Stuart monarchy and its parliamentary opposition and discontented subjects, Hobbes said that the conclusions of his doctrine were such that "for want of them, government and peace have been nothing else to this day, but mutual fear." Hence, he added, "it would be an incomparable benefit to the commonwealth, if every man held the opinions concerning law and policy here delivered."[36] This benevolent aim remained a constant theme of Hobbes's thought in all of his expositions of the law of nature and his writings on moral and political theory.

The State of Nature or Man's Natural Condition

Following his treatment of human nature, Hobbes next proceeded to imagine human beings, as he had previously described them, living in the state of nature without an organized political society, government, or civil laws. This notion of a prepolitical and precivilizational state of nature was an old one in Western moral and political thought and had been sketched out vaguely by numerous authors, who pictured such a condition in different ways.[37] In Greco-Roman antiquity, conceptions of this kind often reflected the widespread belief in an early golden age when men were still entirely simple and good and lived in ease without toil or sin. The Roman Stoic Seneca described a primitive era of innocence in which mankind, not yet corrupted, lived according to nature, ruled by the best and wisest, and slavery, private property, and coercive government were unknown. Eventually, however, moral deterioration, private property, and avarice appeared, putting an end to this condition, which was one of primitive innocence rather than perfection.[38] Similar ideas persisted in the Middle Ages, such as the account in Gratian's *Decretum* of the emergence of government after the period of innocence preceding the Fall of Adam. Following the Fall, men lived at first as scattered individuals guided only by natural law, until they began to form communities in the time of Cain, who built the first city. This era was succeeded by one of customary law and eventually by an age of actual legislation dating from the period of Moses. As part of this change from an early primitive condition, Gratian and other canonists included the development of private property, which occurred after Adam's sin, when the world lay open for appropriation ratified by natural law, which granted ownership to the first occupants of the soil.[39]

Discussing the sixteenth-century Spanish school of scholastic theologians and philosophers such as Vitoria, Soto, Luis de Molina, and Suárez, who were generally Thomists, Quentin Skinner has pointed out that they had a clear concept of the state of nature, even though they made little use of the phrase.[40] In their view, prior to the creation of civil societies men were never solitary wanderers but naturally social, desirous of a communal life and subject to the law of nature in the absence of civil law. A basic conviction of these authors was that human beings in their original natural condition were free, equal, and independent. They traced the origin of government to the realization that without the existence of civil rule and human positive law, men as creatures of sin would be exposed to increasing injustice, insecurity, and internal conflicts, owing to human selfishness.[41]

That men were free and equal in their prepolitical condition and that civil society and government were a natural product of men's innate sociability and mutual needs, which made them interdependent, were common assumptions of many early modern theorists of natural law, including some of Hobbes's immediate predecessors. Richard Hooker imagined a primitive state in which there were no civil societies or any form of public regiment, and explained that the imperfections of this condition and men's natural desire of fellowship caused them to unite in political societies and create government by their consent.[42] Suárez held that man was free by nature and subject only to God, and stated that civil magistracy arose as a further stage after the formation of families and domestic government because man as a social animal cherished a natural desire to live in a political community.[43] The important Dutch political theorist Johannes Althusius (d. 1638) described how the social nature and mutual need of human beings brought them together first in villages and then in commonwealths. His presupposition of an original freedom is clear from such observations as that the efficient cause of political association was the consent and agreement of the participating citizens.[44] Grotius declared in his Prolegomena to *The Law of War and Peace* that "the very nature of man" was what led human beings "into the relations of society" and was therefore "the mother of the law of nature."[45] Aside from some scattered observations he did not say much about the state of nature, to which he never devoted a particular discussion, although he took its existence for granted, but in explaining the origin of the right of private ownership, he referred to a primitive state in which men lived in great simplicity and enjoyed a common right to all things. As examples of common or universal possession, he mentioned certain tribes in America that lived in this way without inconvenience, as well as the Jewish sect of the Essenes and the first Christians in Jerusalem, who held everything in common.[46] The general assumption of an original freedom underlay his characterization of the state as "a complete association of free men, joined together for the enjoyment of rights and for their common interest."[47] In the previous chapter I quoted similar comments by Grotius on the origin of political society, when men who lived in isolated households joined together to resist attack and thereby gave rise to civil power. From the people who associated themselves in this way, he said, derives the right that passes into the hands of those that govern.[48]

Some conception of or allusion to men's natural or prepolitical condition prior to the emergence of civil society, settled government, and private property was thus almost a commonplace in political philosophy and the theory of natural law prior to Hobbes. The latter accordingly did nothing new or unusual in including a description of the state of nature in his political treatises. What made his version of the subject so original and unconventional in comparison with accounts by previous authors was his negative portrait, with its graphic power and detail, of the state of nature, in which the antisocial character of human beings was set forth in some of the best English prose of the seventeenth century.

For Hobbes, the state of nature, which was devoid of government, political or social institutions, laws, or legally enforceable agreements, allowed absolute freedom to individuals while it also condemned them to perpetual war with one another, so that they were compelled to live at all times in great insecurity and fear of violent death. But what did Hobbes intend by the concept of the state of nature he thus exhibited? Did he mean it to describe an actual epoch or stage of human history, or simply to serve as an abstract thought experiment? François Tricaud, who has written one of the best analyses of the Hobbesian state of nature, has very correctly termed it a model and a conceptual artifact whose function was not to reproduce but to illuminate the natural condition.[49] We could likewise apply to it Max Weber's sociological notion of an ideal type, which is designed to identify in a complex social situation, process, or phenomenon its essential features. Hobbes did not neglect to point out that the state of nature corresponded historically to various actual cases, among which he cited the ancient Germans and the savage peoples of his own time who lived in many places in America, although he also admits that such a condition had never existed all over the world.[50] But historical instances of this kind were not really the issue, and he conveys the essential clue to his interpretation of the state of nature when he tells the reader, "Let us return again to the state of nature, and consider men as if but even now sprung out of the earth, and suddainly (like Mushromes) come to full maturity without all kinds of engagement to each other."[51] This statement indicates pretty clearly that he envisaged the state of nature largely as a hypothetical condition, schema, or model, one, to be sure, that plainly referred to the real world and made it possible to elucidate the logical consequences of humans with the nature he attributed to them placed in a situation without a sovereign power to rule, govern, and protect them.

Hobbes offers a variety of reasons why men are at enmity with one another in the state of nature. These include the conflicts that result from their diverse passions, their self-love, vainglory, and desire for precedence and superiority, and their appetite for the same things that can't be divided or enjoyed in common and must therefore go to the strongest as decided by the sword.[52] Their differing appetites and aversions cause them to hold clashing opinions on what is good and evil, one commending what another condemns, thereby producing discord and strife.[53] The equality of men with respect to their ability to kill one another creates diffidence and fear between them; "and from this diffidence," Hobbes observes, "there is no way for any man to secure himself so reasonable as anticipation, that is, by force or wiles to master the persons of all men he can, so long till he sees no other power great enough to endanger him."[54] In *Leviathan* he lists the three causes in the nature of man that inevitably breed conflict as competition, diffidence, and glory: "the first maketh men invade for gain; the second, for safety; and the third for reputation."[55] It has been suggested that Hobbes's source for this comment may have been the first book of Thucydides' *History*, which depicts the motives of the Athenians in building their empire as fear, honor, and profit.[56]

Hobbes gives little consideration to possible developments not difficult to think of that would complicate the state of nature as he describes it, such as alliances between individuals and groups, defensive agreements between the more moderate kind of men, temporary conquests, leaders and followers, truces, and so on. He does mention how one man might subdue another and then exact some caution from him for future security.[57] In general, however, he appears to hold that the insecurity of the natural condition is so great that it excludes any likelihood of reliable agreements or arrangements to reduce fear and enmity between individuals. Even a conqueror would be exposed to so much danger that his survival for many years would be a miracle.[58] The conclusion Hobbes reaches is that the state of nature, in which "men live without a common power to keep them in awe," is a state of war "of every man against every man." This state of war exists not only in times of actual combat but also during the entire period of insecurity in which the disposition and will to fight are dominant among men, with no assurances of any developments to the contrary.[59]

Hobbes emphasizes that the state of nature is antithetical to civilization and a reversion to barbarism. In such a condition, he points out,

> there is no place for industry, because the fruit thereof is uncertain, and consequently no culture of the earth, no navigation, nor use of the commodities that may be imported by sea, no commodious building, no instruments of moving and removing such things as require much force, no knowledge of the face of the earth, no account of time, no arts, no letters, no society, and which is worst of all, continual fear and danger of violent death, and the life of man solitary, poor, nasty, brutish, and short.[60]

This memorable picture conflates images of primitive ignorance and barbarism with images of the retrogression that might afflict a civilized society when subject to prolonged internecine war. Hobbes is thus at pains to liken this "brutish" state to "the manner of life which men that have formerly lived under a peaceful government use to degenerate into, in a civil war." He adds that the relations between independent kings and states, who are constantly on their guard, with their weapons aimed against one another, resemble the state of nature, since all of them are always in a posture of war.[61]

In showing what human life would be like in the state of nature, Hobbes also delineates the moral situation that defines the natural condition. It is one in which human beings have a natural right to all things and hence the right to do anything and use all means that will in their own judgment conduce to their self-protection and self-preservation. I discussed in the previous chapter the Hobbesian concept of a right and the right of nature. As he understands it, a right means freedom from law and legal obligation. The right of nature is a right in a double sense. It is a subjective right, an inherent freedom belonging to individuals in the state of nature, that is grounded in their need and desire to defend and preserve their lives. It is also objectively right, a moral entitlement grounded in reason, which is therefore the right thing to do. As he comments in *The Elements of Law*, "that which is not against reason, men call RIGHT, or *ius*, a blameless liberty of using our own power or ability."[62] He sometimes also speaks of the right of nature as a power men have to preserve themselves. "It is therefore a right of nature," he says, "that every man may preserve his own life and limbs, with all the power he hath." He concludes that "irresistible might in the state of nature is right."[63] This last may seem a hard thought, but it follows logically and underscores the fact that right and power are equivalent in the natural condition, in which each person has the right to exert all his strength, force, and cunning in the preservation of life and body.

Hobbes best sums up in *Leviathan* the remaining features of the state of nature. In consequence of the perpetual war between men, "nothing can be unjust," and there is accordingly no place for ideas of right and wrong or of justice and injustice. "Where there is no common power," he says, "there is no law; where no law, no injustice." Because of the condition of war there is also no property or dominion, no valid distinction between mine and thine; and whatever a man can get is his as long as he can keep it.[64] In *De Cive* he describes this extreme situation in the following way: "What any man does in the bare state of Nature is injurious to no man; not that in such a State he cannot offend God, or break the Lawes of Nature; for Injustice against men presupposeth Humane Lawes, such as in the State of Nature there are none." He also notes that a man could offend against the laws of nature in the state of nature by pretending that something "tend[s] necessarily to his preservation, which yet he himself doth not confidently believe so."[65]

Hobbes rules out injustice and injury in the state of nature because he relates them by definition to the breach of human laws. It would be quite wrong, however, to suppose that the Hobbesian state of nature is completely lacking in moral norms or principles. As his account just cited makes clear, the law of nature and the law of God exist in the state of nature, and men can be cognizant of them. The problem is that these laws set a standard very difficult to follow while men remain in a state of unceasing war and insecurity.

Hobbes's analysis of the natural condition in which every individual has a right to all things ends in a paradox. The paradox is that when everyone has a right to all things, then no one has this right. In *The Elements of Law*, the philosopher states the consequence:

> But that right of all men to all things is in effect no better than if no man had a right to anything. For there is little use and benefit of the right a man hath when another as strong, or stronger than himself, hath right to the same.[66]

De Cive formulates the point in an almost identical way, noting that "the effects of this Right are the same, almost, as if there had been no right at all."[67] This paradox constitutes the conclusive reason for the state of war that characterizes men's natural condition before they enter into society; for as Hobbes points out, given the "naturall proclivity" of human beings "to hurt each other which they derive from their Passions," and adding to it "the right of all to all, wherewith one by right invades, the other by right resists," the result must be "a War of all men, against all men."[68]

The Precepts of the Law of Nature

The law of nature makes its entry to resolve this paradox and rescue mankind from its natural condition. This involves instructing men in the way to peace through the creation of the commonwealth and sovereignty, and showing them the vast superiority of the commonwealth compared to a life without government. Men can leave the state of nature, Hobbes points out, partly through their passions and partly through their reason. The passions he relies on for this purpose are those that "incline men to peace," in particular the "fear of death, desire of such things as are necessary to commodious living, and a hope by . . . industry to attain them." Reason, he adds, then suggests "convenient articles of peace upon which men may be drawn to agreement," and these articles "are called the Law of Nature."[69] In *The Elements of Law* he explains that reason "is no less of the nature of man than passion, and is the same in all men, because all men agree in the will to be directed in the way to that which they desire to attain, namely, their own good, which is the work of reason."[70] From these considerations he derives the law of nature, which is defined in *Leviathan* as a "precept or general rule, found out by reason, by which a man is forbidden to do that which is destructive of his life or taketh away the means of preserving the same, and to omit that by which he thinketh it may best be preserved." *De Cive* puts the definition slightly differently as a "Dictate of right Reason, conversant about those things which are either to be done, or omitted for the constant preservation of Life, and Members, as much as in us lyes."[71] He then proceeds to formulate the first and fundamental law of nature as the general rule or precept of reason "to seek peace and follow it." Otherwise stated, it ordains that "every man ought to endeavour peace as far as he has a hope of obtaining it." Correlative to this first natural law is the fundamental right of nature that if a man seeks peace but cannot obtain it, then he may defend himself by all means.[72]

Hobbes presents a list of the laws of nature in all three of his political treatises. Their number increases somewhat in the successive versions, but despite this and a few other differences, they are substantially alike and similarly grounded.[73] All of them reflect the moral principle of reciprocity based on natural human equality, which mandates that every person should treat others as they would want others to treat them. Hobbes gives cogent expression to this idea in *The Elements of Law*, where he offers an easy rule to decide whether or not an action is against the law of nature: "That a man imagine himself in place of the party with whom he hath to do, and reciprocally him in his. . . ."[74] The second law of nature flows directly from the first and consists of the precept that men should divest themselves of their right to all things; in the words of *Leviathan*, that "a man be willing, when others are so too . . . to lay down [his] right to all things and be contented with so much liberty against other men as he would allow other men against himself."[75] In order for this law to take effect, Hobbes includes a technical discussion, to which I shall return, of how men can enter into agreements to divest themselves of their natural right to all things by means of contracts and covenants.[76] The third law of nature then enjoins that men should perform the covenants they have made.[77] Among the other natural laws is the ninth, which requires that despite civil inequalities, "every man acknowledge other for his equal by nature."[78] *Leviathan* sets forth twenty laws of nature altogether, whose purpose is to dictate peace as "a means of the conservation of men in multitudes" and that, according to Hobbes, concern only "the doctrine of civil society," not any particular human vices. He sums up all of these laws in the Golden Rule of the New Testament, "Do not that to another, which thou wouldst not have done to thyself," a saying understandable, he declares, even to the least intelligent mind.[79]

The law of nature as an injunction to seek peace is a moral law sanctioned by right reason, objectively right, and addressed to the rational self-interest of every individual. This self-interest, however, is also, as Hobbes argues, a common or universal interest, since the good desired by all men includes their self-preservation and commodious living. To the extent that individuals act rationally, therefore, they will want to obey the Hobbesian laws of nature. The character of these laws shows plainly that despite their appeal to self-interest, they are genuine moral principles intended to promote and facilitate peaceable social and other-regarding behavior between people, and that anyone who strives to abide by them would be a moral or virtuous person. The fourth law of nature, for example, enjoins gratitude for the benefits one individual freely gives another, for if ingratitude prevailed and givers had reasonable cause to repent of their good will, Hobbes noted, "there will be no beginning of benevolence or trust; nor, consequently, of mutual help, nor of reconciliation of one man to another." The fifth law of nature prescribes complaisance or sociability, meaning that every man should try "to accommodate himself" to others. Other laws of nature require pardoning people for past offenses if they show signs of repentance; the infliction of punishments not for revenge but for the future correction of offenders; the avoidance of all expressions of contempt or hatred of others whether in words, deeds, or gestures; the avoidance of arrogance in the divestment of rights by claiming more for oneself than one is willing to grant to others; and the observance of equity, which orders that judges should treat individuals equally and impartially in deciding controversies between them.[80] I need not mention all the laws of nature as set forth in *Leviathan*, since their moral purpose and relevance to peaceful coexistence in society is obvious. It is indicative, moreover, of his predominantly moral perspective in framing the laws of nature that Hobbes considers a just or righteous person as one, he says, whose "manners"—that is, his conduct in life—conforms to reason, and "who taketh all the care he can that his actions may be all just." A righteous man, he points out, does not lose this character even if he should commit a few unjust actions that proceed from sudden passion or a mistake regarding things or persons.[81]

Hobbes also explains that in the state of nature, the laws of nature are obligatory and binding in conscience (*in foro interno*) but not necessarily in external actions (*in foro externo*). The reason for this important qualification is that a "modest and tractable" person who keeps his promises when nobody else does so would only make himself "a prey to others, and procure his own ruin" if he acted in accordance with the natural law. To do so in such circumstances would thus be "contrary to the ground of all laws of nature, which tend to nature's preservation." In the state of nature, therefore, where there is no security, the law of nature obliges only to a constant and sincere desire and endeavor to fulfill its precepts.[82]

Hobbes's discussion of the laws of nature is part of a single bloc of argument intended to show the way of egress from the state of nature to a condition of civil peace. It culminates in an account of the creation of the commonwealth by means of covenants that men make with one another to relinquish a large part of their natural right to all things and subject themselves to a sovereign power and its laws. In his account of the origin of the commonwealth or body politic as something made by men, Hobbes belonged to the contractual tradition of political philosophy, which reached its height of influence and theoretical elaboration in the seventeenth and eighteenth centuries. Although there were different versions of the contractual idea in this tradition, they all generally postulated the existence of human beings in an original or primeval condition of freedom and their subsequent decision to create and empower government. Two separate stages are analytically distinguishable in the contractual perspective on how government comes into being. The first is the theory of the social contract, by which men, abandoning their prior individual freedom and independence, agree to enter into the relations of civil society. The second is the theory of the contract of rulership, by which men consent to establish a government over themselves possessed of the powers they agree to give it. Hobbes's treatment of these two contractual stages uniquely combined them into a single continuous process that, by the supposition of a covenant that men make with one another in the state of nature, gives rise at the same time both to civil society as a genuine union of previously separated individuals and to the commonwealth based on subjection to the government of the sovereign.[83]

A number of Hobbes scholars have questioned whether such self-interested human beings as the philosopher pictures them, bent on their own aggrandizement and defense, vainglorious yet diffident, capable of reason but susceptible to passion, and placed in a natural condition of permanent insecurity, could ever achieve an agreement enabling them to escape from the state of nature. They have examined his discussion of the making of covenants and the problem that arises when one party to a covenant performs and must trust that the second and other parties will likewise perform. Hobbes observes that in the state of nature, if a covenant is made between two parties in which neither presently performs and both trust one another, the covenant is void "upon any reasonable suspicion" of nonperformance. He notes also that the man who performs first has no assurance that the other party will perform, "because the bonds of words are too weak to bridle men's ambition, avarice, anger, and other passions, without the fear of some coercive power; which in the condition of mere nature, where all men are equal and judges of the justness of their own fears, cannot possibly be supposed."[84] Such difficulties have led some scholars to doubt that the creation of the commonwealth by rational individuals is explicable in Hobbes's political theory.[85]

There is no necessity to examine this debatable issue, which is historically irrelevant in following and analyzing Hobbes's thought concerning the law of nature and its role in his moral philosophy. He believed and stated explicitly that men could be "drawn to agreement" on the basis of "the convenient articles of peace" contained in the natural law, and that fear of death and desire of things necessary for commodious living were the passions that inclined men to peace.[86] We should not forget that the Hobbesian state of nature is largely a model and imaginary hypothetical condition demonstrating what the case would be in the absence of a coercive political order. Hobbes knew and pointed out at a later stage of his discussion that, historically, most governments owed their existence not to the agreement of absolutely free individuals in the state of nature to institute a sovereign to rule over them but to forcible conquest and the submission in the form of a presumed covenant by the conquered to the conqueror's power in return for sparing their lives. "There is scarce a commonwealth in the world," he commented, "whose beginnings can in conscience be justified."[87] One of the most important points, however, that I think he sought to bring out by the painstaking account in *De Cive* and *Leviathan* of contracts, covenants, oaths, and the relinquishing and transfer of rights was that civil society and government, whatever their historical origin might be, are logically and essentially the products of human will and consent, as are likewise the obligations of obedience to its laws that individuals assume when they become members or citizens of the commonwealth.

The Hobbesian laws of nature are not innately known to human beings because engraved by God and nature in their minds and hearts. They are the conclusion of a chain of reasoning that starts with what Hobbes insists is an empirically accurate description, confirmable by the personal experience of all his readers, of the propensities of human nature and its basic desire and passion for self-preservation as the prerequisite of all the other varied goods human beings may strive to obtain. From there it leads on to the rational judgment expressed in the first and fundamental natural law that men should seek peace if they can obtain it. These preliminaries lay the groundwork for the subsequent rationalization and validation of the existence of the commonwealth or political society, the necessity of the institution of sovereignty in the commonwealth in order to achieve peace, order, and security, and the requirement that subjects agree to give up the total freedom and unlimited natural right they possess in the state of nature and consent to render absolute obedience to the sovereign as the sole way of escaping from the miserable condition of the war of all against all that is the lot of mankind without government. Hobbes thus traces the origin and justification of the commonwealth to "the final cause . . . or design of men, (who naturally love liberty and dominion over others)," but who nevertheless, "in the foresight of their own preservation, and of a more contented life thereby," consent to the restraint of government and a visible power over them "to keep them in awe, and tie them by fear of punishment to the performance of their covenants and the observation of [the] laws of nature."[88]

A certain portion of Hobbes's discourse of natural law was substantially a continuation of language and principles that had long been a part of the natural law tradition. He was merely repeating the common view of both pagan and Christian thinkers when, like Cicero, for instance, he described the laws of nature as "immutable and eternal," because, as he explained, their opposites, "injustice, ingratitude, arrogance, pride, iniquity, and [exception] of persons . . . can never be made lawful," and "it can never be that war shall preserve life, and peace destroy it." In accord with earlier natural law theorists, he equated the law of nature with a number of "moral virtues" such as "justice, gratitude, modesty, equity, mercy," and others.[89] In affirming that the law of nature could be summed up in the biblical Golden Rule, he was following the thought of the church fathers, Gratian, Aquinas, and other Christian jurists and theologians who believed that the natural law is contained in the law and the Gospel.[90] Important also is the fact that like a long line of previous writers, Hobbes saw the essence of the law of nature in right reason, or *recta ratio*, a normative concept in moral philosophy whose origins lay in the Socratic-Platonic teaching equating virtue with knowledge and in the philosophy of Stoicism, which associated reason, virtue, and nature. Reason was termed right reason because it pointed to right or just action and united truth and goodness.[91] Cicero declared that "virtue itself can best be summed up as right reason" and called law "the highest reason, implanted in Nature," commanding what ought to be done and forbidding the opposite. The Stoic Seneca said similarly that "virtue is nothing other than right reason."[92] Medieval scholastics identified good actions with *recta ratio*, and Aquinas asserted that "in human affairs, a thing is said to be just, from being right, according to the rule of reason," adding that "the first rule of reason is the law of nature."[93] Richard Hooker wrote that "the lawes of well doing are the dictates of Right Reason."[94] Adopting the same language, Hobbes stated, in a sentence I have already quoted, that because men naturally shun death as the worst of evils, it is "neither absurd nor reprehensible" nor "against the dictates of true reason for a man to use all his endeavours to preserve and defend his Body, and the Members thereof from death and sorrows; but that which is not contrary to right reason, that all men account to be done justly and with right."[95]

Despite the similarities and continuities that associate him with the natural law tradition, Hobbes broke with this tradition in several major ways that define his subversive character and originality as a theorist of natural law. The first was the exceptional meaning he gave to the right reason of natural law by the priority and tightness of the connection he posited between it and the individual's passionate desire for self-preservation and the need for peace. As J.W.N. Watkins put it in his excellent study, *Hobbes's System of Ideas*, Hobbes based morality on men's interest and "deepest wants."[96] Many Hobbes scholars have noted the novelty and importance of this view linking the law of nature to the common human interest in self-preservation, but have often failed to perceive its full historical significance and implications.[97] The question that has mainly occupied their attention is whether and how the Hobbesian theory of natural law can possibly qualify as a *moral* theory when it commends as good only such actions as reason shows to be in the self-interest of individuals and in conformity with their desire.[98] The putting of this question, however, which has received different answers, neglects to take into account that the Hobbesian law of nature, as I have emphasized, incorporates a large body of moral values and virtues, including peace and peaceableness, a concern for life, civility, benevolence, and equal consideration for others, that would have to be a part of any true system of morality, irrespective of its underlying philosophic principles.[99] The question in any case, moreover, tends to slide over an absolutely vital prior point. For if we recall Hobbes's critique that natural law had become the most obscure of laws and that previous philosophers had built its foundations in the air, then it should be clear that his primary purpose was to give it a firm, unshakable foundation. This is the problem he thought he had solved by basing the law of nature on the observable universal human desire for self-preservation and what must rationally follow from this truth.

His formulation of the natural law is accordingly much more rigorous than the conception advanced by earlier natural law theorists such as the Stoics and the scholastics. The right reason he invokes is not a product of nature immanent in the world order but a foresighted pragmatic calculation, the mental "act of reasoning" or "true ratiocination" by individuals who perceive from clear principles of reason the means most conducive to their preservation. "[T]he whole breach of the Lawes of Nature," he therefore concludes, "consists in the false reasoning, or rather folly of those men who see not those duties they are necessarily to perform toward others in order to their owne conservation."[100] As I have previously pointed out, moreover, no preceding political theorist or writer on natural law had ever depicted human nature and man's condition in the state of nature so fully and vividly as Hobbes did, or with the unqualified negative conclusion that mankind's existence in this condition was solitary, nasty, brutish, and short. Unlike Hobbes, other Christian philosophers of natural law commonly held that God created men to fulfill certain ends proper to their nature as rational agents. They also supposed with little or no argument that although humans might be partially self-interested and were entitled to defend themselves, they were nevertheless endowed by nature with a benevolent sociability toward their fellow beings.[101]

For Hobbes, the chief rationale and purpose of political society is to enable men to live in peace and security under the protection of the sovereign's law. He fully realized, however, that the commonwealth exists not only for life but also for the sake of additional goods that human beings desire but cannot attain in the state of nature. These goods were the products of civilization, among which he mentions "commodious" and "contented" living, the various arts and sciences, happiness, and even living delightfully.[102] The first and basic precept of the law of nature, nevertheless, bids men to seek peace, and from this one moral rule he derived a number of other natural laws that were all instrumental to the achievement and maintenance of peace. The definition of the law of nature by other theorists, although it usually makes reference to the preservation of life and society, tends in comparison to be quite vague, low in content, and even somewhat question-begging. Aquinas, for example, who discussed the essence and different kinds of law in his *Summa Theologiae*, held that natural law is innate in human beings, and defined its first precept as "good is to be done and pursued and evil avoided." Noting that men have an inclination to good in that, like all substances, they seek their own preservation, he then affirmed that "natural law contains all that makes for the preservation of human life."[103] Suárez's treatise *On Laws and God the Lawgiver* defined the law of nature as a law of right reason that indicates what is good and evil and contains its own prohibition of evil and command of good. He also said that the precepts of natural law, which proceed from nature and from God as the author of nature, all tend to the same end, the due preservation and natural perfection or felicity of human nature.[104] Grotius's *Law of War and Peace* shared the common view that the law of nature consisted of self-evident principles and laid down the following definition: "The law of nature is a dictate of right reason, which points out that an act, according as it is or is not in conformity with rational nature, has in it a quality of moral baseness or moral necessity; and that in consequence, such an act is either forbidden or enjoined by the author of nature, God."[105] If natural law can be said to exist at all, then by affiliating it so immediately and instrumentally to the individual's need for self-preservation and the attainment of peace, Hobbes gave this concept a stronger grounding, greater clarity, and more substance than did any previous thinker.

Hobbes's second and most significant departure from the natural law tradition has to do with the legal status of the law of nature. He denies that it is properly or really law except if it is seen as the command of God. He makes this point at the conclusion of his account of the law of nature in all three of his major political treatises and most fully in *Leviathan*, which declares that the theorems of reason conducive to men's conservation cannot properly be called laws, because "law, properly, is the word of him that by right hath command over others. Yet if we consider the same theorems, as delivered in the word of God, that by right commandeth all things, then are they properly called laws."[106]

I noted in the first chapter the disagreement among Hobbes scholars as to whether or not Hobbes was a legal positivist. In my opinion, his definition of the natural law as theorems of reason in contrast to the definition of law as a command, and his claim that to speak of the law of nature as genuine law is improper unless this law is considered as God's command, brings Hobbes's legal positivism clearly into view as a new development in legal and political philosophy. The natural law tradition contained no precedent for the suggestion that the law of nature was not in itself law.[107] Prior theorists of natural law had no doubt that it was truly law and also considered it to be a higher law than human positive law, for which it set a standard of justice. Aquinas stated that "the validity of human law depends upon its justice" and that every humanly enacted law "possesses as much of the nature of law as the extent to which it is derived from the law of nature. If in any point it is at variance with the law of nature, it will no longer be law but the perversion of law."[108] The legal status of natural law was thus ascribed to its content as a morally just ordinance of right reason whose origin was traceable to nature and the reason or will of God. Its character as indisputable law, however, was distinct from the question of what made it obligatory. The usual answer was that God, the creator of both nature and reason, was the ultimate lawgiver who made the law of nature obligatory. It was in this sense that Richard Hooker stated that the laws of nature "do bind men absolutely, even as they are men."[109] Suárez, whose jurisprudence held that will, reason, and justice were necessary requirements of both natural law and law in general, stated that God's decree was the final source of the law of nature, and agreed with what he called "the common opinion found not only in the words of the Doctors, but also in the canon and civil law, that the body of natural law is a true body of law, and that the particular natural law is true law."[110]

How, then, does God fit into Hobbes's conception of the law of nature? A half-century ago A. E. Taylor and Howard Warrender were the best-known advocates of the position that God's command was essential for the Hobbesian law of nature to be a law and obligatory. Both held that Hobbes's moral philosophy was untenable unless the laws of nature derived their legal character from being the commands of God.[111] In his interesting essay, "God and Thomas Hobbes," Willis Glover argues similarly that Hobbes "recognized a general moral obligation to obey natural law as the command of God."[112] Frederick A. Olafson expressed the same view that God's command was necessary to give the law of nature its obligatory character.[113] More recently the issue has been discussed at length in A. P. Martinich's book, *The Two Gods of Leviathan*, a controversial defense of the religious against the secularist interpretation of Hobbes that tries to prove that God's command was a "necessary condition for a law of nature" for Hobbes and that he regarded the laws of nature as "literally" and "properly speaking, laws" because they are "divine laws."[114] Martinich advances several reasons for this opinion, none of which is persuasive. One is the name "law" in "law of nature," which he thinks must have been meant literally, since Hobbes never says he is using it figuratively. Yet the philosopher does plainly state that considered as theorems of reason conducing to men's preservation, the law of nature is not properly called a law, which surely does away with its literal meaning. The second of Martinich's arguments is that Hobbes's law of nature implies a commander, as indicated by its phrase, "by which a man is forbidden to do that," and by the fact that reason as such is powerless to forbid or do anything. In this case, though, Hobbes was probably speaking as people often do in common speech, when they forbid themselves from doing something they think wrong or unreasonable without supposing that anyone other is commanding them. A third reason offered by Martinich is that Hobbes's laws of nature are not merely descriptive or prudential but genuinely deontic, in conformity with the philosopher's distinction between a law and a right, which describes law as imposing obligation and abridging liberty.[115] This particular argument seems, however, to be question-begging, since it simply assumes that the obligation to obey natural law comes from God. Later, however, as will shortly be seen, Hobbes explains that this obligation derives from the civil law of the sovereign. A singular omission in Martinich's discussion of the Hobbesian laws of nature is that it pays almost no attention to Hobbes's account of the relationship between the natural and the civil law, even though this subject is essential to an understanding of the meaning and status of natural law in Hobbes's political and moral philosophy.[116]

Hobbes goes to considerable pains to prove that his laws of nature are a moral law whose precepts can all be confirmed in Scripture, and are therefore also divine law.[117] What he nevertheless refrains from saying is that all human beings owe obedience to these laws because they are God's commands. We should remember that Hobbes called natural law eternal and immutable, which means that it must antedate Scripture and the incarnation of Christ.[118] There would also be many people in different parts of the world who had never heard of the Christian God or the Scriptures. Hobbes's position thus appears to be that all who believe in God and scriptural revelation should obey the law of nature as God's command, since this law is confirmed in Scripture.[119] These believers would no doubt have included nearly all of Hobbes's contemporary readers; but he knew of course that there were atheists who would not have accepted that the law of nature came from God, and other people who, while they might acknowledge that God exists, did not believe that he took any interest in the affairs of men.[120] As a moral philosopher, Hobbes based his arguments on reason, although he also sought analogies and support for his conclusions in the Bible, because he was addressing Christian readers. It was chiefly on the foundations of reason and logic, nevertheless, that he strove to persuade.[121] Essentially, he intended his doctrine of natural law for all rational persons, whether religious Christians or not, and he never himself endorses the proposition that the law of nature as the conclusion of right reason is genuinely law to which obedience is due by everyone because it is the command of God.

How, then, does the law of nature become actual law in Hobbes's moral philosophy? At the beginning of part two of *Leviathan*, entitled "Of Commonwealth," he declares that since the laws of nature are contrary to such natural passions as partiality, pride, and revenge, they would fail to take effect "without the terror of some power to cause them to be observed." With respect to his third law of nature, which stated that covenants should be kept, he points out in the same place that "covenants without the sword are but words, and of no strength to secure a man at all." The conclusion he draws is that "notwithstanding the laws of nature," it is necessary for men to erect a power over themselves great enough to give them security and keep them in awe.[122] These remarks indicate that neither the rational content of the law of nature as a way to peace nor the belief in it as the command of God suffices to establish its status and obligatory force as actual law. They likewise indicate that the will and command of a visible sovereign power are necessary to convert the laws of nature from dictates of reason into true and enforceable law. In other words, for natural law to take effect, the commonwealth ruled by a sovereign invested with great power, including the power to legislate and inflict punishment on lawbreakers as a necessary attribute of sovereignty, must come into existence. In part two of *Leviathan*, Hobbes attempts to show how this can be done by means of mutual covenants made between the members of society, who create the commonwealth by consenting to renounce some of their rights and confer their power on one man or an assembly of men whom they authorize as sovereign to maintain internal peace and defend against foreign enemies.[123]

When his discussion of the commonwealth brings him to the analysis of civil law, Hobbes makes the novel claim that the civil law and natural law "contain each other and are of equal extent."[124] After first explaining that "law in general" is manifestly a "command" and an expression of will, he then defines civil law as the rules the sovereign as legislator of the commonwealth commands to every subject "for the distinction of right and wrong, that is to say, of what is contrary, and what is not contrary to the rule."[125] He insists that natural law and the civil law of the sovereign "are not different kinds, but different parts of law, whereof one part (being written) is called civil, the other (unwritten) natural." His justification for merging the two laws, as he reminds the reader, is that the moral virtues comprised in the law of nature "are not properly laws, but qualities that dispose men to peace and obedience." Hence, only when the commonwealth exists are the laws of nature "actually laws, and not before, as being then the commands of the commonwealth and therefore also civil laws; for it is the sovereign power that obliges men to obey them." The conclusion of this crucial argument is that "the law of nature is part of the civil law in all commonwealths of the world," and conversely, that "the civil law is part of the dictates of nature" that require "obedience to the civil law."[126]

Hobbes's remarkable discussion of civil law in chapter 26 of *Leviathan* sometimes refers to the law of nature as unwritten law, as law from all eternity, and as a moral law consisting of such virtues as justice and equity.[127] It also distinguishes natural law from positive law, the latter consisting of laws not from all eternity but made by the will of the sovereign power.[128] His fusion of the law of nature and the civil law as being parts of one law, however, was a radical innovation in the theory of natural law. While previous authors held that natural law and human positive or civil law are related and that natural law sanctions and enjoins obedience to civil law, they considered the two as different kinds of law and never affiliated them in the way Hobbes did. Grotius describes human law as municipal law emanating from the civil power of the state. He makes a careful distinction between natural and municipal law, noting that the obligation to obey the latter derives its force from natural law.[129] He also declares that "municipal law cannot enjoin anything which the law of nature forbids, or forbid what the law of nature enjoins."[130] Aquinas was even more explicit about the relationship between the two laws. He defined law in general not as a command but as "an ordinance of reason for the common good," and distinguished human law from other kinds of law as being the enactment of a human legislator who had the care of the community. Natural law authorized and justified the moral obligation of obedience to human positive law, whose validity depended on its consonance with natural law and therefore on its conformity to justice, as well as on its being properly promulgated.[131] Aquinas also makes it clear that because the precepts of natural law are very general, they need to be supplemented by the particular determinations of civil law in order to provide legal solutions to specific problems of regulation and coordination in the varied circumstances of human communities. "These particular determinations," he said, "devised by human reason, are called human law, provided the other essential conditions of law be observed."[132] In Aquinas's theory of law, therefore, the law of nature as a higher law and human positive law as a derivative law are distinct though complementary laws.[133]

Hobbes's conception was directly contrary to that of Grotius, Aquinas, and other philosophers of natural law. By absorbing natural law into civil law, he made the law of nature into a pillar of political absolutism in the state and affirmed the validity of all civil law in the strongest possible terms. "It is not possible," he says in *De Cive*, "to command aught by the civill Law, contrary to the Lawes of nature."[134] The explanation of this extreme position, which has no parallel in the previous theory of natural law, lies mainly in Hobbes's fear of the danger of private judgment as a threat to the stability and existence of the commonwealth. The state of nature as he depicts it is essentially one in which anarchic private judgment prevails and everyone is free by natural right to decide what is just and unjust and good and evil according to their own personal reason. That is why men's natural condition is a state of war. The law of nature requires that private be superseded by public judgment for the sake of peace, and with the institution of the commonwealth, all private judgment as to what is equity, justice, and moral virtue must submit to the public reason and will of the sovereign, which is contained in the civil law.[135] In discussing the causes that weaken and tend to destroy a commonwealth, Hobbes includes the seditious doctrine that "every private man is judge of good and evil action." This would be true, he says, "in the condition of mere nature, where there are no civil laws," but under government "the measure of good and evil actions is the civil law" and the legislator is the judge.[136] It becomes the case, therefore, that the civil law of the state is to be accepted as right reason in the decision of controversies.[137]

Natural law in Hobbes's moral philosophy therefore appears to efface itself, as Sharon Lloyd has aptly put it.[138] Absorbed by civil law, it seems to become relativized to conform in every state to whatever the civil law commands. This is not the whole story, however, and we must ask if Hobbes left any role at all for the law of nature to serve as an independent standard for judging the sovereign's laws and actions as ruler. I believe he does leave space for it to play a role of this kind, as will be shown later in this essay, and it is surprising that Hobbes scholars have paid so little attention to this aspect of his philosophy of natural law. In keeping with his legal positivism, however, a judgment founded on the law of nature could only be a moral, not a legal, judgment. It is thus by converting natural law into a set of purely moral principles that Hobbes, as I have suggested earlier, could be at the same time both a legal positivist and part of the natural law tradition.[139]

Natural Rights and the Creation of the Commonwealth

In his excellent study *The Idea of Natural Rights*, Brian Tierney devotes very little space to Hobbes. He summarily dismisses Hobbes's conception of natural rights as an aberration from the mainstream of natural rights thinking that flowed from medieval jurists and scholastic philosophers to seventeenth-century thinkers such as Locke and to the subsequent writers of the Enlightenment.[140] This seems to me to be a mistaken judgment, for it is arguable that Hobbes's discussion of natural rights is one of his most original and significant contributions to political philosophy, even if he had no use for the concept of natural rights as a justification for resistance to rulers or for setting political limits on government and making it accountable.

Let us keep in mind that Hobbes conceived of a right and a natural right as synonymous with the freedom to act or to forbear. For him, law, as he always stressed, whether natural or civil, is the opposite of a right, a restriction or infringement on freedom that imposes the obligation either to do or to refrain from doing something. In the development of the theory of natural rights, as I pointed out earlier, most political philosophers understood natural rights to be the offspring of natural law. For all these thinkers the law of nature logically precedes rights and, in accord with reason, creates and confers such rights on individuals as the right to defend themselves, to acquire ownership of land, and to establish and appoint governments to which the people or society convey or transfer specific powers. In the Hobbesian scheme, however, natural rights do not derive from natural law; they have an independent existence as a primordial entitlement to freedom bestowed equally by nature on every individual and fully operative in the state of nature. According to this right, human beings living in a condition without government or civil laws have an unlimited freedom, sanctioned by reason, to do or use everything they deem needful to protect their lives and bodies. As far as I know, Hobbes was the first political philosopher to give the concept of the right of nature a status prior to and independent of the law of nature.

Having shown that the natural right of individuals to all things must produce a condition of permanent war in which no one has a right to anything, Hobbes then faced the challenge of explaining how men could divest themselves of a portion of their natural rights, as the law of nature instructed them to do, and create a common power over themselves to give them peace, security, and political order under the rule of the sovereign. To grasp Hobbes's thought, it is necessary to realize that despite his basing the existence of the commonwealth on the rational human desire for self-preservation and the need for peace, he placed only a partial reliance on the effect of reason. While the moral law of nature taught men to seek peace and the means to attain it, and was binding on conscience even in the state of nature, Hobbes never forgot that certain passions springing from pride and partiality could often deflect the human will from consistently pursuing the path to peace that reason pointed out. It was necessary, therefore, to supplement the rational precepts of the law of nature with the fear of institutionalized coercion. "[T]he bonds of words," as Hobbes typically says, "are too weak to bridle men's ambition, avarice, anger, and other passions, without the fear of some coercive power."[141] This power to compel and enforce is embodied in the commonwealth and its sovereign.

In *The Elements of Law* and *De Cive*, Hobbes had spoken of the origins of sovereignty in connection with the way men could relinquish, transfer, or convey a right to one person or a council of men by means of contracts and covenants.[142] *Leviathan* contains the fullest description of the process of relinquishing rights, basing it on the novel conception of authorization, representation, and artificial person, which Hobbes here introduces into his political theory for the first time, and on a "covenant of every man with every man."[143] In the sixteenth chapter, entitled "Of Persons, Authors, and Things Personated," he presents an elaborate account of how it is possible for a multitude of individuals to become a united entity or one people by designating and authorizing a person to act for and represent them. A multitude of men, he argues,

> are made one person, when they are by one man, or one person, represented so that it be done with the consent of everyone in that multitude in particular. For it is the unity of the representer, not the unity of the represented, that maketh the person one.[144]

They accomplish this purpose of representation through a covenant which is more like a hypothetical contrivance than a literal fact, because it is made, Hobbes says,

> in such manner *as if* [my italics] every man should say to every man I authorize and give up my right of governing myself to this man, or to this assembly of men, on this condition, that thou give up thy right to him, and authorize all his actions in like manner.[145]

By this compact with one another, individuals confer all their power and strength on one man or an assembly of men, to whom they consent to submit their wills and judgment in everything that concerns "the common peace and safety." In so doing, they reduce their separate individual wills to a true unity in a single will, thus becoming at once both a civil society and a body politic represented by the sovereign, whom they authorize to "bear their person" and of whose actions in relation to the common peace and safety every particular man "acknowledge[s] himself to be the author." Despite the origin of the commonwealth in the act of a multitude of individuals, Hobbes calls their agreement "more than consent or concord," since by its means they are absorbed as a people into the state personality of the sovereign, who represents them and whose will and acts in matters of state are both logically and legally their own. This, the philosopher says in a memorable passage, "is the generation of that great Leviathan, or rather (to speak more reverently) of that Mortal God to which we owe, under the Immortal God, our peace and defence."[146]

"Leviathan," Hobbes's extraordinary symbol of the commonwealth and absolute sovereignty, was the name of the mighty sea monster described in the biblical book of Job. In the introduction to his treatise, however, Hobbes likened Leviathan not to a mortal god but to an artificial man fashioned by human art, but far greater and stronger than a natural man, in which sovereignty was the "artificial soul . . . giving life and motion to the whole body."[147] The Hobbesian commonwealth seems therefore to be a mechanical organism made by men. It is pictured in the famous and frequently reproduced engraving on the title page of the original edition of *Leviathan*, the upper half of which shows the image of the colossal artificial man Leviathan looming hugely over a peaceful landscape of country and city, crowned and bearing a sword and crozier as the signs that he is the imperial ruler of state and church, his arms and body composed of a mass of tiny human figures who are looking up at him and united in his person. Written above his head is the Latin Vulgate text from the book of Job: "There is no power on earth like unto him" (Job 41:24).[148] This title page corresponds pictorially to Hobbes's definition of the commonwealth as

> one person, of whose acts a great multitude, by mutual covenants one with another, have made themselves every one the author, to the end he may use the strength and means of them all, as he shall think expedient, for their peace and common defence. And he that carrieth this person is called Sovereign, and said to have Sovereign Power; and every one besides, his Subject.[149]

The commonwealth, *civitas*, or political order owes its being, therefore, to the consent and willingness of its individual members to be governed by a sovereign power, a person who may be one or many, to which they have relinquished and transferred their natural right to govern themselves. I have noted earlier that with respect to their origins Hobbes distinguished two kinds of commonwealths. One kind stems from the institution of individuals, who agree between themselves to choose a sovereign, either one man or an assembly of men, and to surrender to it their natural right to all things in exchange for the peace, protection, and security of government. The other kind derives from force, conquest, and acquisition, when men submit to a sovereign power to preserve their lives.[150] In the case of the latter, Hobbes is emphatic that "it is not . . . the victory that giveth the right of dominion over the vanquished, but his own covenant."[151] Hence even government by conquest rests ultimately on consent, and the obligation of obedience in the defeated people originates in their voluntary submission and consequent relinquishment of rights to the victor.

Grotius had devoted a historical and comparative discussion in *The Law of War and Peace* to the subject of sovereignty, which he defined as "a power whose actions are not subject to the legal control of another, so that they cannot be rendered void by the operation of another human will."[152] Hobbes's treatment of sovereignty gave prominence to the sovereign's will but dealt with the concept mainly analytically. In whatever way the commonwealth and sovereignty originated, the rights of the sovereign are said by Hobbes to be the same, and they are very extensive.[153] The sovereign has made no contract with its subjects, who have created the sovereign power by agreements between themselves to acknowledge its acts as their own.

Therefore it cannot commit a breach of contract, or forfeit its power, or be accused by any of its subjects of an injury; it cannot be punished by its subjects; it is the sole judge of what is necessary for their peace and defense and of what doctrines are to be taught; it determines the rules of property by which subjects know what is their own, and the rules of good, evil, lawful, and unlawful that are contained in the civil laws of the commonwealth; it is the sole legislator and supreme judge of controversies; it decides the times and occasions of war and peace; it is the supreme commander in war; it appoints all magistrates, officers, ministers, advisers, and commanders; it is the source of all rewards, punishment, and public honors; its rights are indivisible, inseparable, and inalienable.[154] Each of these attributes of sovereignty and all of them together may be regarded as an analytic deduction from Hobbes's theoretical construct of the sum of powers necessary in government for the maintenance of the commonwealth's peace and stability.

Because he was so convinced of the necessity of absolute government, Hobbes was incapable of conceiving sovereignty in other than indivisible and unitary terms as the wielder of a comprehensive authority. He recognized, however, the objection to his doctrine of sovereignty that the condition of subjects under such an "unlimited power" would be "very miserable" because of their vulnerability to its "lusts and other irregular passions." To this argument his main answer was that life could never be without some inconveniences, and that the worst thing that could befall a people under any type of government amounted to little compared with the miseries and calamities incident to a civil war, the death of sovereignty, and the "dissolute condition of masterless men, without subjection to law and a coercive power to tie their hands from rapine and revenge." Noting the restiveness of subjects when pressured by government to contribute taxes for their own defense, he observed that

> all men are by nature provided of notable multiplying glasses (that is their passions and self love), through which every little payment appeareth a great grievance, but are destitute of those prospective glasses (namely moral and civil science), to see afar off the miseries that hang over them, and cannot without such payments be avoided.[155]

Hobbes would have written these lines with the memory still fresh in his mind of the popular complaints in the later 1630s against Charles I's financial exactions, in particular ship money, and the ensuing revolution and bloody civil war in England during the 1640s, with its great losses of life and property and its overthrow of kingship. In exalting sovereignty with such a panoply of powers, however, he could not have foreseen or imagined the incarnation of its will in the unspeakable terror, repression, violence, mass slaughter, and genocide brought upon their own peoples and the world by the leviathan fascist, Nazi, and communist states of the twentieth century.

The principle of the right of nature runs through Hobbes's moral and political philosophy and has by no means finished its work with the creation of the commonwealth. Despite the range of rights and powers possessed by the sovereign, its subjects have not parted with all their rights and retain certain ones that nature has given them. These are largely rights that are not possible for an individual to renounce or alienate by any covenant. Hobbes explains that the renunciation or transfer of rights is a voluntary act, and "of the voluntary acts of every man the object is some good to himself." He never loses sight of the fact that the motive and object of human beings in surrendering rights to the sovereign is to assure themselves of a number of goods, beginning with security of person, life, and "the means of so preserving life as not to be weary of it." Hence, among the natural rights retained by subjects is the right of resisting and defending oneself to save one's life from death, wounds, or imprisonment, and the right not to incriminate oneself under questioning or to be accused by testimony obtained through torture.[156] He names additional reserved rights in his discussion of the liberty of subjects, which states that "every subject has liberty in all things the right whereof cannot by covenant be transferred."[157] Thus, a subject may resist being killed at the sovereign's command, even though justly condemned. He is also not bound to confess to a crime done by himself or obey a command to kill himself or another man. He may refuse to fight against an enemy of the commonwealth, although such refusal may justly be punished by the sovereign with death, but the subject will be guilty of no injustice if he finds a sufficient soldier to take his place in war.[158] Should many men join together to resist the sovereign or commit a crime punishable by death, they have the right to persist in their resistance once begun and to defend their lives, unless they are offered a pardon, in which case they are obliged to desist from their actions taken in self-defense.[159]

With respect to the natural rights remaining in the subject, Hobbes makes two significant general comments. The first is that if the sovereign commands a subject "to execute any dangerous or dishonourable" duty, the subject may refuse if the command is contrary to the purpose for which sovereignty was created. The rule Hobbes accordingly lays down is that "when . . . our refusal to obey frustrates the end for which the sovereignty was ordained, then there is no liberty to refuse; otherwise there is."[160] The second comment points out that the obligation of subjects to the sovereign is understood to last no longer than the sovereign's power to protect them: "the right men have by nature to protect themselves," he says, "when none else can protect them, can by no covenant be relinquished," because "the end of obedience is protection." Sovereignty is mortal, and should it be overthrown in a foreign or internal war, its subjects are absolved from obedience to it.[161]

Despite the tight structure of sovereignty and obedience Hobbes built into his political theory, his own logic, as the above statements indicate, made it impossible for him to avoid leaving an opening for the natural right of self-preservation and its ramifications that human beings retain under government. It cannot escape notice that only the personal judgment of the individual subject is capable of deciding whether a command of the sovereign is contrary to the end for which sovereignty was ordained and therefore may be refused or resisted, and whether in a war or rebellion the sovereign still has the power to protect its subjects. There are also other aspects of government in the Hobbesian commonwealth in which decision by the personal judgment of the subject cannot be excluded. I return to this topic in the next chapter.

Consent, Fear, Obligation, and Populism

Hobbes is a philosopher of natural right not only because the right of nature plays such a prominent role in the generation of the commonwealth but because of the large significance his political philosophy assigns to rights and consent. A commonwealth by institution presupposes the consent by covenant between free individuals to renounce their right to all things and authorize a government and sovereign power to rule over them. A commonwealth by acquisition seems more problematic, but here too Hobbes is quite definite that "it is not . . . the victory that giveth the right of dominion over the vanquished" but the latter's "own covenant" and "consent." Nor is the vanquished, he adds, "obliged because he is conquered . . . but because he cometh in and submitteth to the victor."[162] I don't think it an exaggeration to say that all obligation in Hobbes's moral and political theory derives initially or originally from the consent of the individual based on rational, passional, and moral considerations. At a later stage obligation may be imposed by the civil laws, but its beginning lies in the assent of the individual subject to live under the government of the sovereign. "[I]n the act of our submission," Hobbes declares, consists "both our obligation and our liberty . . . there being no obligation on any man which ariseth not from some act of his own; for all men are equally by nature free."[163] This proposition is a strong confirmation of Hobbes's membership in the natural rights tradition, and it also subverts the transcendental grounding of moral and political obligation in the law of nature and decree of God by locating the ultimate source of such obligation in the consent and voluntary action of each individual person.

Hobbes's emphasis on consent raises the issue of the place of fear and coercion in his view of obligation. He addresses this subject, which is a general problem in moral philosophy, in all three of his political treatises and refers to it as the "usuall" and "often moved question" of "Whether Compacts extorted from us through fear, do oblige or not."[164] Grotius had dealt with the same question in *The Law of War and Peace* in a chapter on promises. There the Dutch jurist stated that "on the whole I accept the opinion of those who think that a person who makes a promise under the influence of fear is bound by it. . . . For in such a case there is a consent, not conditional . . . but absolute."[165] Hobbes's position was similar and articulated most fully and relentlessly in *Leviathan*. Essentially he held that "fear and liberty are consistent," meaning that fear does not preclude voluntary action.[166] Both he and Grotius cited the well-known instance, first mentioned in Aristotle's *Nicomachean Ethics*, of the man who throws his goods into the sea to save his ship from sinking. Hobbes commented that since the man could have refused to do this action but did it very willingly, it was a free action.[167] In another example he maintained that even in the commonwealth a man forced to redeem himself from a thief by promising him money was obligated to pay unless the civil law absolved him.[168] In general he observed that all actions men do in the commonwealth for fear of the law are actions they had "liberty to omit."[169] Among the most important of the laws of nature for Hobbes and all theorists of natural law was the injunction to abide by covenants (*pacta sunt servanda*).[170] This is one of the reasons why he held that covenants made from fear are binding in the state of nature.

If such covenants, "entered into by fear, in the condition of mere nature," weren't obligatory, he said, it would be hard to understand how individuals in the state of nature could emerge from this condition.[171] Hobbes decisively rejected the view that covenants proceeding from fear of death or violence were void. If this were true, he said, no man in any kind of commonwealth could be obliged to obedience."[172] He sometimes distinguished between being obliged to obey the law, which required obedience because one has promised, and being also tied to obey it, the tie being the compulsion on the person "to make good his promise, for fear of the punishment appointed by the Law."[173] I do not believe he deserves any criticism for stressing the role of fear in the compliance with law, since in all legal systems the laws, especially the criminal law, are enforced by punitive sanctions a potential lawbreaker may fear. He did allow, however, that following the establishment of the commonwealth, the civil law of the sovereign might prohibit or cancel certain kinds of promises extracted by fear.[174] "We are oblig'd," he said in *De Cive*, "by promises proceeding from fear, except the Civill Law forbid them, by vertue whereof, that which is promised becomes unlawfull."[175]

Hobbes's concern with fear and the enforcement of promises and covenants was centered less, however, on the private transactions between subjects than on the problem of ensuring the obedience of subjects to the sovereign's law. In his discussion of covenants, he reiterated his belief that the force of words was "too weak to hold men to the performance of their covenants," but suggested that human nature contained two possible helps to strengthen their force. These were men's "fear of the consequence of breaking their word" and "a glory and pride in appearing not to need to break it." The latter quality, he thought, was too rare to be counted on, and he therefore concluded that in the case of most people "the passion to reckon on is fear," both fear of God and invisible spirits, and fear of the power of those offended by promise-breaking.[176]

Since Hobbes's focus on covenant associated him with the contractual tradition in political philosophy, certain of his concepts and political language involving men's original freedom, natural rights, and the foundation of the state in consent and contract were similar to those of the populist and revolutionary theorists of the sixteenth and seventeenth centuries, the forerunners of a later liberalism and constitutionalism, who defended the doctrines of popular sovereignty and the right of resistance to unjust kings and rulers. Gierke and J. N. Figgis pointed out many years ago that the Monarchomachs, the antimonarchical writers of the early modern period, generally based their claim to resist the monarch on the notion of an original contract. All of these writers agreed that men were originally free, that the ruler is contractually appointed to govern by the people, and that the ruler's authority was limited by the rights of the governed. They accordingly also insisted on the people's right in the case of misgovernment to forcibly resist and depose a king who became a tyrant.[177] In *Vindiciae contra Tyrannos* (1579) (*A Defense of Liberty againt Tyrants*), one of the most famous revolutionary tracts of the age and a work Hobbes may have known,[178] the contractual principle was invoked to support the claim that kings were originally created by the people and that their rule is based on a compact with the people by which they are obliged to govern justly. "In all legitimate governments," the *Vindiciae*'s author maintained, "a compact is always to be found."[179]

Some of the English political writers of the mid-seventeenth century who justified the revolt against the Stuart monarchy and the political changes that accompanied it similarly tended to base their argument on the notion of a political contract and the right of the people. Henry Parker, one of the most prominent publicists on the parliamentary side, claimed that all power "is originally inherent in the people" and derived by "common consent" from pacts and agreements by which the people conferred authority conditionally upon rulers.[180] The Levellers, a democratic movement of populist radicalism that sprang up during the English revolution, seized on the principle of the individual's native right to freedom to justify their entire program of political reform and equality. "By naturall birth," one of them wrote, "all men are equally and alike borne to like propriety [property], liberty, and freedome, and as we are delivered of God by the hand of nature into this world, everyone with an innate natural freedome . . . even so are we to live, every one equally and alike to enjoy his Birthright and priviledge."[181] The poet Milton's revolutionary tract *The Tenure of Kings and Magistrates*, published in 1649 to justify the accountability of kings and the execution of Charles I, declared that "No man who knows aught, can be so stupid to deny that all men naturally were born free." It was manifest, Milton maintained, that all government originated in the consent of the governed and that "the power of kings and magistrates is nothing else but what is only derivative, transferred, and committed to them in trust from the people to the common good of them all, in whom the power yet remains fundamentally and cannot be taken from them without a violation of their natural birthright."[182]

Hobbes was of course familiar with these populist conceptions, which he could have encountered in the political literature of the sixteenth century and in the debates that preceded and accompanied the English revolution. He could equally have found some of them in the natural law tradition itself, which was in general incapable of imagining that any earthly power could be above the law, as the Hobbesian sovereign was. Not many years before Hobbes wrote, the eminent philosopher and jurist Suárez stated his agreement with the "common opinion of the jurists" and Aquinas that all power resides immediately in the community and that in order to be justly transmitted to a given individual or prince, it must be bestowed by the community's consent. And even after power has been transferred, Suárez maintained, the community always remains its immediate possessor by virtue of being its source.[183]

Hobbes regarded the revolutionary principles of his time as poisonous, seditious doctrines that contributed to the dissolution of government. Among them were such opinions as the pretence of a right to resist the sovereign, that liberty is every man's inheritance and birthright, that the sovereign is subject to the civil law, that every subject has an absolute right to his property that excludes the sovereign, and that it is lawful and praiseworthy to kill tyrants.[184] His own political theory succeeded in adapting the language of contract and rights to his advocacy of authoritarian government and in canceling the populist and revolutionary implications of this language by his concept of absolute sovereignty. The sovereign power, as he expounds its genesis, is not a party to a contract with its subjects and therefore cannot commit any breach of legal obligation to them. The people cannot be counterposed to the sovereign as a separate and superior political entity, because without the sovereign in which it is collectively merged, the people does not even exist and is merely a number of dissociated individuals. This was the ground of Hobbes's insistence on the difference between a multitude and the people and of his claim that the people cannot be a body "distinct . . . from him or them that have the sovereignty over them." The same reasoning enabled him to maintain by a logical and verbal sleight of hand that the people rules in every form of government, even in a monarchy, because the sovereign always represents its will.[185] As I have already mentioned, in *Leviathan* Hobbes developed this argument further with the help of his new notion of authorization, representation, and artificial person, which made the theoretical bond and identity between the sovereign and its subjects as close as it could possibly be. He might have come by this idea as an extension of the legal doctrine, to which he refers in his previous treatises, that conceived of the corporation as a single person.[186] Quentin Skinner has recently suggested, however, that Hobbes was indebted for this new way of explicating the covenant to the language of the parliamentarian and radical political writers of the 1640s. One of its possible sources, as he notes, was Henry Parker, who in 1642 wrote that "God is the free and voluntary Author" of the powers "derived" into the hands of kings and magistrates and that the people are always "the Authors, or ends of all power" and therefore "the finall cause of Regall Authoritie."[187] Parker, however, hardly intended the same meaning as Hobbes did, and if the latter did make use of some of these writers, he harnessed their thoughts to his authoritarian theory of government.

Despite its relationship to the right of nature and the presupposition of consent and authorization, Hobbes's doctrine of absolute and indivisible sovereignty left no room for the limits on government that populist and contractual theorists postulated. He ridiculed the idea that a commonwealth could be constituted in such manner as to limit and moderate the sovereign power.[188] Taking into consideration the quite influential theory of a mixed monarchy or government whose virtue was supposed to lie in its balance of regal, aristocratic, and democratic elements, he pronounced a polity of this kind to be untenable and impossible. A mixed monarchy, he said, "is not government, but division of the commonwealth into three factions." If there had not first been in England a widely received opinion, he pointed out, that the sovereign power was divided between the king, the House of Lords, and the House of Commons, the civil war could not have occurred.[189] In opposition to the notion of a divided sovereignty, he maintained that there were only three separate forms of commonwealth, namely, monarchy, aristocracy, and democracy, each of which was defined by its different kind of sovereign power, either a single person, or an assembly of part of the people, or an assembly of all the people. Terms like oligarchy and tyranny, he believed, which were mentioned in histories and books of policy, were not names of other forms of government but simply names of the same forms when they are "misliked." Hence, subjects discontented under a monarchy called it a tyranny, those displeased with aristocracy called it oligarchy, and those grieved under a democracy called it anarchy.[190] This was Hobbes's incisive rhetorical and deconstructive analysis of the language of political sedition and rebellion.

He admitted that the greatest objection to his theory of sovereignty was its actual practice or instantiation, "when men ask where and when such power has by subjects been acknowledged." His answer to this question was another question: "when or where has there been a kingdom long free from sedition and civil war." For him, any government that lacked an absolute sovereign with all the combined rights and powers he attributed to it was built on fragile foundations, fashioned contrary to the rules and principles of civil science and prone to dissolution.[191]

CHAPTER 3

The Sovereign and the Law of Nature

Thomas Hobbes's moral and political philosophy is an intricate system of interrelated concepts that are designed to support one another in demonstrating the causes and nature of the commonwealth and the inestimable benefits it brings to human beings. The capstone of his political theory is the doctrine of sovereignty, which postulates that a commonwealth in any of its three forms, whether a monarchy, aristocracy, or democracy, necessitates the existence of a supreme sovereign power possessed of a comprehensive authority to govern its subjects. To this sole power the subjects have relinquished or transferred a significant portion of their natural rights as individuals in authorizing it to represent them and bear their person. By means of this transfer, they have ceased to be a multitude of separate beings and become a commonwealth, body politic, or state united by a single will expressed in the will of the sovereign to which they owe absolute obedience.

The Theory of Sovereignty

When Hobbes conceived the extraordinary image of the monstrous artificial man Leviathan as the personification of sovereignty, he rose to a visionary height of insight in creating a lasting symbol of the omnipotent state. Although he did his best to demonstrate that the sovereign with its extensive powers was an office confirmed by the Scriptures and stood as "God's vicegerent on earth" with the authority "under God . . . of governing Christian people,"[1] Leviathan in his political philosophy was a contrivance made by men, a work of human reason independent of divine grace whose powers were instrumental to its function of providing the members of the commonwealth with peace and protection. I have touched in the preceding chapter on the various powers of the sovereign, to which Hobbes devotes a great deal of attention and whose importance in his political theory it is impossible to exaggerate. He insists that they can be neither limited nor divided without endangering political stability. In claiming to have shown, as he said, that "a commonwealth without sovereign power is but a word without substance, and cannot stand,"[2] he could not of course ignore the fact that few if any polities in recorded history actually possessed the fully achieved absolute sovereignty with all its attributes that he posited as fundamental to and constituting the soul of government. In consequence, he may at times seem to waver between the idea that sovereignty constitutes the defining feature of any body politic, even though in many instances its powers are less than the total he considers to be logically requisite to it, and the idea that sovereignty will be found to exist in its complete and necessary panoply of attributes only in a body politic that has been well constructed according to the principles of civil science and hence is capable of lasting indefinitely.[3]

Hobbes was not the first political thinker to put forward a doctrine of sovereignty. Medieval popes, canonists, and theorists had adumbrated this concept in developing a juridical and theological interpretation of papal authority as consisting of a divinely bestowed plenitude of power by which every pope as the immediate successor of St. Peter and vicar of Christ is the supreme legislator for the church.[4] In the later sixteenth century the noted French lawyer, political theorist, and polymath Jean Bodin explicitly defined the principle of sovereignty in his treatise, *Six Livres de La République* (1576), which no lawyer or political philosopher, he said, had yet done. He described it as "the most high, absolute, and perpetual power over the citizens and subjects in a Commonweale," unrestrained by laws, and "as the greatest power to command." In favor of killing witches but also a believer in religious tolerance, Bodin (d. 1596) lived through France's destructive civil wars between Catholics and Huguenots lasting more than three decades, which brought the authority of the French monarchy to a low point and threw the kingdom into anarchy. He was therefore profoundly concerned with the idea of sovereignty as a supreme ordering power. He saw its essence and highest mark in the sovereign's position as the state's sole legislator who makes and gives law to all and is itself above and not subject to positive law. He also held that sovereignty was indivisible and its powers inalienable and perpetual. While accepting that there were only three types of state, monarchy, aristocracy, and democracy, each defined by its form of sovereignty, he nevertheless distinguished several different kinds of monarchy, which he called legitimate or royal, lordly, and tyrannical. Despite the unitary conception of absolute power, which shaped his view of sovereignty and kingship, he maintained that all sovereigns were bound by the law of nature, and that in a legitimate monarchy, such as the monarchy of France, the sovereign was also obligated to respect the private property and natural liberty of its subjects.[5] In the case of France, moreover, the sovereign was also obliged to observe the fundamental constitutional laws of the kingdom, which regulated the succession to the throne and prohibited alienation of the royal demesne. Because of these immanent limits in certain instances, scholars have questioned the consistency of Bodin's theory of sovereignty.

Bodin's treatise, which exerted a wide influence, was included in the Hardwick library and was familiar to Hobbes, who cited it in *The Elements of Law* to support his argument that the rights of sovereignty are indivisible.[6] Unlike Hobbes, however, Bodin's analysis of sovereignty and other aspects of government was embedded in a great mass of historical erudition and empirical examples, which made it a veritable political encyclopedia. Despite the amplitude of his conception of sovereignty, he qualified its powers in several respects. Hobbes's theory of sovereignty, in contrast, was clarity itself and logically consistent as an analytic deduction from his understanding of the nature and function of government. It differed from Bodin's, moreover, in that his sovereign as supreme power and commander was not subject to any legal limits in the state that it ruled. As I show later in this chapter, the Hobbesian sovereign's relationship to the law of nature was not one of legal but of moral obligation.

Unique to Hobbes as a theorist of sovereignty was also the ingenious argument he developed in *Leviathan* that since its subjects have authorized the sovereign power to represent and bear their person, its actions are likewise theirs; they therefore contradict themselves should they oppose an action of the sovereign, because its will contains and expresses their will also. As Hobbes put it in his discussion of the institution of sovereignty in *Leviathan*,

> because every subject is by this institution author of all the actions and judgments of the sovereign . . . it follows that, whatsoever he doth, it can be no injury to any of his subjects, nor ought he to be by any of them accused of injustice. For he that doth anything by authority from another doth therein no injury to him by whose authority he acteth; but by this institution of a commonwealth every particular man is the author of all the sovereign doth; and consequently he that complaineth of injury from his sovereign complaineth of that whereof he himself is the author, and therefore ought not to accuse any man but himself; no nor himself of injury, because to do injury to one's self is impossible.[7]

This argument, in which the implicit meaning of injury is a breach of covenant, may seem too good to be true and would fail to convince those who could not conceive that by creating sovereignty, they had agreed to authorize all of the sovereign's actions. It is nevertheless fully compatible with the premises from which Hobbes deduces the necessity of sovereignty.

In the Hobbesian scheme, the sovereign is the commonwealth's absolute ruler and sole lawmaker, legally unaccountable to its subjects, who can neither accuse nor punish it. "Power unlimited," he says, "is absolute sovereignty."[8] He also avers that in his understanding, it appears from both reason and Scripture that the sovereign power in any of the three forms of government "is as great as possibly men can be imagined to make it," and, moreover, that while men may fancy many evil consequences from such an unlimited power, the consequences of its absence in the perpetual war of all against all would be far worse.[9] In a brief summary of "the notes of supreme command," he includes the making and abrogation of laws, the determination of war and peace, the judgment of all controversies personally or through appointed judges, and the choice of all magistrates, ministers and counselors.[10] This listing does not exhaust the powers of sovereignty, which are set out more fully in the eighteenth chapter of *Leviathan* and are also explicated in other parts of that work.

The core of Hobbes's doctrine of sovereignty as the soul of the state is the sovereign's unrestricted power to make and abrogate law. *Leviathan*'s masterly chapter 26 on the civil laws, which delineates their distinction from other kinds of law and their essential nature as the sovereign's command, amounts to a small treatise and is one of the most important in the work. Committed to the imperative theory of law, Hobbes thinks of civil law entirely as an act of will expressing the sovereign's reason. The sovereign is accordingly the supreme judge and interpreter of the law. Hobbes understood that all laws "have need of interpretation," and while agreeing with the doctrine of the lawyers that the law can never be opposed to reason, he explains that the only reason to be considered in construing the law is the will and intention of the sovereign, not the reason of lawyers, legal commentators, moral philosophers, or any private reason.[11] When custom and long usage have acquired the authority of law, it is due not to prescription of time but to the presumption that the sovereign has tacitly accepted and consented to them as law.[12] Hobbes was critical of the English common law as a law founded on precedent and judicial decisions. He denies the opinion of the famous English jurist, judge, and legal commentator Sir Edward Coke (d. 1634), a champion of the supremacy of the common law and judicial independence, that the sort of reason required for the understanding the law is not natural human reason but the "artificial perfection of reason" of the lawyer that is attainable only by long study, observation, and experience. Long study of the law, Hobbes comments, if built on false grounds, will simply increase and confirm erroneous sentences. It is not the wisdom of subordinate judges, therefore,

> but the reason of this our artificial man the commonwealth, and his command that maketh law; and the commonwealth being in their representative but one person, there cannot easily arise any contra-

diction in the laws; and when there doth, the same reason is able, by interpretation or alteration, to take it away. In all courts of justice, the sovereign (which is the person of the commonwealth) is he that judgeth; the subordinate judge ought to have regard for the reason which moved his sovereign to make such law, that his sentence may be according thereunto; which is the sovereign's sentence.[13]

I shall return to Hobbes's discussion of the civil law when examining his conception of its relationship to the law of nature.

No less radical and uncompromising in Hobbes's thought on sovereignty is a corollary of the sovereign's sole legislative power, its right to determine and prescribe the rules of private property by which citizens and subjects know what is their own and what belongs to another. The right and the definition of property in particular commonwealths, Hobbes held, can only be the creation of the civil law.[14] Thus he comments that although theft is forbidden by the laws of nature,

> what is to be called Theft . . . is not to be determined by the naturall, but by the civill Law; for not every taking away of the thing which another possesseth, but onely another mans goods is theft; but what is ours, and what anothers, is a question belonging to the civill Law.[15]

While subjects have rights of property against one another that are enforceable by law, they have none that can compel the sovereign power. In one of his boldest moves, one that deviated markedly from the law and tradition of the European states of his time, he maintained that the sovereign possesses a supreme dominion over private property that empowers it to take the property of subjects, whose rights it can override, and that includes the power to tax.[16] This claim was at variance with the practice in England, where property was safeguarded by law from arbitrary seizure and all direct taxes levied by the monarch required the consent of parliament, as well as with that in other countries, where some form of consent to certain kinds of taxes was usual even in monarchies that tended toward absolutism. C. H. McIlwain, a great medieval constitutional scholar and historian of political thought (and one of the present author's teachers), once stated that the living political conceptions of the later Middle Ages could best be summed up in the maxim of the Roman philosopher Seneca that "to kings belong authority over all; to private persons, property."[17] Hobbes's political theory brushed aside this vital principle of ruler limitation with respect to the right of private property as being wholly out of keeping with the logic of absolute sovereignty.

Hobbes also claimed for the sovereign the right to control the public expression of thought and opinions, explaining that since men's actions proceeded from their opinions, "on the well governing of opinions consisteth the well governing of men's actions, in order to their peace and concord." It is quite obvious that he disliked and feared the effect of popular oratory and of free public political and religious controversy and debate, which could adversely affect the authority of the sovereign. The latter must therefore have the sole power to judge and decide what opinions and doctrines were adverse or conducive to peace, to determine which men were permitted to speak to numbers of people and on what occasions, and to examine the doctrines in books before they were published. One of Hobbes's justifications for this sovereign right was the pragmatic but sophistical argument that while only the truth should be regarded in matters of doctrine, this requirement would not be repugnant to the regulation of doctrines in relation to peace, as a doctrine opposed to peace could no more be true than peace and concord could be opposed to the law of nature.[18] In Hobbes's time, as well as before and after, it was common for governments, as well as the Catholic Church, in the interests of political and social stability and the dominant religion, to exercise some degree of censorship of books and publications and regulation of the press and the pulpit. It was therefore not a novel power that Hobbes attributed to the sovereign, although he formulates it in an explicit and rather extreme form. It is worth noting that contrary to his view, the poet Milton in his tract of 1644 entitled *Areopagitica*, published during the English civil war, strongly condemned book censorship prior to publication as a relic of the Catholic Inquisition and called for freedom of the press in the expression of ideas.[19]

Hobbes's expansive theory of sovereignty also entailed the complete subjection of the church and clergy, religion, and religious teaching to the state and sovereign. The chapters in the third part of *Leviathan* on the Christian commonwealth drove home this conclusion with a wealth of argument in a tour de force of exposition and doctrinal interpretation of a large number of scriptural texts and examples. An Erastian in the fullest sense of the term as it was understood in his time, Hobbes maintained that the church in a Christian state was not an independent or autonomous institution but a part of the commonwealth and thus under the rule of its sovereign, who is head of the church no less than of the state.[20] He admitted no distinction between "temporal and spiritual government," which he described as "but two words, brought into the world to make men see double and mistake their lawful sovereign."[21] The Hobbesian sovereign is not merely a secular ruler but also the supreme pastor of the Christian church, by whose authority all other pastors, religious teachers, and church officials were appointed.[22]

Included in its powers was the right to judge doctrines and decide which books of the Bible were canonical.[23] Hobbes noted that "subjects owe to sovereigns simple obedience in all things wherein their obedience is not repugnant to the laws of God," and also contended that it is the legislative authority of the sovereign by means of the civil law that makes God's laws and the precepts of the Bible binding upon men.[24] Regarding the question of what was necessary for salvation, he stated that a Christian needed only two virtues, faith and obedience. The required obedience was owed to God and the sovereign, whose command made the laws of God also laws for the commonwealth. As for faith, only one belief was necessary, namely, that Jesus is the savior and king sent by God to bring eternal life to everyone who believes in him.[25] By this simple criterion, Hobbes incidentally reduced the Christian faith to the single proposition that Jesus is the Messiah, which would have made the doctrinal divisions and controversies among Christians over the requirements of salvation into a comparatively minor matter. I return to this topic in the next chapter.

Finally, a very prominent and controversial feature of the Hobbesian theory of sovereignty was its candid affirmation of the total reciprocity between obligation and protection. As was noted in the preceding chapter, Hobbes maintained that "the end of obedience is protection," and that the natural right of subjects to protect themselves when the sovereign was no longer able to do so could not be relinquished in any covenant.[26] For Hobbes, therefore, as we have already pointed out, the initial agreement of subjects to obey the sovereign was ultimately founded in utility and practical reason, not in emotional allegiance, hereditary attachment, or religious duty, and ceased with the inability of the sovereign to protect them. In making so explicit the principle that obligation depends on protection, he was merely being faithful to the original reasons and motives that caused men in compliance with the law of nature to submit to the sovereign's government for the sake of their self-preservation and a secure, peaceful life. At the same time, implicit in this doctrine was the inescapable responsibility of all individual subjects to decide by their own private and personal judgment in various circumstances whether or not the sovereign was still able to protect them.

Modern scholars have called this doctrine the de facto theory of obligation, since it authorized subjects to obey any government in power in exchange for the latter's protection. Hobbes spoke of it in *Leviathan* when he explained that the overthrow of the sovereign power dissolved the commonwealth and left "every man at liberty to protect himself by such courses as his own discretion shall suggest unto him." In a clear allusion to England and the deposition of Charles I after the civil war, he declared that "though the right of a sovereign monarch cannot be extinguished by the act of another, yet the obligations of the members may. For he that wants protection may seek it anywhere" and "is obliged ... to protect his protection as long as he is able."[27] Hobbes reverted to this subject in the final thoughts he inserted in the "Review and Conclusion" at the end of *Leviathan*. It should be recalled that by the time this work appeared in 1651, not only had the civil war in England ended with the king's defeat and execution, but the monarchy and House of Lords had been abolished and a new republican government established, called the Commonwealth, that was ruled by the House of Commons with a much reduced membership. The dead monarch's son and heir Charles II was then living as an exile in France, and in England Oliver Cromwell, the general of the republic's army, had emerged as the most powerful leader who in the next several years would assume a quasi-monarchical office. With the establishment of the English Commonwealth, former supporters of the king faced the decision of whether they should or could in conscience conform to the new regime. This question became even more pressing with the enactment of a law in 1650 requiring all men of eighteen or older to subscribe to an Engagement promising to be "true and faithful to the Commonwealth of England as it is now established, without a king or House of Lords."[28] Hobbes's discussion of obligation and protection is directly relevant to this Engagement, whose imposition provoked considerable political controversy.[29] In the conclusion of *Leviathan* he introduces two points connected with this crucial issue. The first adds a further law of nature to his original list, stating that nature obliges every man to do his utmost "to protect in war the authority by which he is himself protected in time of peace of peace." This precept, although it could be inferred from other laws of nature, provided an explicit natural law justification for the fidelity of the royalists who had aided, fought, and sacrificed for the king's cause in the civil war. With regard to the second point, Hobbes noted that recent English publications (this was an allusion to the Engagement controversy) had shown that men were still uncertain what conquest is and when a subject becomes obliged to a conqueror and must obey the latter's laws. His answer to this uncertainty was that an individual becomes obligated to a conqueror when, having the liberty to submit, he consents by express words or other sufficient sign to be the conqueror's subject. He elaborates this point in some detail, but stresses that it is not the conqueror's victory that makes the conquest but the submission and promise of obedience by the individual, who in return for being given his life and liberty becomes the conqueror's subject. One of the most striking aspects of this discussion is Hobbes's caution that submission by the conquered entails only a promise of future obedience, not approval of the conqueror's past actions. He adds that there is hardly a commonwealth in the world whose beginnings can be justified in conscience, and that a principal seed of the death of any state is when conquerors require not only future submission but endorsement of acts done in the past.[30]

It is evident that Hobbes attached the greatest importance to the dependence of obedience on protection and to the timeliness of this proposition as presented in *Leviathan*. In the latter's final paragraph, he states that he has completed his discourse of civil and ecclesiastical government "without other design than to set before men's eyes the mutual relationship between protection and obedience, of which the condition of human nature and the laws divine (both natural and positive) require an inviolable observation."[31] In a later work of 1656, he actually claimed, in spite of having been a royalist, that his *Leviathan* had persuaded "the minds of a thousand gentlemen to a conscientious obedience to [the] present government, which otherwise would have wavered in that point."[32]

Leviathan was very offensive to royalists and pious readers of various persuasions for a number of reasons, not least because its doctrine of the mutual dependence of obligation and protection seemed to identify political legitimacy simply with the de facto possession of state power apart from any question of justice or right.[33] Many considered him a traitor who had written *Leviathan* to justify the new government's and Cromwell's usurpation of power. Hobbes's old friend from the period before the civil war, Edward Hyde, Earl of Clarendon, a longtime servant and principal minister of both Charles I and his son Charles II, wrote a large critique of *Leviathan* that denounced this doctrine, along with various others in the work. Calling it "the most contagious poison that runs through the Book," he charged that it served

> to absolve all men from their Allegiance [to the king], and industriously perswaded all sorts of men, that Cromwell was their true and lawful Soveraign, and that it was folly and guilt, and inevitably deserved ruin, not to adhere to him, and assist him against any opposition soever.[34]

Another typical response was the comment of the nobleman Viscount Saye and Sele, a former supporter of parliament against the king, who criticized those that like "weathercocks" turn with the wind, and for whom

> whear there is might thear is right, it is dominion if it succeed, but rebellion if it miscarry, a good argument for pyrates upon the sea, & for theeves upon the high way, fitter for Hobbs & atheists then good men and Christians.[35]

The Liberty of Subjects

The right of nature or unlimited natural freedom of individuals to act to preserve and protect their lives and bodies is the primordial and fundamental concept in Hobbes's moral and political philosophy. It is the first human entitlement and logically precedes his other foundational concept, the law of nature, a theorem of reason whose first and foremost precept bids men to seek peace by agreeing with one another to renounce their unlimited but totally insecure freedom in the state of nature and create a sovereign power that will govern and protect them. Subjectively, the right of nature originates as a naturalistic fact that springs from deep human (and one could also say animal) instinct, or as Hobbes describes it, from "a certain impulsion of nature, no lesse then that whereby a Stone moves downward," to avoid death and maintain one's existence. Objectively, the right of nature is also a normative moral claim because it is in accord with right reason and is therefore justifiable and right "for a man to use all his endeavours to preserve and defend his Body, and the members thereof from death and sorrowes."[36]

But fear of death and the desire for self-preservation, although the first and most elemental of motives and reasons that cause men to create the commonwealth, are not the only ones that direct them toward this end. From time to time Hobbes mentions additional motives and reasons. Not only for their safety but for their "happiness," he remarks, "did men freely assemble themselves, and institute a government, that they might, as much as their humane condition would afford, live delightfully." He speaks also of their desire for commodious and contented living, and when picturing the grim condition of the state of nature as a permanent state of war, he refers to the many things men want that cannot be attained in it that are among the fruits of civilization—thus the absence of agriculture, industry, navigation, and imported commodities, of commodious building and appliances for moving and removing objects requiring great force, of knowledge of the earth and an account of time, and of arts and letters.[37]

In dealing with the creation of the commonwealth, however, Hobbes gives comparatively little attention to the further ends men might have in view beside self-preservation, peace, and security, although we should keep these ends in mind when we reflect on his conviction of the superiority of the political order compared with the total freedom of the state of nature. He discusses the position of individuals in the commonwealth under the sovereign's absolute government from two theoretical perspectives: first, their liberty as subjects, and second, the duties owed them by the sovereign. These topics are treated in each of his political treatises with some variations but also, I think, in a similar way. Here I concentrate mainly on the fullest account of them as set forth in chapters 21 and 30 of *Leviathan*.

Although Hobbes's concept of liberty has been quite widely discussed, one may wonder whether it has been adequately or altogether fairly understood. There has been a common impression, for example, that he was an enemy of liberty, although this is either a misconception or at most a very partial truth. In an essay of 1990 Quentin Skinner devoted a careful examination to the subject but overlooked his approval of a "harmless liberty," which comes out, among other places, in his discussion of the sovereign's duties.[38] Hobbes's idea of liberty is couched exclusively in terms of what has become known as negative liberty and provides no place for a separate conception of political liberty that recognizes various affirmative rights of subjects in the political realm.[39] It fits into the now familiar distinction between positive and negative liberty such as was expounded in 1958 by Isaiah Berlin in his well-known Oxford inaugural lecture, published as *Two Concepts of Liberty*, which provoked a large amount of subsequent discussion among political theorists on the nature of liberty that has continued up to the present day. In that discourse, in which he referred to Hobbes, Berlin defined negative liberty as follows: "I am normally said to be free to the degree to which no human being interferes with my activity. Political liberty in this sense is simply the area in which a man can do what he wants. If I am prevented by other persons from doing what I want I am to that degree unfree."[40] Save for the comment on political liberty, to which Hobbes attached no special or distinct meaning, this formulation comes fairly close to his understanding of liberty.

Quentin Skinner has given more attention than any other historian to the development of Hobbes's concept of liberty and has made an admirable attempt to follow its convolutions and explain their contexts in his most recent book, *Hobbes and Republican Liberty*.[41] An opponent of the theory of negative liberty, he subscribes to what he has alternately called the neo-Roman and the republican theory of liberty, which he draws on in this latest work as the basis for an examination and indictment of Hobbes's view of liberty.[42] The republican theory of liberty stemmed chiefly from sources in Roman law, historiography, and political writers. In the Renaissance and early modern era it influenced the European advocates of republican rule, popular government and ruler accountability, and the right of resistance to unjust monarchs. As Skinner depicts it, the republican theory conceived of liberty as a state of nondomination, or not being in any way subject to another's will. It therefore considered slavery the opposite of liberty and held that a condition of servitude exists not only when persons are forced to act in obedience to another's will but also if they are obliged to live with either the threat or even the mere possibility of such domination. Even if they should have a benign ruler who scarcely interferes with them and leaves them a large freedom of choice in their actions, they are nevertheless enslaved, because they remain subject to the arbitrary will of another whenever that other chooses to exercise it. "The nerve of the republican theory," according to Skinner, "is thus that freedom within civil associations is subverted by the mere presence of arbitrary power, the effect of which is to reduce the members of such associations from the status of free-men to that of slaves."[43] If the republican theory offered as sound an understanding of liberty as Skinner believes, then the citizens or subjects of Hobbes's commonwealth ruled by an absolute sovereign power whose will makes law would be nothing more than slaves. Hobbes, however, knew the difference between freedom and slavery, and the subjects of the commonwealth as he conceives them are most definitely not slaves but free human beings endowed with a number of rights.

One of Skinner's major claims is that Hobbes's theory of liberty was a conscious response to the republican theory, of which he was "the most formidable enemy," and that his attempts to discredit it, especially in *Leviathan*, "constitute an epoch-making moment in the history of Anglophone political thought."[44] I believe this statement overestimates very considerably both the importance of the republican theory of liberty in English politics in the earlier seventeenth century and its significance in the formation of Hobbes's political thought. Before the 1650s there was no body of political thought in England that could be identified as republican. Prior to and during the civil war, most of the arguments the parliamentary opponents of Charles I advanced in attacking his policies and government were not derived from the republican theory of liberty but were based primarily on such principles as the supremacy of law, the inherited legal rights and liberties of subjects founded on medieval precedents, and the necessity of parliament's role in consenting to royal financial exactions, plus an increasing appeal in the 1640s to the ideas of contract and individual natural rights proclaimed by such radical groups as the Levellers. When the House of Commons took the revolutionary step in 1649 of making England a republic, most of its members were motivated in their abolition of kingship primarily by pragmatic considerations lying in the immediate political situation, not by a commitment to republicanism and its theory of liberty. In the later 1650s, the foremost English republican theorist, James Harrington, author of *Oceana* (1656), although a critic of Hobbes's absolutism and theory of sovereignty, was in many respects his disciple. Esteeming him one of the greatest thinkers of the age, Harrington stated that "his treatises of human nature, and of liberty and necessity . . . are the greatest of new lights, and those which I have follow'd, and shall follow."[45]

Of course, Hobbes was strongly opposed to republicanism and the republican tradition, as he often stated. He framed his own theory of liberty, however, not as an answer to the republican theory but as a development of his civil science, and chiefly in relation to the fundamental importance his natural philosophy assigned from an early date to the phenomenon of motion and to his theory of the will and belief in universal determinism. In the dedicatory epistle to the Earl of Devonshire in *De Corpore* (1655), the treatise on body that constituted the first section of his tripartite division of philosophy, Hobbes praised Galileo as "the first that opened ... the gate of natural philosophy universal, which is the knowledge of the nature of motion."[46] In his materialist and mechanical conception of nature, he identified motion as the universal cause of any kind of change, including the most subtle psychological changes, maintaining that all change was due to the impact of the motion of one body on another even when the bodies and the space in which their impact occurred were far too small to be sensed or observed. He regarded the imagination and the passions of human beings, their appetites and aversions, as effects of motion.[47] It is no wonder, then, that he should have placed such an emphasis on the existence of impediments to motion in his theory of liberty. With regard to the will, he did not regard it as a distinct faculty but defined it as the last act in a process of deliberation involving an alternation of desire and fear or aversion. The will, he argued, was not free but always determined in its choice by antecedent causal necessity. Freedom accordingly consisted not in having a free will, which was impossible, but in being unprevented from doing or acting as one wills.[48]

In *The Elements of Law*, Hobbes dealt very sketchily and unsatisfactorily with the idea of liberty, which he discusses in a chapter devoted mainly to masters and servants. He says there what he always maintained, that liberty isn't an exemption from subjection and obedience to the sovereign power. He adds that a free man is someone who hopes to receive better treatment than other subjects because he placed himself voluntarily under the sovereign rather than being compelled to do so, and that in all other senses, "liberty is the state of him that is not subject."[49]

De Cive offers an improved, more precise discussion of liberty. Here Hobbes notes that no writer has fully explained what liberty and slavery are, implying that he is the first to do so. He then defines liberty "as nothing else but an absence of the lets [obstacles] and hindrances of motion." He elaborates somewhat on this formulation, but its essential point is the association of liberty with the lack of impediments to motion.[50] In a subsequent chapter he makes the observation that it is not possible for laws to circumscribe all the many varied motions and actions of subjects, and that there are "infinite cases which are neither commanded nor prohibited" in which men may either do or not do, as they please. In these cases, Hobbes says, each man is said to enjoy his liberty, "and in this sense liberty is to be understood ... for that part of naturall Right, which is granted and left to Subjects by the civill Lawes."[51] This statement conforms to Hobbes's concept that a right and natural right are synonymous with freedom and the absence of obligation. It can also be related indirectly to the idea that freedom means being able to do what one wills to do without any hindrance or impediment.

In 1646, Hobbes wrote some remarks concerning liberty and necessity that originated in a discussion he had held on this subject with the Anglican bishop John Bramhall. These remarks, which were later published in 1654, convey an understanding of his idea of liberty in the 1640s prior to the publication of *Leviathan*. Respecting necessity, he states that "nothing taketh beginning from itself, but from the action of some other immediate agent without itself." Hence, if a man has an appetite or will to something, to which he immediately before had no will or appetite, the cause of his will is not in the will itself but in something exterior to it. It follows therefore that while the will is the cause of voluntary actions, the will itself is necessarily caused. Summarizing his conception of liberty, he declares that "will is the last act of our deliberation," that "a free agent is he that can do if he will," and that "liberty is the absence of external impediments."[52]

Chapter 21 of *Leviathan* contains Hobbes's fullest treatment of liberty in the context of the commonwealth and the obedience subjects owe the sovereign power. For the first time he devotes an entire chapter to the liberty of subjects. Although Skinner takes great pains to analyze Hobbes's thought on liberty in this last of his major political treatises, I cannot agree with his claim that in this work, Hobbes changed his view of liberty and repudiated his earlier opinions.[53] It is true that he adds some important new points and elaborations, but his idea of liberty nevertheless remains continuous with the previous conceptions he had held for a number of years. I will give a condensed account of his position because I have touched on certain aspects of it elsewhere in this book. It is apparent that he wants his account in *Leviathan* to deal with liberty in the widest philosophical sense connected with the will and motion. He therefore first equates what is "properly called liberty" with the simple notion of a "natural liberty" applying no less to irrational and inanimate creatures than to rational humans, and which he defines as the absence of opposition or "external impediments of motion." These impediments must be external, he notes, for if they lay in the constitution of the agent, we would not say that the latter lacks the liberty but rather the power to move, as in the case of man fastened to his bed by sickness. He then defines a free man "in its proper and generally received meaning" as he "that in those things which by his strength and wit he is able to do is not hindered to do what he has a will to."[54] Skinner's partisan judgment is obvious in his barbed comment at this point that Hobbes's description of his definition of a free man as its generally received meaning is "perhaps the most outrageous moment of effrontery in the whole of *Leviathan*." He calls this definition a "sensationally polemical one," because if there was any generally received meaning of the term at the time, it was that a free man is someone who lives independently of the will of others.[55] Hobbes, however, was offering a general philosophical, not simply a political definition of freedom and a free man. It is doubtful, moreover, as I have already suggested, that the republican theory of liberty should be considered as the then generally received conception. Hobbes's definition is a clear expression of the idea of negative liberty, which, though he never used this phrase, he may have been the first to formulate. It presumes the basic distinction, on which he always insisted, between the human will, which itself is never free but always determined in its deliberations by exterior physical causes, and the freedom to act or not as the will dictates if the person is not prevented by external interference or force. The freedom to act would also, of course, be described by Hobbes as voluntary action.

When he next turns specifically to the liberty of subjects, he observes first that they are held by the "artificial chains" of the civil law, which they have tied by means of their mutual covenants to the sovereign's lips at one end and to their own ears at the other. It is only in relation to these bonds, he explains, that he proposes to deal with the liberty of subjects. He points out that the chains of the law, although inherently weak, are nevertheless dangerous to break. This danger obviously arises from the deterrent fear of the sovereign's penalties on lawbreakers, but as we might recall from our discussion in the previous chapter, Hobbes denied any inconsistency between fear and liberty, affirming that "all actions men do in commonwealths for fear of the law are actions which the doers had liberty to omit."[56] Skinner protests that Hobbes attributes far too much liberty to subjects in suggesting that the laws of the sovereign are easily broken, and states that "his basic strategy in attempting to discredit the republican theory of liberty remains that of trying to lay as much emphasis as possible on the persistence of our freedom even under government."[57] Hobbes does seem to be saying that laws do not restrict the liberty of those affected by them because it is possible to break them. This opinion is surely mistaken, however, because any law that is legally enforced will act as a restriction on the liberty of those whom it affects.[58]

Since no commonwealth can possibly have rules that regulate everything its subjects do and say, Hobbes followed out his own reasoning to conclude that liberty under government consists of the indefinitely many actions the civil law of the sovereign leaves subjects free to do or not, as their own minds and wills decide. Among such actions he instances buying, selling, and the making of contracts, the choice of where to live and what to eat, choosing a trade, educating children as the parents see fit, and other similar freedoms.[59] In *De Cive* he expresses this same thought in the statement I have already quoted that the liberty of subjects does not lie in exemption from the laws but in the "infinite cases" that are neither commanded nor prohibited in which everyone can do or not do as they "list." In all such cases, everyone is said to enjoy their liberty, which is thus understood for "that part of naturall Right, which is granted and left to Subjects by the civill Lawes."[60]

It was consequently Hobbes's view that the liberty of subjects in the commonwealth is partly derived from the silence of the law. This liberty seems to be mainly associated, moreover, with the private sphere of civil society in which individuals, in the absence of legal commands and rules, remain free to do as they please in their own personal affairs. Such freedom, he emphasizes, does not abolish or limit in any way the power of the sovereign, including its power of life and death over subjects.[61] This concept of what it means to be free ignores the political dimension of life and enables him to claim that men have been deceived by "the specious name of freedom" to look upon it as "their private inheritance and birthright,"[62] not understanding that the only right of freedom is the public right of the commonwealth or state itself. Hence he contends, most implausibly, that the freedom of individuals is the same in every form of government, whether monarchical or democratic. The reason men think otherwise, he maintains, is that "in these western parts of the world" they have taken their opinions about commonwealths from Aristotle, Cicero, and other Greek and Roman authors who mistakenly taught that some states are freer than others and that in monarchies, all men are slaves. Owing to their influence, men have contracted the habit "under a false show of liberty" of favoring tumults and "licentious controlling the actions of their sovereigns," which must lead to civil war and much bloodshed. Hobbes concludes this exaggerated indictment of the republican and democratic political sentiments, which he believed were instilled by a classical education, with the notorious comment that "there was never anything so dearly bought, as these western parts have bought the learning of the Greek and Latin tongues."[63]

Although it proceeded from his own logic and definitions, Hobbes's claim that individuals possessed an identical freedom in every type of polity is one of the worst defended in his work. He must have known that by any sensible account, subjects are more free in a commonwealth where the sovereign cannot take their property without due process or tax them at will or make law without their consent, or in which they have some participation in their government and some political means of holding it accountable. Hobbes offered a brief comparison of the three basic forms of government and their inconveniences in each of his political treatises.[64] While he favored monarchy, he acknowledges that some people considered it more grievous than democracy because it affords less liberty. Citing the common belief as expressed in the sixth book of Aristotle's *Politics* that liberty exists only in a popular state, he observes that the reason people are deceived into holding this erroneous opinion is because a popular state provides for equal participation in ruling and in public offices and for equal voices in choosing magistrates and public ministers. Despite such apparently good grounds for thinking that freedom is greatest in a popular state or democracy, Hobbes never ceased to argue that when men call for more freedom, they are really demanding sovereignty for themselves, and that "single persons have no lesse liberty under a Monarch, then under the People."[65]

In spite of the importance he assigns to the silence of the law in the first part of his treatment of the liberty of the subject, Hobbes attributes an even more significant role in that freedom to the original right of nature, to which he recurs when he proceeds to describe the "particulars of the true liberty of the subject" and how this liberty "[is] to be measured." We have reviewed these particular liberties in the last chapter but must take notice of them here as well. They are traceable, as we have seen, to the unrestricted freedom of individuals in the state of nature, of which they retain a residue even when as subjects they have surrendered most of their rights with the establishment of the commonwealth. Hobbes declares in this connection that since all men are equally free by nature, their obligation and liberty as subjects must be understood in relation to the end for which they have instituted sovereignty, namely, internal peace and defense against a common enemy.[66] The innate natural rights that remain to them constitute a freedom they cannot renounce or transfer by any covenant and entitle them to refuse, without committing any injustice, the commands of the sovereign in a number of matters. These latter pertain mainly to the inherent right of subjects singly or together to preserve and defend their lives, bodies, and means of life in various circumstances and even against the lawful action of the sovereign. This liberty includes the right not to accuse oneself or confess to a crime when questioned and not to serve in war if one finds a substitute to fill one's place. Hobbes grants this liberty a surprising amount of latitude, allowing that in the case of a large number of men who have unjustly united to resist the sovereign power or committed crimes that incur the penalty of death, they may nevertheless continue to resist and to help one another in defense of their lives. "[T]hey but defend their lives," he says, "which the guilty man may do as well as the innocent." He adds that for them to go on maintaining what they have wrongly begun is not a new unjust action, and moreover, "if it be only to defend their persons, it is not unjust at all."[67]

Hobbes's approval of certain liberties that permitted subjects to defy the commands of the sovereign appears to stand in close relationship to his pervasive psychological naturalism with its emphasis on self-preservation, although these liberties also possess a normative character as rights. We must imagine him as thinking that when human beings face a threat to their physical survival or bodily well-being, or are ordered or forced to accuse themselves of some offense or crime, they are apt to try to defend themselves and can hardly help doing so. In such cases, even those of wrongful action, he recognizes that resistance is justifiable and may therefore also be considered as a right, although he equally recognizes the sovereign's superior right to repress and punish such resistance. He reminds the reader that the subject's obligation to the sovereign depends on the purpose for which sovereignty was created. The rule he proposes for determining when disobedience is justifiable, which I have mentioned previously, is accordingly the following: "when our refusal to obey frustrates the end for which the sovereign was ordained, then there is no liberty to refuse; otherwise there is." Depending on its interpretation, this rule seems to leave a considerable space for disobedience. Even more striking is that despite Hobbes's insistence on the necessity of the supremacy of the sovereign's judgment in all controversies in the commonwealth, the rule he lays down regarding the refusal of obedience makes sense only if it is applied according to the personal judgment of each individual subject.

Seventeenth-century royalist and religious critics of Hobbes's work complained that *Leviathan*'s explanation of the liberty of subjects was nothing else than a justification of resistance and rebellion against the sovereign. In his attack on *Leviathan*, his old antagonist Bishop Bramhall asked why the book should not be renamed "the Rebell's Catechism." Similar comments were made by Sir Robert Filmer and the Earl of Clarendon.[68] Jean Hampton, who cites these criticisms in her important study of Hobbes's political thought, perceived in his account of the subject's liberty the concession of a subversive "self-defense right" that seemed to her to completely undermine and destroy his theory of sovereignty. Although she does not refer to the republican theory of liberty, she pictures the condition of subjects in the Hobbesian commonwealth as one of slavery and of being enslaved to the sovereign, but argues at the same time that "as long as subjects retain the right to preserve themselves in a commonwealth, they cannot be said to have surrendered *anything* to the sovereign." She also contends that if subjects have the right to decide whether or not to obey any of their ruler's commands, "*private judgment* has not been destroyed in the commonwealth."[69]

While I would not minimize the significance of the space for private judgment Hobbes permits in his discussion of the liberty of the subject, and will return to this matter in due course, it seems to me, nevertheless, that Hampton's critique is greatly exaggerated. For one thing, it is quite mistaken and very misleading to describe the sovereign's subjects in the commonwealth as slaves. Hobbes, who touched on slavery in his work, understood how a subject differed from a slave.[70] A slave is a chattel that can be bought and sold, who may have been taken in war and can be kept in fetters, and is entirely at the will of the master, who owes him nothing. Hobbesian subjects, however, are free individuals who can do as they like over large areas of their lives; they are endowed with rights, capable of owning and bequeathing property, and, as I shall presently note, the sovereign not only has genuine duties to them but governs them not by arbitrary and unpredictable fiat but very largely by formal laws, properly promulgated, whose reasons are made known to them and that are to a very considerable extent intended for their benefit. For another thing, just as Hobbes once pointed out that a sovereign who set forth a law "Thou shalt not rebel" would effect "just nothing,"[71] so he would doubtless have considered it equally futile to pass a law that prohibited subjects from attempting to preserve themselves or from exercising their private judgment. His discussion of the liberty of subjects simply acknowledges the human desire to avoid death and physical harm as a basic fact and specifies conditions in which action to this end may be legitimate even in the case of disobedience to the sovereign's law. It also recognizes that individuals cannot avoid having their private opinions irrespective of the laws, although they may not voice them. Hobbes's sovereign is invested with very ample powers, and so long as a great number of its subjects are unwilling or afraid at any one time to try to coordinate their actions in a common resistance to the sovereign, which is usually likely to be the case, or to join together to manifest an adverse judgment on the sovereign's law, it would offer no serious threat to the condition of sovereignty that subjects possessed the rights and liberty Hobbes attributed to them.[72]

Hobbes's Very Moral Sovereign

Given the common impression that Hobbes's political theory is centered on the power and unity of the state, the title of this section may seem a misnomer. I believe it is entirely accurate, however, and that Hobbes's concept of the sovereign included stringent moral standards and obligations When reading his discussion of the duties of the sovereign, one might at times have the impression that it belongs in certain respects to the broad genre of European literature of statecraft and advice to princes, which combined political wisdom, practical suggestions, and moral instruction. A somewhat conventional instance of this genre is the famed humanist scholar Erasmus's *The Education of a Christian Prince* (1516), which Hobbes may or may not have known, addressed to the Habsburg sovereign the Archduke Charles, the future Holy Roman Emperor Charles V and inheritor, among other realms, of the rule of the Netherlands and the crowns of the Spanish kingdoms of Castile and Aragon. Erasmus was of course an ethical as well as pragmatic teacher, an advocate of moderate government and a hater of war, whose precepts sought to impress on the young Prince Charles the difference between a true king and a tyrant and exhorted him to be a virtuous Christian and just ruler.[73] Contemporaneous with Erasmus's treatise was the more celebrated and very different sort of book, Machiavelli's notorious *The Prince* (c. 1513), a contribution to reason of state that lauded war and advised the prince to pretend rather than to be good, and to pay no heed to morality when it stood in the way of the preservation and pursuit of power. We can be reasonably sure that Hobbes was well acquainted with the literature of statecraft and civil knowledge going back to Plato and Aristotle and including among the moderns the writings of Machiavelli and others. Thucydides' *History*, which Hobbes had translated, contained many political lessons that confirmed his dislike of democracy as practiced in Athens and the demagogic influence of popular orators on the conduct of government. He would have known the Greek historian Polybius, the chronicler of Rome's rise to world power, and the *Annals* by the great Roman historian Tacitus, who exposed the secrets of empire in relating the rule and crimes of the emperor Tiberius and his immediate successors.[74] In *De Cive* Hobbes referred to the historian Sallust's account of the conspiracy of Catiline against the Roman republic, of which he said that "there never was a greater Artist [than Catiline] in raising seditions."[75] All of these works, as well as a number of sixteenth-century commentaries on Tacitus dealing in part with political questions and methods of government, were contained in the Hardwick library. In his very recent account of an astute political pamphlet of the Thirty Years' War whose English translation he attributed to Hobbes, Noel Malcolm has noted the philosopher's acquaintance with various early modern writings, also part of the Hardwick library, on politics, reason of state, and the interest of states by English, Italian, French, and other authors, including not only Machiavelli and Guicciardini but also Botero, Sarpi, Boccalini, Lipsius, and La Noue, among others.[76]

Just as Hobbes associated the liberty of the subject with the end for which sovereignty was ordained, so in *Leviathan* he begins his discussion of the duty of the sovereign, whether a monarch or an assembly, by relating it to "the end for which [the sovereign] was trusted with ... power."[77] Although he had always made clear that the sovereign had no contractual obligations to its subjects, it is noteworthy that he nevertheless described its powers as a trust, a term that seems to imply that the sovereign was in some moral sense accountable for their use. The purpose of sovereign power, he says, is to procure "the safety of the people," to which the sovereign is obliged by the law of nature and for which it will have to render an account to God. The safety of the people, he likewise explains, does not mean "a bare preservation, but also all other contentments of life, which every man by lawful industry, without danger or hurt to the commonwealth, shall acquire to himself." This end should be accomplished, he then adds, by the sovereign's general oversight of the polity in the form of public instruction based on both doctrine and example, and by the making and execution of good laws.[78]

Before proceeding further, we need to consider for a moment Hobbes's definition of counsel and the distinction he drew at an earlier point between counsel and command. On this subject he says in *Leviathan* that whereas counsel to do or not to do something is intended for the good and benefit of the person counseled, a command is directed to the benefit of the person who commands, "for the reason of his command is his own will only, and the proper object of every man's will is some good to himself."[79] Since the Hobbesian sovereign is the supreme commander in the commonwealth, must we therefore suppose that its commands are directed exclusively to its own benefit? And if that is the case, how can the safety of the people, meaning their good and benefit, be its basic purpose? I believe Hobbes's answer to these questions is that his sovereign identifies its own good entirely with the good and safety of the people. Thus he affirms in *The Elements of Law* that "the profit of the sovereign and subject goeth always together" and that "governing to the profit of the subjects, is governing to the profit of the sovereign." In another formulation he maintains that "the general law for sovereigns [is] that they procure, to the uttermost of their endeavour, the good of the people."[80] Hobbes's position on this point provides further proof that he was not an adherent of psychological egoism who saw personal self-interest as the sole motive of action, and shows pretty clearly that his conception of human nature and human relationships does not in any way exclude the possibility of altruism and human beings seeking the good or happiness of others as a part of their own good. This is discussed further in the next chapter

The first part of Hobbes's examination of the sovereign's duties concentrates mainly on what it must do to secure its position. He stresses its obligation to keep its essential rights intact, since on these rights depends the peace of the society, and to instruct and indoctrinate its subjects in the principles of reason that justify the existence of absolute sovereignty. He insists that these principles represent a progressive advance in the knowledge of how commonwealths should be constructed to make them more perfect and possibly everlasting, unless destroyed by external violence. He likens the doctrines the sovereign should take care to instill in the people to the Ten Commandments. Thus, they should be taught not to prefer another form of government to their own, nor to dispute or speak evil of the sovereign power or show it any disrespect, and to obey and honor their parents and their fathers, who were absolute sovereigns over their offspring prior to the institution of the commonwealth. They should also be taught to act justly toward everyone, taking from no man what is his, avoiding fraud and violence, private revenges, violations of conjugal honor, and corruption of judges and witnesses. In this connection Hobbes warns of the need to prevent the people from being infected by the many opinions contrary to the peace of mankind, such as that men should decide what is lawful by their private judgment and conscience rather than by the law, or that subjects need not obey the commonwealth's commands unless they first judge them lawful, or that the sovereign has no dominion over property, that it is lawful for subjects to kill tyrants, and that sovereignty may be divided. Although he attributed these errors concerning justice and other principles to the immediate influence of preachers and lawyers, Hobbes, who was himself an Oxford graduate, identified their main source as the universities and the books read there. It was therefore manifest, he believed, that "the instruction of the people dependeth wholly on the right teaching of youth in the universities." One of his intentions, he frankly admits, is to teach the universities.[81]

The remainder of his account of the sovereign's duties is concerned largely with particular policies and actions that contribute to the safety of the people. It is hardly possible to read this discussion without gaining an enhanced respect for Hobbes as an advocate of the rule of law (excluding the sovereign) and of civil equality before the law.[82] He begins by declaring that the safety of the people requires the sovereign to administer justice equally to all degrees of its people without distinction of status, to the poor and obscure as well as to the rich and mighty. Despite the years he had spent as tutor and secretary in a great noble household, he deplores any partiality of the law to great persons, observing that the latter are to be valued "for their beneficence and the aids they give to men of inferior rank, or not at all," while the violence, oppressions, and injuries they commit "are not extenuated, but aggravated by the greatness of their persons, because they have least need to commit them." He also recommends as related to equal justice the equal imposition of taxes, which the sovereign has the right to demand for the common defense, and should be levied upon poor and rich in proportion to what they consume. For what reason can there be, Hobbes asks, "that he who laboureth much, and sparing the fruits of his labour, consumeth little, should be more charged than he that living idly, getteth little and spendeth all he gets? . . ." Addressing the problem of poverty, he urges public charity and support for poor people unable to work and compulsory labor for able-bodied idle persons unwilling to work. He also suggests the transplantation of the growing surplus of poor people to colonies, where they were to cultivate the land and not exterminate the natives but live in peace with them as far as possible.[83] Hobbes had of course some knowledge and experience of colonization projects through his involvement with his employer the Earl of Devonshire in the affairs of the Virginia Company.[84] His recommendations with regard to the relief of poverty, public charity, unemployment, and colonization mainly reflect the mercantilist policies that sixteenth- and seventeenth-century governments generally tried to promote.[85]

Hobbes next addresses the sovereign's responsibility to make good laws, which are not the same, he points out, as just laws, since all the sovereign's laws, being authorized by the commonwealth, are just. He then defines a good law as "that which is needful for the good of the people, and withal perspicuous." Along with its necessity as a criterion of a good law, he stresses that the use of laws "is not to bind the people from all voluntary actions" but to direct them in such a way "as not to hurt themselves by their own impetuous desires, rashness, or indiscretion." He remarks on the error of thinking that a law is good if it is for the sovereign's benefit but not necessary for the people, and insists that "the good of the sovereign and people cannot be separated." A law's perspicuity, he states, consists of its declaration of the reasons for which it was made and thus shows the meaning of the legislator. He worried about the ambiguity of language and noted that "the multiplication of words in the body of the law is multiplication of ambiguity," which, by making evasion easier, was the cause of many unnecessary legal processes. Hence he maintained that laws should be brief and contain as few words as possible.[86]

Hobbes's discussion also dealt with the sovereign's duty to make the right use of punishment and rewards. He was quite unusual in arguing that the purpose of punishment should not be revenge or the expression of anger but correction.[87] The heaviest punishments, in his view, should be inflicted on crimes most dangerous to the public. These included malice toward the established government, contempt for justice, and crimes that aroused popular indignation because committed by persons who enjoyed the protection of men in authority. In comparison with such offenses, he mentioned "crimes of infirmity," which sprang from great provocation, great fear, great need, or ignorance. Concerning these latter, he held that "there is place many times for lenity, without prejudice to the commonwealth; and lenity, when there is place for it, is required by the law of nature."[88]

Hobbes concludes his survey in *Leviathan* of the sovereign's duty with some comments on the distribution of rewards so as always to benefit the commonwealth and on the choice of good counselors and military commanders. He observes that the best counsel concerning the ease and benefit of the subjects is to be taken from the general information and complaints coming from the people in different regions of the country, "who are best acquainted with their own wants, and ought therefore, when they demand nothing in derogation of the essential rights of sovereignty, to be diligently taken notice of." Possibly thinking of republican Rome and generals such as Julius Caesar or of Oliver Cromwell in his own time and country, Hobbes speaks also of the danger to the sovereign power from army commanders who become too popular. He pointed out, however, that when the sovereign itself is popular, there is no danger from the popularity of a subject. In passing he also offered some interesting obiter dicta, such as that politics is a "harder study" than geometry and that "the greatest and most active part of mankind has never hitherto been well contented with the present."[89]

In the account he gives of the sovereign's duty in his earlier treatises, Hobbes casts some additional light on his conception of this vitally important topic. Because eternal is better than temporal good, he declares in *The Elements of Law* that the law of nature obliges the sovereign to ordain in accord with its conscience such doctrines, rules, and actions as it believed would constitute the true way to the subjects' eternal good. Presumably this injunction to provide for the salvation of their subjects would affect only Christian sovereigns. In *De Cive* Hobbes attributes this same duty to the sovereign, but much more tentatively.[90] In *Leviathan*, by contrast, he does not mention this duty at all. Among the temporal goods of the people, *The Elements of Law* names "commodity of living," which consists of liberty and wealth. Respecting liberty, Hobbes prescribes that there should be

> no prohibition without necessity of any thing to any man, which was lawful to him in the law of nature; that is to say, that there be no restraint of natural liberty, but what is necessary for the good of the commonwealth; and that well meaning men may not fall into the danger of laws, as into snares, before they be aware.

Enlarging on this point, he adds that natural liberty requires being able to move easily and safely from place to place, and that the law of nature obliges the sovereign to make laws to this effect.[91] *De Cive* mentions "a harmlesse liberty" among the benefits included in the safety of the people.[92] In all of his recommendations on liberty, Hobbes ignores its political dimension. The Hobbesian commonwealth focuses on the authority and duty of the sovereign, while the foremost duty of the subject is obedience. No provision is made for the participation or distinct consent of subjects in their government.

Nevertheless, Hobbes's discussion of the sovereign's duties leaves no doubt that it has genuine obligations that constitute a moral trust, and that in performing its functions it ought to manifest a continuous concern for its subjects' good and happiness, particularly in the making and execution of law. This is a consequence not only of the moral responsibility he attributes to the sovereign but of his claim that the good of the sovereign and of its subjects coincide. But then the question inevitably arises, how can the sovereign have moral obligations to its subjects, and whence do these obligations derive? It is obvious that in some sense they must come from the law of nature, but how? This is an absolutely essential question, and we have to consider whether Hobbes provided us with a coherent or consistent answer.

In his account of the relationship between civil and natural law, as was pointed out in the previous chapter, Hobbes was unique in positing a complete merging of the two laws once the commonwealth comes into existence. The law of nature and the civil law, he declares in *Leviathan*, "contain each other" and "are of equal extent." For the laws of nature, "which consist in equity, justice, gratitude, and other moral virtues," are "not properly laws, but qualities that dispose men to peace and to obedience." It is not until they are promulgated as commands of the commonwealth that they actually become laws, being then civil laws which "the sovereign power obliges men to obey." He concludes from these propositions that "the law of nature therefore is a part of the civil law in all commonwealths of the world" and that "reciprocally also, the civil law is part of the dictates of nature." "It is not possible," he comments in *De Cive*, "to command aught by the civill law, contrary to the Lawes of nature."[93]

According to this analysis, it would seem that the law of nature and the civil law can never be in conflict, and that the first is always compatible with and reinforces the second as a fundamental moral sanction and support. Yet there are numerous instances in Hobbes's treatment of the sovereign power where he speaks of its obligations under natural law and envisages the possibility of its violation of the law of nature.[94] He says, for instance, that the sovereign can never lack a right to anything except as it is itself "the subject of God and bound thereby to observe the laws of nature." He also says that whatever is not against the law of nature can be made law by the sovereign, and that all punishments of innocent subjects are against the law of nature.[95] In *De Cive* he notes very clearly that the sovereign "may diverse wayes transgresse against ... Lawes of nature, as by cruelty, iniquity, contumely, and other like vices, which come not under [the] strict and exact notion of injury."[96] He observes as well that while sovereigns are not subject to the civil law, they "are all subject to the laws of nature, because such laws be divine, and cannot by any man or commonwealth be abrogated." The first thing he says in beginning his discussion of the sovereign's duties is that it is "obliged by the law of nature" to procure the safety of the people.[97]

These passages are taken mainly from *Leviathan*, but we find comments to the same effect in Hobbes's previous treatises. According to *The Elements of Law*, when acts of the sovereign power "tend to the hurt of the people in general, they be breaches of the law of nature, and the divine law; and consequently, the contrary acts are the duty of sovereigns, and required at their hands to the utmost of their endeavour by God Almighty, under the pain of eternal death." The civil law, this work also says, cannot make that to be done *jure* [i.e., according to law], "which is against the law divine, or of nature."[98] In *De Cive* Hobbes explains that while sovereigns cannot be subject to the civil law, they must as much as possible yield obedience to "right reason, which is the naturall, morall, and divine Law," and that those in authority who use their power other than for the safety of the people will be acting "against the reasons of Peace, that is to say, against the Lawes of nature." He goes on to add that that "Princes are by the Law of Nature bound to use their whole endeavour in procuring the welfare of their subjects."[99]

It is very interesting that in passages like those above, Hobbes holds the sovereign answerable not only to the law of nature but also to divine law, with the possibility of eternal death for failing to perform its duty in procuring the safety of the people. Having invested the sovereign, whether ruling by institution or by conquest, with such great and comprehensive powers and rights, he would have been a very impractical and careless thinker not to take account of the fact that sovereigns, who were no more than human beings, could be guilty of great wrongs in their government and do very evil things. In our own time, sovereign dictators such as Hitler, Mussolini, Stalin, Mao Tse-Tung, and a number of African and Asian despots have been amoral monsters and world-scale criminals. Although Hobbes stated on more than one occasion that tyranny was not a type of rule but merely a term of discontent used by those who disliked a particular government, he also recognized that a legitimate monarch who failed to govern well might be called a tyrant.[100] He might therefore have conceded that sovereigns who thought only of themselves and separated their own interests in power and wealth from the good of their subjects could properly be described as tyrants. He was also fully aware, as I noted in an earlier chapter, that one of the strongest objections to his theory of sovereignty was that it rendered "the condition of subjects ... very miserable, as being obnoxious [i.e., vulnerable] to the lusts and other irregular passions of him or them that have so unlimited a power in their hands." To this objection, his answer was always the same, namely,

> that the estate of man can never be without some incommodity or other, and that the greatest that in any form of government can possibly happen to the people in general is scarce sensible in respect of the miseries and horrible calamities that accompany a civil war (or that dissolute condition of masterless men, without subjection to laws and a coercive power to tie their hands from rapine and revenge.[101]

Was Hobbes, then, guilty of a manifest inconsistency or contradiction in his description of the relationship between natural and civil law when he affirmed on the one hand that the sovereign's civil law and the natural law contain each other and are of equal extent, and on the other hand that the sovereign was under an obligation to obey the law of nature, which imposed on it the duty of governing its subjects with their safety, welfare, and happiness as its foremost aim? It is difficult to believe that he would not have perceived and avoided such an obvious paralogism. I think, however, that we may find the solution to this problem of his apparent inconsistency with regard to the sovereign's subordination and obligation to the moral law of nature by looking at his conception of equity.

Equity is frequently mentioned by Hobbes not only in his political treatises but also in a later work on law, *A Dialogue Between a Philosopher and a Student of the Common Laws of England*, probably written in the 1660s.[102] A concept in ethics, law, and jurisprudence that the Greeks called *epieikeia* and the Romans *aequitas*, equity was discussed by Plato and Aristotle, by Cicero and Roman lawyers, and by Christian theologians, philosophers, and canonists. Christopher St. German, a prominent common lawyer in the reign of Henry VIII, dealt with the common law and its relationship to equity, conscience, and natural law, which he termed the law of reason, in his well-known *Dialogue Between a Doctor of Divinity and a Student of the Laws of England* (1530).[103] Suárez's treatise on law and God the lawgiver touches on equity and its relationship to justice, law, and the law of nature, with many references to earlier authorities.[104] Grotius occasionally refers to equity in *The Law of War and Peace*, and also wrote a short treatise on the subject that is printed in some of the later editions of this work.[105] Equity could signify fairness, impartiality, equality, what is fair and right, interpretation, and general principles of justice that correct an injustice caused by a literal interpretation of the law. Probably the most common and perdurable meaning of equity was expressed in the classic discussion in Aristotle's *Nicomachean Ethics*, which identifies the just with the equitable, but observes that while both are good, "the equitable is superior," because it is not the legally just but "a correction of legal justice." He explains that this correction may be necessary in those cases that inevitably occur that do not fit the universality of the law. He thus defines "the nature of the equitable" as "a correction of the law where it is defective owing to its universality." He also notes that the equitable man exemplifies this kind of justice because he is not "a stickler for his rights in a bad sense, but tends to take less than his share though he has the law on his side."[106]

Hobbes spoke of equity in a variety of ways in several different contexts. He would have been familiar with the term partly because the great English Court of Chancery was a court of equity presided over by the Lord Chancellor, an essential part of whose jurisdiction consisted of providing equitable relief to aggrieved litigants who claimed to have suffered injury from the application of the rules of common law in other courts. One of the primary meanings Hobbes gives to equity is equality, the principle of treating equals equally, which he says is the same as distributive justice. He also says that "equity, justice, and honour, contain all virtues whatsoever."[107] Equity as a precept of equality is a Hobbesian law of nature. According to this law, "we are forbidden to assume more Right by nature to ourselves, then we grant to others," and this is called "Equity." He avers further that the natural and moral law are the same because both are necessary means to peace, as is also equity, together with modesty, trust, humanity, and mercy. He identifies the character of equity as a natural law mandating equality with the biblical injunction to love thy neighbor as thyself. He also allows that the citizens of the commonwealth may sometimes go to law against their chief or sovereign, an action, he explains, that belongs not to "to Civill Right, but to Naturall Equity." Hobbes often uses the phrase "natural equity" to designate an evident type of justice, such as the judge's obligation by equity to judge equally between parties, or the "naturall equity" of imposing the burden of taxation equally.[108]

References to equity appear more frequently in *Leviathan* than in any of Hobbes's earlier writings. There he declares that the law of nature always prescribes equity, and because equity is a law of nature, "a sovereign is as much subject to it as any . . . of his people." He acknowledges cases in which "commands of the sovereign" are "contrary to equity and the law of nature." He also notes that violations of the law that harm private persons cannot be pardoned by the sovereign without a breach of equity except with the consent of and satisfaction made to the injured party.[109] In classifying laws as either natural or positive, he describes the former as moral laws and laws from all eternity consisting of virtues such as justice, equity, and all habits of mind that conduce to peace and charity. The chapter of *Leviathan* on civil law also refers often to equity in relation to judges and legislation. The first thing that makes a good judge and interpreter of the laws, according to Hobbes, "is a right understanding of that principal law of nature called equity." Since the intention of the legislator, as he points out, is always supposed to be equity, when the literal words of the law do not fully authorize a reasonable meaning, the judge's duty is to supply it with the law of nature, or if it is a difficult case, to respite judgment until he receives fuller authority.[110]

A Dialogue Between a Philosopher and a Student of the Common Laws of England includes some comments on equity in its discussion of legal and political issues and its criticisms of the common law and the opinions of the eminent English lawyer Sir Edward Coke.[111] The philosopher of the dialogue, who is Hobbes's spokesman, argues that while a statute of the sovereign is always just, it may be guilty of iniquity, and that the difference between injustice and iniquity is that the first is a transgression of a statute law, while the second violates the law of reason. He claims that the only law by which the king as sovereign is bound is the law of equity. He also identifies equity with the law of God and notes that it must deal with the "many reasonable Exceptions" that can be made "almost to every General Rule, which the makers of the Rule could not foresee'" and with the "very many words in every Statute . . . that are . . . of Ambiguous signification." He defines equity in relation to law as "a certain perfect Reason" that "amends . . . Judgments . . . when they are Erroneous."[112]

It appears from these various statements that equity may be described, as Larry May has correctly said, as "the dominant moral category in Hobbes's political and legal philosophy."[113] Equity appears to represent at once the fullest expression of equality and fairness in the treatment of human beings, the clearest manifestation of justice, and the highest standard of moral reason and rectitude, from which neither the sovereign nor the civil law can be excepted. Not only is equity one of the laws of nature, for Hobbes it seems to be the very essence of this law that infuses all of its dictates as moral laws. When he speaks of natural equity, he seems sometimes to have in mind an almost immediate or intuitive moral and rational perception of what is fair and just. It is because of the supreme position of equity in both the moral and legal order that it is possible for him to acknowledge that the sovereign, despite the fact that all of its laws are said to be just in a stipulated or definitional sense, can be guilty of iniquity and of a breach of the law of nature. The principle of equity, I believe, thus exists in Hobbes's political philosophy as a genuine and significant moral limit on the rights of the sovereign and the absolutism of the state. Hobbes remains a legal positivist in his concept of law, but he is far from denying the relevance of moral standards in appraising the sovereign's government and legislation.

In *Leviathan*, he declares that

> a sovereign monarch, or the greater part of a sovereign assembly, may ordain the doing of many things in pursuit of their passions, contrary to their own consciences, which is a breach of trust, and of the law of nature.

But having made this admission and others like it already quoted, which Hobbes scholars have largely tended to ignore, he immediately adds:

> but this is not enough to authorize any subject, either to make war upon, or so much as to accuse of injustice or any way to speak evil of, their sovereign, because they have authorized all his actions, and in bestowing the sovereign power, made them their own.[114]

Hobbes seems unduly optimistic in supposing that by reason of his theory of representation and authorization, subjects who perceive the evils committed by their sovereign as a breach of trust and the laws of nature will refrain from accusations of injustice or thoughts of revolt. This is an area from which personal judgment cannot be excluded, and unhappy subjects who feel oppressed will surely consider themselves justified in making such accusations or contemplating resistance. But notwithstanding the prominent role of equity and the law of nature as a moral standard in the Hobbesian commonwealth, Hobbes never countenanced the slightest compromise in condemning rebellion as always wrong and never legally or morally justified. He had at least a plausible argument for this position in the conviction that revolution and civil war were always far worse for human beings than a sovereign's misgovernment.

But while he did not recognize the legitimacy of rebellion, he did point out that there were such things as natural punishments that were a part of the natural law. All human actions, he remarked, gave rise to a long chain of consequences, the end of which no one could foresee. Acts done for pleasure must incur the pains that may be part of their natural consequences and do more harm than good. Thus, intemperance is naturally punished with diseases, injustice with the violence of enemies, pride with ruin, and cowardice with oppression. In the same way, Hobbes concludes, "negligent government of princes" is punished "with rebellion; and rebellion, with slaughter.

For seeing punishments are consequent to the breach of laws, natural punishments must be naturally consequent to the breach of the laws of nature, and therefore follow them as their natural, not arbitrary effects."[115]

Hobbes lived in an age of revolutions and revolutionary ideologies, as he was well aware, one in which many countries and the greatest European states, including the Spanish, French, and English monarchies, were smitten by violent internal conflicts ranging from peasant and urban revolts to provincial insurrections and nationwide civil wars springing from deep religious and political divisions.[116] In the preface to the English translation of *De Cive* he recorded that his country "some few yeares before the civill Warres did rage, was boyling hot with questions concerning the rights of Dominion, and the obedience due from Subjects, the true forerunners of an approaching War." He lamented the influence of populist and revolutionary doctrines that had cost the lives of so many kings and men—doctrines holding it lawful to kill tyrant kings, that kings could be deposed for certain causes, and that private men had the right to judge whether the commands of kings were just or not before obeying them.[117] Throughout his intellectual life, therefore, the strongest motive of his political philosophy was to contribute to the peace and stability of states by fashioning a civil and moral science that would expose the errors and consequences of these dangerous opinions. Since such opinions arise daily, he said in his preface to *De Cive*,

> if any man now shall dispell those clowds, and by most firm reasons demonstrate that there are no authenticall doctrines concerning right and wrong, good and evil, beside the constituted Lawes in each Realme, and government; and that the question whether any future action will prove just or not, good or ill, is to be demanded of none, but those to whom the Supreme hath committed the interpretation of his Lawes; surely he will not only shew us the high way to peace, but will teach us how to avoyd the close, dark, and dangerous by-paths of faction and sedition, then which I know not can be thought more profitable.[118]

With beliefs like these, no major thinker of the seventeenth century ever accorded a higher validation to civil life and organized political society, the rule of law and duty of obedience, and the mutual respect of subjects for one another's rights than did Hobbes. The notion of nostalgia for an early golden age in which a benign nature allowed human beings to live spontaneously without government in freedom, peace, and plenty was totally alien to him. His concept of the state of nature, though somewhat tinged with associations of primitivism, connoted essentially a condition, which he believed could occur in any era, in which the collapse of effective rulership and law through an imperfect constitution and civil strife brought on a war of all against all that threatened the fruits and existence of civilization. The contrast between Leviathan and the state of nature was thus fundamentally a contrast between civil peace and the benefits of civilization, on the one hand, and fear, insecurity, violence, and reversion to barbarism on the other. Hobbes, who, like his older contemporary and friend the lawyer-philosopher Francis Bacon, was a firm believer in the possibility of intellectual and scientific progress, never doubted that the existence of an absolute sovereignty, and the subordination and limitations on individual freedom it entailed, was a rational and moral necessity and a huge gain for human beings.

Although Hobbes is not mentioned, the British legal philosopher H.L.A. Hart's discussion of law and morals in his classic work, *The Concept of Law*, expresses essential elements of the Hobbesian view so well that it is worth quoting his remarks in full as the conclusion of this chapter:

> The facts that make rules respecting persons, property and promises necessary in social life are simple and their mutual benefits are obvious. Most men are capable of seeing them and of sacrificing the immediate short-term interests which conformity to such rules demands. They may indeed obey, from a variety of motives: some from prudential calculation that the sacrifices are worth the gains, some from a disinterested interest in the welfare of others, and some because they look upon the rules as worthy of respect in themselves and find their ideals in devotion to them. On the other hand, neither understanding of long-term interest, nor the strength or goodness of will, upon which the efficacy of these different motives towards obedience depends, are shared by all men alike. All are tempted at times to prefer their own immediate interests and, in the absence of special organizations for their detection and punishment, many would succumb to the temptation. No doubt the advantages of mutual forbearance are so palpable that the number and strength of those who would co-operate voluntarily in a coercive system will normally be greater than any likely combination of malefactors. Yet, except in very small closely knit societies, submission to the system of restraints would be folly if there were no organization for the coercion of those who would try to obtain the advantages of the system without submitting

to its obligations. "Sanctions" are therefore required not as the normal motive for obedience, but as a guarantee that those who would voluntarily obey shall not be sacrificed to those who would not. To obey, without this, would be to risk going to the wall. Given this standing danger, what reason demands is voluntary cooperation in a coercive system.[119]

CHAPTER 4

Hobbes, the Moral Philosopher

Self and Others

From his own time to the present, there has been a persisting misconception of Hobbes as a thinker for whom the calculation by each individual of his self-interest and advantage is the predominant and determining feature in human relationships and moral decision making. This view has been thought by its proponents to be justified by Hobbes's depiction of human nature as innately unsociable, competitive, and generally aspiring to outdo or dominate others, and by the precedence he assigned in the scheme of human life to self-preservation as an essential motivational force, a primordial right, and a primary goal of moral reason. The host of Hobbes's English critics in the seventeenth century and early eighteenth century, who included royalists, philosophers, theologians, and secular thinkers and publicists, despite the fact that some of them were influenced by certain of his political ideas, frequently accused him of atheism and irreligion on such grounds as his philosophical materialism and determinism, his theological unorthodoxy with respect to various Christian doctrines, and his teachings on the state of nature, law, and sovereignty.[1] Commonly included in this indictment was also the priority he gave to the principle of self-preservation. The Anglican bishop Richard Cumberland in his anti-Hobbesian treatise *A Philosophical Inquiry into the Laws of Nature* (1672) maintained that Hobbes made self-preservation man's chief aim, to be pursued at any price, and that while with one hand he offered kings and princes the gift of the great powers of sovereignty, in the other hand he held "a sword ready to pierce their breast," because by his principles they could never be safe from their successors, who might kill them to take their place.[2] The philosopher Locke was probably thinking primarily of Hobbes when he alluded in his unpublished *Questions Concerning the Laws of Nature* to those

> who refer the entire law of nature to the self-preservation of each individual and seek no deeper foundation for it than self-love and that instinct by which each man cherishes himself and looks out, so far as he is able, for his own safety and preservation.

Locke rejected this position, on which he commented that

> if the care and preservation of one's self should be the fountain and beginning of this entire law, virtue would appear to be not so much man's duty as his interest, and nothing would be right for a man were it not useful.[3]

In 1683, Oxford University took notice of this alleged Hobbesian view in a decree condemning "certain pernicious books and damnable doctrines destructive to the sacred persons of princes, their state and government, and of all humane society," which included political works by Hobbes. Of the twenty-seven propositions the university condemned, six were charged to the philosopher, the first of which stated that "Self-Preservation is the fundamental law of nature and supercedes the obligation of all others, whenever they stand in competition with it."[4]

Modern scholars have often concurred with this traditional misinterpretation of Hobbes's thought in accepting it as a matter of fact that his moral and political theory was anchored in the supremacy of the principle of self-interest. A highly competent contemporary moral philosopher takes it for granted in a recent essay that "Hobbes . . . relied on self-interest in constructing his view" of human life and that an "implicit contrast" exists in his work "between self-interest (to which Hobbes assigns the motivational power) and altruism that was, and still is, largely endorsed by common sense."[5] The moral philosopher David Gauthier is one of a number of Hobbes scholars who have denied that Hobbes had a concept of moral obligation, since to be obliged means there is something one ought to do even though it may conflict with self-interest, and, according to Gauthier, acting against self-interest is not a possibility within Hobbes's reading of human nature.[6] Thomas Nagel has expressed the similar view that man as Hobbes describes him "can never perform any action unless he believes it to be in his own best interest. . . . He is susceptible only to selfish motivation and is therefore incapable of any action which could be clearly labeled moral. He might, in fact, be best described as a man without a moral sense."[7] S. A. Lloyd's summary of what she calls the standard philosophical interpretation of Hobbes includes the opinion that moral considerations could not possibly have played any functional role in his political theory, because self-interest was for him the motivating ground of all obligation.[8]

It is weird that modern philosophical critics, generally free of the religious and political biases of their seventeenth-century predecessors, could have considered themselves so much wiser than Hobbes that they did not hesitate to insist, however wrongly, that he had no theory of moral obligation and attributed all human actions to self-interest. In his own mind, this charge could not have possibly been true. For as we have seen, the foundational concept of his moral and political theory, along with the right of nature, was the law of nature, and he had no doubt that this law and the moral law were identical, that the natural law was a science of virtue and vice and of good and evil, and that its rules of human conduct deriving from reason were not only self- but other-regarding, affecting the conscience and promoting various traditional virtues in human beings. It is not surprising that certain present-day Hobbes scholars, reacting against the imputation to him of a moral system allowing for nothing but self-interest, have depicted him instead as a virtue theorist concerned with the formation of moral character and instructing individuals to become right-acting people.[9]

Given the constitution of human nature as analyzed by Hobbes, which highlights partiality to self, self-interest does, of course, play a prominent part in his moral philosophy, but it is also transmuted by him into something much wider that transcends the limited good of single individuals and expands into a common or general good. Some confusion has been caused by his statements to the effect that individuals regard whatever they desire as good, so that good and the object of desire are the same for an individual. He frequently declares, for example, that "necessity of nature makes men to will and desire . . . that which is good for themselves, and to avoid that which is hurtful," that "every man, by naturall necessity desires that which is good for him," and that "whatsoever is the object of any man's appetite or desire that is it which he for his part calleth good, and the object of his hate and aversion evil."[10] One wonders how different these propositions are from the opinion of Socrates that "no man voluntarily pursues evil, or that which he thinks to be evil."[11] In his later treatise on man, *De Homine*, Hobbes repeats the point that "the common name for all things that are desired, insofar as they are desired, is good," and connects this view with that of Aristotle, who, he said, "hath well defined good as that which all men desire." The same work avers that "nature is so arranged that all desire good for themselves," and that "the greatest of goods for each is his own preservation."[12] These statements can all be associated with Hobbes's belief that nothing is "simply good" in itself, that the words "good" and "evil" are "ever used with relation to the person that useth them," and that men always equate good with what they desire and pleases them.[13]

What all these propositions affirm is that human beings always act to satisfy their own desires, which by necessity they define as good, or, alternatively, that all human beings desire the object of their desire. They do *not* state that human beings act solely for personal self-interest or that their desires are exclusively self-regarding.[14] The philosopher Bernard Gert has offered the best critique of the theory that Hobbes based his moral philosophy exclusively on self-interest. He distinguishes between psychological and tautological egoism: the first holds that human beings act only from self-interest and never from moral reasons respecting the good or needs of others, the second holds that all human actions are necessarily motivated by the agent's desires. Gert argues that Hobbes was essentially a tautological but not a psychological egoist.[15] A tautological statement, however, is one that is true by definition, and I am not sure that Hobbes thought himself to be offering a purely definitional, not an observational or empirical, proposition in maintaining that what human beings desire they call good. In any case, however, he surely never meant to suggest that human beings are so formed by nature that they are entirely limited in their desires by what is good only for themselves and can never be motivated to desire the good of others. Such a view, which excludes the possibility of altruistic behavior, is very obviously false, and Hobbes's psychological naturalism would have rejected it as completely counter to human experience and observation. Most individuals may perhaps act a good deal of the time according to what they deem their self-interest, as Hobbes believed, but they may also be influenced to act at times for non-self-interested reasons, as he also understood, and make sacrifices for others. It is not uncommon to know men and women who devote part of their lives to helping other people even at a personal cost because they desire the good of these others; such individuals may also feel that their own good is tied up with the good of others and that they become better and kinder persons by helping the latter. In his dedication of *Leviathan* to the memory of Sidney Godolphin, a royalist who fell in the civil war, Hobbes's description of Godolphin belies any notion that self-interest is the sole spring of action. He pictures this aristocratic gentleman as possessing all of the virtues that dispose a man "either to the service of God or to the service of his country, to civil society or private friendship" and as having these virtues inherent in him and "shining in a generous constitution of his nature."[16]

It is important to note, incidentally, that self-interest as a motive for action cannot be thought inherently antithetical to or incompatible with a moral point of view. The moral philosophy of Joseph Butler (d. 1752), cleric, theologian, philosopher, and one of the foremost British thinkers of the eighteenth century, assigned an important place to self-love, which included the desire of happiness, in the composition of human nature and sought to demonstrate the harmony that commonly existed between virtue and self-interest.[17] A recent volume of essays by a number of contemporary philosophers on the relationship between morality and self-interest shows how complex the concept of self-interest can be and how it can interfuse quite naturally with moral obligations and actions that may relate to self but are consciously associated with specific virtues and the good of others. This is particularly demonstrated in an insightful article by W. D. Falk, who offers a critique of the deprecation of what he terms "the personal ought" of one's own interest, in which he observes that "men often have cause to be temperate, courageous, and wise for their own good" and also notes the pointlessness of then complaining that such men act solely for their own sake.[18]

Hobbes stated at the conclusion of *Leviathan* that "I ground the civil right of sovereigns, and both the duty and liberty of subjects, upon the known natural inclinations of mankind, and upon the articles of the law of nature."[19] This means that he based his moral and political theory on the empirically observed nature of man as both the matter and the maker of civil society and human morality and on the ethical precepts contained in the law of nature. Human nature was thus both the material and the creator of the artificial man Leviathan, the symbol of the sovereign power from which men derived their peace and security.[20] This approach not only conformed to his methodological conception of moral and political philosophy as sciences dealing with natural and artificial bodies, which he outlined in the ninth chapter of *Leviathan*, it also fulfilled the aim I have attributed to him in his critique of the natural law tradition of supplying the moral law of nature with a firm nontranscendental, nonsupernatural, and nonteleological origin and grounding. Grotius, Hobbes's eminent predecessor, never presented a systematic account of the law of nature, and although he described human nature as the "mother of the law of nature," all that he meant by this was the inherent sociability of human beings, an idea that was a truism in the natural law tradition.[21] Hobbes undertook the far harder task of explaining how a moral and political order could be fashioned and carried on by human beings who were in a high degree self-centered individuals. He nevertheless stated unambiguously that "there is . . . no inconsistence of human nature with civil duties, as some think."[22] I think we may say, moreover, that he believed he had shown in his account of the laws of nature and their relation to a peaceful, secure, commodious, and possibly happy existence that not only had rational human beings very good reasons to be moral but that among these reasons was that attempting to live by the laws of nature made for virtuous people and was the right thing to do. In explaining the distinction between just and unjust, he emphasizes that these terms apply less to particular actions than to persons and their general disposition and mind-set; hence, to be just, he said, "signifies . . . to be delighted in just dealing, to study how to do righteousnesse, or to indeavour in all things to doe that which is just."[23]

Hobbes's refusal, as I have previously noted, to condemn human nature and the passions as either evil or sinful,[24] his profound recognition that the drive to go on living is both a compulsive instinct and a rightful human desire, and his acceptance of desires and interests as necessary and inevitable features of man's existence and moral world that could be trained and educated but not suppressed or abolished testify not only to his psychological naturalism and the realism of his moral philosophy but in particular to its humanity and the charitable allowance it makes for the needs of human nature. If we compare Hobbes for a moment with that great and most exacting of European moral philosophers, Immanuel Kant (d. 1804), we can at once see the difference. A mind less like Hobbes's can hardly be imagined.[25] In his political conceptions and values, Kant was a republican, a liberal, a strong sympathizer with the French Revolution, and a profound believer in personal moral autonomy and civil and religious freedom. His concept of the state and sovereignty required the strict rule of law and equal citizenship. Whereas Hobbes viewed the international system of independent sovereign states as necessarily constituting a hostile condition analogous to the state of nature, Kant envisaged the possibility of a peaceful international order among states founded on law. Kant nevertheless admired Hobbes as a man of genius and an original, paradoxical thinker, and discussed his work in several different connections.[26] Hobbes would certainly have agreed with Kant's comment that from "the crooked timber of humanity nothing perfectly straight could ever be made," as well as with his further statement in the same work that man "certainly abuses his freedom with respect to other men, and although as a reasonable being he wishes to have a law that limits the freedom of all, his selfish animal impulses tempt him, where possible, to exempt himself from them."[27] But Kant's moral philosophy laid a heavy unremitting burden of duty on individuals in the process of living. His universal rules of human conduct, framed as categorical imperatives conformable to reason, required every person in their dealings with others to treat these others as ends in themselves, never as a means to further ends, and to act only in accord with those maxims or principles that one could will to be a universal law for all mankind.[28] Kant's moral theory not only is debatable, it is not wholly clear, and it is difficult if not impossible in many instances to know how to apply. It makes the moral life a severe trial of rule following and continual duty, in contrast to Hobbes, whose laws of nature are intended to appeal to and promote the rational desires and needs of human beings for peace, security, commodious living, and happiness.

To Hobbes, it was obvious that each person cannot help being by nature in a certain sense the center of his universe around which everything else revolves and that the thing closest to every human being is the consciousness of his own self, with its incessant stream of desires and needs. For him these are ineradicable characteristics of human nature that moral philosophy must take as its point of departure. In their natural condition, without government or law, men are in a continually hostile state and have the natural right and complete freedom to use any means they judge necessary to secure their own survival and bodily protection against the threat of death and violence. The first and fundamental law of nature as a deliverance of reason instructs them, however, to seek peace, from which is derived a second law ordaining that they be willing to renounce their unlimited rights when others are also willing to do so, and to be contented with as much freedom against other people as they would allow to other people against themselves.[29] Here already we have a moral principle of equality and reciprocity that may owe its original motivational force to the interest every individual has in his own personal survival but that has become enlarged, mutual, and social by comprehending the interest and needs of everyone who desires peace. To be sure, covenants will be necessary to give effect to these two laws of nature and others that follow. But Hobbes underscores their unmistakable moral character in three distinct ways. One is to equate the laws of nature with their "easy sum," which is the other-regarding precept, "Do not that to another, which thou wouldst not have done to thyself." Not mentioning here that this rule is to be found in the Scripture, he simply explains that it will negate the effect of an individual's own passions and self-love in weighing the actions of other people.[30] The second way is to point out that the laws of nature always oblige the conscience to put them into effect if possible.[31] The laws of nature as moral rules thus always exert a claim on the human conscience to be disposed to comply with them, which can hardly be true of the motive of self-interest. The third way in which Hobbes shows that the laws of nature are moral directives is to identify them with a number of what he calls "moral virtues" such as justice, gratitude, equity, and others, all promoting peace.[32] Hobbes scholars and readers of the philosopher frequently take little notice of the various precepts set forth in the fifteenth chapter of *Leviathan,* entitled "Of Other Laws of Nature," although these are essential to his conception of morality and what it means to be a moral person. A number of them are rules of individual conduct that mandate such requirements as a general willingness to accommodate oneself to other people, a readiness to pardon past offenses when the offender is sorry, the infliction of punishments not as retribution but for the sake of deterrence and the future correction of the offender, and the avoidance of all expressions or signs of hatred and contempt for others. In passing, Hobbes also mentions the prohibition of things tending to the destruction of individuals, such as drunkenness, which are also forbidden by the law of nature.[33]

Hobbes did not question the existence of a common good or interest that unites people despite a presumption that every individual acts for his own benefit.[34] The fundamental assumption that grounds the laws of nature as moral directives and precepts of action in human relationships is that reason recognizes them as means to peace and therefore as a common good from which everyone gains. In the case of the creation and maintenance of the commonwealth, personal interest and the common good coincide in the need and rational desire for peace. Hobbes's political theory has no difficulty in distinguishing between private interest and the common good. Thus he points out that when men have once consented "for the common good, to peace and mutuall help," there will still be need of a sovereign power to restrain them by fear, lest they should afterward dissent "when their private Interest shall appear discrepant from the common good."[35] In comparing forms of government, he considered monarchy superior to all the others because it united the public interest and the private interest of the sovereign most closely in a single individual, and where this was the case, he stated, the public interest was most advanced.[36] Speaking of the sovereign's obligation to make good laws, he explains that a good law is one that is necessary for the good of the people.[37] The theme that runs through his entire discourse on the duties of the sovereign is its responsibility to procure the people's good and safety.[38] There are for Hobbes quite obviously not only individual and personal but common, collective, and public good and interests.

Obligation

Modern political theorists generally mean by political obligation a moral requirement to obey the law.[39] Hobbes made frequent references to obligation, which he defines as being obliged or bound to do or not to do something. An obligation is always a restriction on the liberty of the agent, and men become bound or obliged when they agree to transfer or renounce a right.[40] It seems to be Hobbes's view that obligation is created by or originates in contracts or covenants.[41] The sole exception is the obligation of human beings to obey God, which is not due to a covenant or relinquishment of rights but to God's omnipotence. Hobbes is clear that God's right of sovereignty in his natural kingdom of the created world (as distinct from the unique covenantal relationship he had with his chosen people the Jews, as described in the Old Testament), and the obedience men owe him are entirely based on God's irresistible power.[42] He is also clear that because all men are "equally by nature Free," no man has any obligation "which ariseth not from some action of his own," which is to say that all obligations have their original beginning as voluntary acts.[43]

It might be possible to classify the three kinds of obligation, namely, moral, legal, and political, that come within Hobbes's purview, in which case the first would be the obligation of obedience to the law of nature, the second of obedience to the civil law, and the third of obedience to the sovereign in everything except the various freedoms not transferable by covenant and necessarily retained by subjects as part of their natural rights. He does not analytically distinguish these three types of obligation, however, but treats them as intertwined, overlapping, and reinforcing one another.[44] It seems to me, moreover, that the basic and primordial obligation in Hobbes's political theory is moral and springs from the law of nature, which incorporates the precepts leading to the establishment and preservation of peace. It is in compliance with the moral law of nature as a product of right reason that men consent by covenants and contracts to renounce their unlimited natural rights for the sake of peace and a secure life. This renunciation entails the assumption of a lasting voluntary obligation by subjects to obey the civil law of the sovereign as long as the latter is capable of protecting them. The moral obligation to obey the law of nature consists in the individual's conscientious desire and effort even in the state of nature to put this law into effect if possible. The law of nature becomes true law and therefore legally as well as morally obligatory when it is ordained by the civil law. "The Law of nature," Hobbes states, "commands us to keep all civil Laws," and he points out that the obligation to obey these laws is more ancient than their promulgation because it is contained in the very constitution of the commonwealth.[45] The civil law, in turn, being the measure for the sovereign's subjects of right and wrong and good and evil, incorporates the law of nature and makes it enforceable through legal sanctions and the power of the sword.[46] Hobbes takes great pains in *Leviathan*'s fourteenth chapter to deal with questions such as how and between whom the agreements are made that create the commonwealth, what might invalidate them, and the problems of performing first, mutual trust, and nonperformance. Following on the dictate of the first two laws of nature to renounce those rights that, "being retained, hinder the peace of mankind," the third law of nature decrees that "men perform their covenants, without which covenants are in vain, and but empty words." This particular law of nature, according to Hobbes, is the fountain and origin of justice, the definition of injustice being "the not performance of covenant."[47] By forbidding breach of covenant, the law of nature also undergirds the moral obligation to obey the civil laws.[48] In stressing the obligation to abide by covenants, or *pacta sunt servanda*, Hobbes was reiterating an essential precept that was continuous within the natural law tradition and also came to be accepted as one of the fundamental principles of international law.[49]

Some scholars who doubt that Hobbes had a genuine moral theory and contend that human beings as he conceives them act exclusively from self-interest have introduced the notion of a prudential obligation to define the sort of obligation propounded in his moral and political philosophy. J. W. N. Watkins argued that Hobbes's laws of nature are not moral but prudential, and resemble a doctor's orders to a patient rather than moral rules.[50] Philip Pettit in a recent book endorses Watkins's view of prudential obligation applied to Hobbes, which he describes as more or less accepted at present as the orthodox doctrine.[51] A. E. Taylor, in attempting to make a separation between the psychological egoism he attributed to Hobbes and what he believed was the philosopher's genuinely ethical doctrine, held that without the command of God to make them obligatory, the laws of nature in Hobbes were only prudential maxims.[52] Stuart M. Brown, Jr., a critic of Taylor's thesis, insisted, however, that Hobbes's psychological and moral principles could not be separated and that his laws of nature were both moral and prudential.[53] C. B. Macpherson seems to waver on whether obligation for Hobbes was moral or prudential, while David Gauthier maintained that his moral system "was nothing more than a system of common, or universal, prudence."[54] S. A. Lloyd's summary of the standard philosophical interpretation of Hobbes lists the opinion that political obligation for him was prudentially based, and that his laws of nature were mere maxims of prudence.[55]

W. D. Falk in a previously mentioned essay on morality and self-interest has remarked that "it is a textbook cliché against Hobbes that his account of morality" comes down to precepts "of prudence or expediency." Falk reminds us that the prudent and the expedient are not the same, and that in various instances doing what is prudent can also be a moral virtue. He notes that when Hobbes said that "men never act except with a view to some good to themselves," this was quite different than if he had said that they never act except with a view to what is expedient.[56]

Almost a century ago a well-known essay on the basis of moral philosophy by the British philosopher H. A. Prichard argued that a prudential motive was not a moral motive and that the only true justification there can be for a moral action is the intuitive understanding that it is the right thing to do.[57]

In classical antiquity and later centuries, philosophers reckoned prudence or practical wisdom (Latin *prudentia*, Greek *phronesis*) as one of the foremost virtues. Aristotle described it as the ability to deliberate about what sorts of thing conduce to the good life in general.[58] Aquinas discussed prudence at length in his analysis of the moral virtues in his *Summa Theolo-*

giae, which defined it as "right reason of things to be done" and "good counsel about matters regarding man's entire life, and the end of human life."[59] So highly did these two thinkers rank the virtue of prudence that no later philosopher who followed their view would have disparaged Hobbes as a moral philosopher if he had attributed a prudential character to the law of nature. In our own time, however, prudence is rarely thought of any longer as a virtue, and its meaning, as our English dictionaries currently define it, commonly refers to such qualities as practical judgment, foresight, sagacity, shrewdness, and circumspection. Hobbes himself took prudence to mean mainly foresight or practical judgment in estimating from experience what would be most likely to happen in the future.[60]

Whatever status we assign to prudence, however, the notion of prudential obligation as used by Watkins and others in reference to Hobbes appears to be a misnomer and a misconception. Whether considered a virtue or not—and Hobbes does not call it a virtue—prudence cannot be obligatory, although a prudent person may think it good to take on some particular moral obligation to himself or to others, such as resolving to stop smoking or drinking or to contribute some of his time to help a human rights organization. There can accordingly be no such thing as a prudential obligation, and since Hobbes has told us that being obliged is the same as being bound, he could not have thought of prudence as obligatory. While his laws of nature do, of course, have an instrumental value in being conducive to peace and security, they are not maxims of prudence but genuine moral principles that make people who strive to live by them both just and good. These laws are also beneficial for people to act on and to which they become obliged when they have recognized the need to renounce a part of the rights given them by nature and accept the terms of living as members of society and the commonwealth under the sovereign's government.

In *Behemoth*, his posthumously published dialogue explaining the causes and reasons of the English civil war, Hobbes provides an illustration of the difference between his understanding of prudence and moral virtue. In reply to his interlocutor's observation that he distinguishes between the ethics of subjects and the ethics of sovereigns, the philosopher comments that

> the virtue of a subject is comprehended wholly in obedience to the laws of the commonwealth. To obey the laws, is justice and equity, which is the law of nature, and consequently is civil law in all nations of the world; and nothing is injustice or iniquity, otherwise, than it is against the law. Likewise, to obey the laws, is the prudence of a subject; for without such obedience, the commonwealth (which is every subject's safety and protection) cannot subsist.[61]

Hobbes's account of the laws of nature in *Leviathan* includes several pages that follow immediately after his presentation of the third law of nature requiring that covenants should be kept. Here he discusses for the only time the question of whether justice actually exists and if it would be conformable to reason for everyone to make or break covenants as they supposed conducive to their benefit.[62] He attributes the view he rejects to "the fool," who "hath said in his heart, 'there is no such thing as justice.'" As Hobbes's readers would have known, this fool's statement was directly reminiscent of the famous sentiment of another fool that appears in the opening line of the Bible's fourteenth psalm: "The fool hath said in his heart, 'There is no God.'" Hobbes cites this latter statement also and declares that the two fools are the same.[63]

Pronouncing the fool's reasoning to be specious and false, he proceeds to define the issue in terms of two alternative situations. The first is under the commonwealth, when one party to a covenant has already performed or a civil power exists to make him perform; in this case, he asks, would it be contrary to reason and against the other party's benefit to perform? Hobbes answers that the second party's nonperformance would be against reason, and explains that when a man does something tending to his own destruction, even if by some unforeseen accident the event turns to his benefit, this cannot make such actions "reasonably or wisely done." The other situation is a condition of war, in which no one can hope to avoid destruction without the help of confederates.[64] In these circumstances, according to Hobbes, a person who says "it is reason to deceive those that help him can in reason expect no other means of safety than what can be had from his own single power." Someone who breaks his covenant, therefore, and states that he may do so with reason could not be admitted to any society formed for peace and defense except through an error, which couldn't reasonably be counted on as a means of security. Such a person, who would perish if cast out of society or survive only because of the errors of other men, has "acted against the reason of his preservation."[65]

Hobbes thus insists that it is in accord with reason to adhere to covenants and to perform as a second party if the first party has performed. What is noteworthy in this instance, however, is that his response to the fool does not invoke any moral principles. But this absence is not because such principles aren't an essential part of his moral and political philosophy but because he is speaking to a moral fool who has already denied the obligatory character of the law of nature in respect to covenants and acts unscrupulously from shortsighted perceptions of supposed advantage.[66] The answer he frames is accordingly one that befits the fool and is largely of a pragmatic character, which shows that even in allegedly rational calculations of personal self-interest and benefit, the fool is mistaken.[67]

Having dealt with the fool, Hobbes then mentions the case of those who might think it reasonable to break a covenant in order to attain sovereignty by rebellion, and others who believe that the laws of nature are rules that conduce not to the preservation of life but to the attaining of eternal felicity after death. To gain heaven, these latter might think it a work of merit to breach a covenant and kill, depose, or rebel against the sovereign power they have themselves instituted by their own consent. Some may also believe that there is no obligation to keep faith with persons they consider heretics. Needless to say, Hobbes rejects all these opinions as contrary to reason. The only imaginable way to secure perpetual felicity, he maintains, is by keeping covenants, and he stresses that the likelihood of attaining sovereignty by rebellion is so small that it can hardly be expected. He adds the further skeptical argument, moreover, that no one can have any natural knowledge of man's estate after death or of any reward to be given in the afterlife for a breach of faith.[68]

Hobbes thus seeks to refute every argument that might be offered as an excuse for noncompliance with a legitimate covenant. It is worth noting, before we leave this subject, the degree of similarity between his answer to the fool and the reflections of the contemporary British moral philosopher Philippa Foot on the question of why be just and the improbability of not being found out if one is unjust. Is it true to say, she asks,

> that justice is not something a man needs in his dealings with his fellows, supposing only that he is strong? Those who think that he can get on perfectly well without being just should be asked to say exactly how such a man is supposed to live. We know that he is to practice injustice whenever the unjust act would bring him advantage; but what is he to say? Does he admit that he does not recognize the rights of other people, or does he pretend? In the first case even those who combine with him will know that on a change of fortune, or a shift of affection, he may turn to plunder them, and he must be as wary of their treachery as they are of his. Presumably the happy unjust man is supposed ... to be a very cunning liar or actor, combining complete injustice with the appearance of justice. ... Philosophers often speak as if a man could thus hide himself even from those around him, but the supposition is doubtful, and in any case the price in vigilance would be colossal. ... As things are, the supposition that injustice is more profitable than justice is very du-

bious, although like cowardice and intemperance, it might turn out incidentally to be profitable.[69]

Is and Ought

Hobbes's political treatises cover a multitude of subjects, but one of their most prominent features is that they are works of moral instruction and prescriptive ethics. They not only tell us a great many things that he believed to be fact and true about human beings and other subjects, they also contain many thoughts concerning duties and what human beings should do. They are, in other words, deeply normative as well as descriptive and analytical. All of his laws of nature are ought statements and value propositions, and he also refers frequently to duty. He equates the concept of obligation with duty and speaks of the people's duty to the sovereign power.[70] The discussion in *Leviathan* on the office of the sovereign is largely concerned with the sovereign's duties to its subjects, for the word "office" as used there has the double meaning of a public or governmental position and a duty as a moral or legal obligation.

This brings up the question of how Hobbes comes by the concept of ought in his moral prescriptions, whence he derives it, and what its status and justification are. This question is prompted by the philosopher David Hume's famous discussion in his *A Treatise of Human Nature* (1740) of the relation of *is* to *ought* in moral discourse. Arguing in that work that moral distinctions are not perceived by reason, Hume pointed to the fallacies of moral philosophers, who invariably first proceeded "in the ordinary way of reasoning" to make various observations on the being of God and human affairs and then suddenly, instead of the usual propositions connected by *is* and *is not*, "I meet with no proposition that is not connected with an *ought*, or an *ought not*. This change is imperceptible; but is, however, of the last consequence." He went on to note that this *ought* or *ought not* expressed a new relationship or affirmation that needed to be explained, and a reason given for what seemed inconceivable, "how this new relation can be a deduction from others, which are entirely different from it." Hume declared that attention to this point "wou'd subvert all the vulgar systems of morality."[71] His comment was more than a critique of the obvious logical error of importing into the conclusion of a syllogism a proposition that was not entailed by its premises. It also implied the fundamental question for moral philosophy of how *ought* could ever be deduced from *is*, and more broadly, how any normative moral proposition could be a deduction from statements of fact. In the twentieth century the logical gap between is and ought and the related distinction between facts and values became one of the mainstays of moral relativism and a major subject of discussion and debate among philosophers, social scientists, historians, and other scholars, who either sought to overcome this gap or maintained that it couldn't be bridged. The fallacy of "ethical naturalism" was ascribed to those who held that moral values could be deduced from facts about the world and who identified moral properties such as goodness with natural facts such as pleasure or utility.[72] If the disjunction between facts and values is valid, then there is no way to prove the truth of moral or other ought propositions relating to values. Such propositions affirming an ought or an ought not have a different status than those, whether true or false, that posit facts to which we attribute an objective existence. While we may offer good reasons for believing the former, they cannot follow simply and immediately as a logical deduction from the facts. Thus, although it is a fact that the Bible condemns homosexuality as evil, this could not license the logical conclusion that homosexual acts should be punished by law. Similarly, while we might state it as a fact that capital punishment is cruel, this would not justify the deductive conclusion that it should be prohibited.

As I noted in an earlier chapter, one of the basic objections that legal positivist critics have raised against the concept of natural law is that it disregards the distinction between facts and values, conflating the two by mistakenly confusing law as it is with law as it ought to be and contending that no purportedly legal enactment can be valid law unless it meets some moral criterion.[73] Natural law, in the words of a contemporary legal philosopher, "emphasizes the ethical dimension of law, which, it asserts, is essential to anything properly called law." Legal positivism, on the other hand, "insists that, although the morality of law is a critical question, law and ethics are distinct," and its core is the claim that "it is in no sense a necessary truth that laws reproduce or satisfy certain demands of morality."[74] Thinkers in the Western and Christian natural law tradition of earlier centuries did not perceive any distinction between facts and values, which to them were on the same footing in a universe possessed of meaning and purpose, and they affirmed the existence of the law of nature as an inherently moral, just, and rational law originating in nature and the reason and will of God. This eternal, immutable law was held to be grounded in a cosmic context that was both ontological and normative and ruled by the providence of God. Philosophers and theologians considered the moral law of nature superior to human positive law and taught that the latter's validity was impaired if it conflicted with natural law by failing to be just. A modern Catholic historian and theorist of natural law reaffirms the Thomistic conviction that the establishment of this law is possible only as "a continuation of metaphysics, the science of being, which, when applied to the free will of rational man, becomes the science of oughtness." On this view, the existence of natural law presupposes the identity of deontology and ontology, or of oughtness and goodness with being.[75] There are some contemporary natural law theorists, however, who, heedful of the Humean problem of is and ought, have attempted to revise the traditional doctrine of the law of nature in a way that does not require it to depend on the existence of God and a normative conception of nature. A notable work exemplifying this approach is the treatise on natural law and natural rights by the Oxford legal philosopher John Finnis, which conceives the law of nature as prescribing the basic forms of human good and argues that it does not presuppose God's authorization or illicitly deduce values from facts.[76] Finnis's claims, which have encountered a variety of criticisms, are debatable, and it seems to me more than doubtful that there could be a moral law of nature without a theistic foundation.[77]

As my previous discussion has shown, Hobbes's originality and subversive character as a philosopher of natural law consisted in his rejection of the grounding of this law in a transcendental, divinely governed, and value-laden cosmic order and his basing it on theorems of human reason whose precepts are not properly or actually law until they become incorporated in the civil law of the state as the command of the sovereign. He would probably have regarded the proposition of the identity of being and oughtness as an example of the senseless speech of scholasticism. He did not see any relationship between the moral law of nature and metaphysics or believe that its precepts were inscribed in the constitution of the universe.[78] Rather, as he explains in *Leviathan* and elsewhere, natural law is the product of human right reason, and its moral rules are ones that human beings could and should follow in fulfillment of their desire for self-preservation and a life of peace and security in civil society. He founded the law of nature on the needs and desires of human nature when instructed by reason. In doing so, he anticipated Hume's view in his *Treatise of Human Nature* that "Human Nature is the only science of man, and yet has hitherto has been the most neglected."[79] His moral philosophy, which he equated with natural law, is closely associated with his science of man and human nature.

One of the frequent indictments brought against Hobbes during his lifetime and afterward was that he was a voluntarist with no fixed moral position who failed to understand that good and evil were absolutes immutably founded in the nature of things and instead referred the definition and judgment of all moral values to the arbitrary will of the sovereign. The Platonist Ralph Cudworth (d. 1688), a leading philosopher of the later seventeenth century and author of the posthumously published *A Treatise of*

Eternal and Immutable Morality (1731), attacked him for maintaining that justice is not inherent in nature but "a mere factitious and artificial thing, made only by men and civil laws." Unable to stomach the thought that moral distinctions might be decided by human definition, Cudworth argued tautologically that just as something is white by its whiteness or alike by its likeness, so actions that are right and wrong or just and unjust possess this character as an eternal necessity of their nature according to the disposition of divine reason. In an echo of the controversy between fourteenth-century voluntarists and intellectualists,[80] he contended that not even the omnipotent will of God could change the moral nature of things, for this would involve a contradiction between God's absolute power and his supreme wisdom and goodness.[81] Samuel Clarke (d. 1729), another eminent thinker, opponent of atheism, and a disciple and popularizer of Newton, accused Hobbes of claiming "that there is no such thing as just and unjust, right and wrong originally in the nature of things; that men in their natural state, antecedent to all compacts, are not obliged to universal benevolence, nor to any moral duty whatsoever," and that "in civil societies, it depends wholly upon positive laws or the will of the governors, to decide what shall be just or unjust." According to Clarke, Hobbes made morality and the distinctions of right and wrong and just and unjust to depend on positive law without a "foundation in the nature of things" and taught that the laws of God and nature "are no further obligatory than the civil power shall think fit to make them so." Critics of this kind, who branded Hobbes an atheistic philosopher, were Christian rationalists convinced that reason could clearly demonstrate God's existence and goodness. Making no distinction between facts and moral values, they ran the two together by assuming that the truths of morality were immanent in nature and the world order. Their endeavor, as Clarke put it, was "to deduce the original obligations of morality, from the necessary and eternal reason and proportion of things." It was Clarke in particular that Hume seems to have been thinking of when he criticized the errors of moral philosophers in their passing imperceptibly from is to ought.[82]

Some scholars have suggested that Hobbes himself, by erecting a theory of moral and political obligation on a number of empirical propositions about human nature, provided an example of the naturalistic fallacy of attempting to deduce moral principles from factual premises. R. S. Peters considered him guilty of this mistake, and J. W. N. Watkins came close to the same view when he stated that Hobbes derived his prescriptions from factual premises but without committing a logical fallacy, because these prescriptions were not moral but prudential, in the manner of doctor's orders.[83] C. B. Macpherson admitted that Hobbes had fallen into what seemed the grave error of trying to deduce ought from is, but defended his procedure nonetheless. In addition to arguing that it was wrong to impose Hume's later logical canons on Hobbes, he contended that Hobbes's postulate of human equality was a radically new position that enabled him to deduce right and obligation from fact by assuming that "right did not need to be brought in from outside the realm of fact, but . . . was already there," because equal need entailed equal right. Macpherson called this a leap in political theory as radical as Galileo's formulation of the law of uniform motion in natural science.[84] Both of these arguments are clearly untenable. If Hume's or any other rule of logic is valid, then it is always in force, irrespective of the time to which it is applied. Hobbes, a logician himself, would also have known perfectly well that anything in the conclusion of a valid syllogism had to be part of its premises. If Hobbes, moreover, as Macpherson believed, posited the existence of right as an original part of a proposition of fact about human equality, then his reasoning would simply have assumed the truth of the conclusion he needed to prove and thus constituted a clear case of the logical error of *petitio principii*, or begging the question.

At one time I myself thought that Hobbes's political philosophy provided an example of the fallacy exposed by Hume, a view I stated in an essay in 1992.[85] I now regard this opinion as mistaken and believe that his moral precepts and theory of obligation should be considered in the main as the teachings and outcome of practical reason in light of the various facts he adduces and takes as true. It is true, of course, as we will recall, that in reflecting on the possibility of moral and political philosophy as a science, he looked upon geometry as a model by which a series of universal truths could be attained in a process of deductive reasoning from definitions.[86] He often claimed that he had proved the truth of his moral and political philosophy. He said in *De Cive* that he had demonstrated from maxims based on the desiring and rational parts of human nature "the absolute necessity of Leagues and Covenants" and "the rudiments of both morall and of civill Prudence." In a passage from *Leviathan* quoted earlier, he explained that he grounded "the civil right of sovereigns, and both the duty and liberty of subjects, upon the known natural inclinations of mankind, and upon the articles of the law of nature."[87] These statements need not signify, however, that he claimed to arrive at his conclusions deductively from factual premises and are best understood, I think, as meaning that they emerge as truths in a continuous process of practical reasoning based on the facts he presents concerning human nature. He did not envisage the three main parts into which he divided philosophy, dealing in successive order first with body in its most general features, next with man as a natural body, and finally with the commonwealth as an artificial body, as forming a single comprehensive deductive system. He declared of *De Cive*, for instance, a treatise first published in 1642 that belonged to the third part of his philosophy, that it was grounded on its own principles "sufficiently knowne by experience" and therefore stood in no need of the two preceding parts concerning body and man, which had not yet appeared.[88] His first law of nature specified "as a general rule of reason that every man ought to endeavour peace, as far as he has hope of obtaining it."[89] The moral obligation implicit in this law is not the product of a syllogism. It is part of a rational reflection on means and ends that instructs human beings, creatures with a natural instinct and compelling desire to preserve their lives, that the surest way of doing so is to seek peace and thereby gain egress from the condition of war of all against all. Hobbes does not conflate is and ought, and when he first introduces the idea that human individuals have a natural right to try to preserve themselves, he finds the origin of this right, a normative principle, not in the fact of desire, need, or human equality but in right reason, another and prior normative principle. What the word "right" signifies, he states, is "that liberty which every man hath to make use of his naturall faculties according to right reason: Therefore the first foundation of naturall Right is this, That every man as much as in him lies endeavour to protect his life and members."[90] Rightness thus constitutes the shared moral quality that joins reason with the human claim to self-preservation as a right of nature. While one might say that the practical reasoning in Hobbes's moral philosophy sometimes brings is and ought in close proximity to one another, the latter is not proffered as a deductive conclusion; rather, it presents itself as a rational instrumental judgment arrived at in relationship to the facts as described, and therefore encourages us to understand that peace is a great common good for human beings and one they have strong reason to pursue. If this argument is correct, then Hobbes's laws of nature are not a fallacious deduction of values from facts but moral truths that emerge in a chain of practical reflection and teach human beings how to attain what all of them desire, namely, civil peace, the prerequisite of security and civilized living.[91]

Religion and Toleration

Hobbes discussed religion in all of his political treatises and in various other works. His fullest account is in *Leviathan*, the last two parts of which contain a series of remarkable chapters dealing with a Christian commonwealth and the perversion of religion by Catholic scholasticism, vestiges of paganism, and false philosophy. He was something of a biblical scholar, and his political writings are full of biblical references and doctrinal interpretations. For the claims he makes about the church, religion, and their relation to the commonwealth, his greatest argumentative resource in confirming his position was the Bible. His religious beliefs have been the subject of extensive discussion and remain in some respects obscure. Externally he conformed to the Anglican state church throughout his life. His treatment of religion conveys the impression that while he might have been in some respects a believing Christian, he was not a man of deep piety or faith.[92] Although often charged with atheism and irreligion, an accusation that could be very dangerous in his time, his own words deny that he was an atheist. He made many statements about God and suggested that it was impossible to avoid the conclusion of God's existence as the first and eternal cause of all things.[93] At the same time, though, he held that God was unknowable, incomprehensible, and all-powerful, a being wholly beyond the realm of philosophy and human reason of whom we can have no conception.[94] God, he said, governs "as many of mankind as acknowledge his providence by the natural dictates of right reason" and reigns over men "not as creator and Gracious" but because of his irresistible power. Both natural and divine law, he held, oblige those who believe in God to honor, worship, and obey him.[95]

A vein of skepticism is frequently apparent in his discussion of religion. A skeptical note seems to underlie his definitions of religion and superstition in *Leviathan*: "Fear of power invisible, feigned by the mind or imagined from tales publicly allowed, Religion; not allowed, Superstition." To be fair, however, we should not omit his conclusion: "when the power is truly such as we imagine, True Religion."[96] While emphasizing that natural reason and the senses were not to be renounced in the study of Scripture, he offered the skeptical advice, when anything in Scripture was too obscure to grasp, "to captivate our understanding to the words," because such mysteries were not comprehensible, adding that "it is with the mysteries of our religion as with wholesome pills for the sick, which, swallowed whole, have the virtue to cure, but chewed, are for the most part cast up again without effect,"[97] a remark that could have been made by Voltaire.

Hobbes held a number of unorthodox beliefs that scandalized and offended many of his readers. Even though discretion and a concern for his safety may have impelled him to withhold some of his thoughts, many of the things he said were bold, courageous, and even daring. His philosophical naturalism, as we have seen, extended to religion, whose "natural seed" in human beings he traced to such things as belief in "ghosts" or spirits and ignorance of physical causes.[98] He considered God a corporeal and material being and thought that incorporeal spirits could not exist. He denied that the soul was immaterial and immortal. He maintained that there was no hell of eternal torment, but that the soul, being mortal, died with the body, and that at the resurrection those who were saved would be bodily restored to eternal life on earth while the damned were condemned to eternal death. He threw doubt on miracles, advanced questionable ideas about the Trinity, and showed that Moses could not have written most of the biblical books, the Pentateuch, generally attributed to him.[99] He inveighed against superstition, of which he seemed to imply that much of religion consists, and attacked the superstitious belief in spirits, prognostications from dreams, and false prophecies.[100] He was highly skeptical of claims by individuals to divine inspiration and personal revelations from or communication with God, and was inclined to treat such claims as most likely untrue. An admirer of Copernicus and Galileo, he pointed out that the Bible was not a book of knowledge about the physical world or nature but was "written to shew unto men the kingdom of God, and to prepare their minds to become his obedient subjects, leaving the world and the philosophy thereof to the disputation of men for the exercising of their natural reason."[101] His biblical exegeses in behalf of his political conclusions and religious beliefs are among the most extraordinary features of his work. In *Leviathan* he acknowledged that his book might most offend because of the "texts of Holy Scripture alleged by me to other purpose than ordinarily they use to be by others."[102] The Earl of Clarendon, author of a large critique of *Leviathan*, complained of the license with which Hobbes used Scripture to justify his arguments, "torturing the texts" by "putting such unnatural interpretations on the words, as hath not before fallen into the thoughts of any other man, and drawing very unnatural inferences from them."[103]

Hobbes's foremost interest in religion as a political theorist and natural law thinker was to prevent it from ever becoming a cause of sedition or political disunity that could threaten the commonwealth's existence. He believed he had proved that "subjects owe sovereigns simple obedience in all things wherein their obedience is not repugnant to the laws of God."[104] To show that such repugnancy need never exist in the case of Christian subjects was his principal aim. The most frequent pretext of sedition and civil war in Christian commonwealths, he declared in *Leviathan*,

> hath a long time proceeded from a difficulty, not yet sufficiently resolved, of obeying at once both God and man, when their commandments are one contrary to the other. It is manifest enough that when a man receiveth two contrary commands, and knows that one of them is God's, he ought to obey that and not the other, though it be the command even of his lawful sovereign . . . or . . . of his father. The difficulty, therefore, consisteth in this: that men, when they are

commanded in the name of God, know not, in divers cases, whether the command be from God, or whether he that commandeth do but abuse God's name for some private ends of his own.[105]

He was almost equally concerned about the ambition of the clergy as a threat to the civil power and insisted that the Christian church and its ministers did not constitute a spiritual power separate from the temporal but were a part of the commonwealth and necessarily subject to the sovereign's authority. It would be difficult to name an English thinker of the seventeenth century who was more anticlerical and Erastian than Hobbes. He detested the pretensions of the clergy to interfere in politics and seemed to regard most clerics as obscurantists who opposed the free interchange of philosophical ideas and hindered the progress of knowledge. In a letter in 1641 to his patron the Earl of Devonshire, he declared that there could be no unity in the church unless its government depended on the state, and that "the dispute for precedence betwene the spirituall and civill power, has of late more then anything in the world, bene the cause of civill warres, in all places of Christendome."[106] He opposed the claims not only of the Catholic papacy to correct and depose kings but of the Presbyterian ministers who replaced the Anglican Church and its bishops during the English civil war and demanded the church's autonomy from the secular authority. His history of the civil war in *Behemoth* denounced the Catholics, the arrogance and ambition of the English bishops, and the seditious Presbyterian ministers, these last of whom he accused of inciting the civil war, the murder of King Charles I, and guilt for the death of all the victims of the war.[107]

Hobbes strove consistently to show that the moral and political principles he advanced were in keeping with the Christian religion and endorsed and sanctioned by Scripture. He stated that the laws of nature, which he had called theorems of reason and included "equity, justice, mercy, humility, and the rest of the moral virtues," were all also "divine laws."[108] He defined a church as a body of Christians "united in one Christian sovereign," so that in principle there could be only one church in every Christian commonwealth.[109] This church, he believed, being the commonwealth's public institution of religion, must be based on a single uniform public worship that everyone would follow.[110] The powers he ascribed to the Christian sovereign covered not only the government of the church but included the status of chief pastor with the authority to decide doctrinal controversies and the canon and meaning of Scripture. Chapter 42 of *Leviathan*, "Of Ecclesiastical Power," the longest in the book, contains an extensive theological analysis of the nature and position of the church and clergy, as well as a critique of the authority of the papacy as set forth in the treatise *De Summo Pontifice* (*On the Supreme Pontiff*) by the Catholic theologian Cardinal Bellarmine. Throughout his treatment of the Christian church and religion, Hobbes strove to frame the position of the sovereign in relation to Christian doctrine and biblical instruction and example in such a way that that no conflict could arise between subjects' moral obligation to obey the sovereign and its laws and their religious obligation to God and personal interest in their salvation.

Hobbes, who died in 1679 at the age of ninety-two, lived through an era in which the question of religious toleration became a great issue of religious and political controversy for the first time in Western history. The Protestant revolt initiated by Luther against Catholicism and the consequent destruction of the religious unity of Europe had brought into being in a number of countries new Protestant religious denominations—Lutheran, Calvinist, Anglican, and others; state churches ruled by princes and governments; and numerous sects. This was the most intolerant period in the history of Christianity, marked by religious wars, fierce confessional hatreds, and relentless persecution by both Catholic and Protestant authorities of individuals and groups who differed from the religion of the state and dominant church. The demand for religious toleration, freedom of conscience, and pluralism, voiced chiefly by members and spokesmen of persecuted religious minorities and radical Protestant thinkers and publicists, arose in reaction to these developments. Among its aspects was a broad critique and condemnation of what I have elsewhere called the Christian theory of persecution, that is, the rationale for and justification of the use of force, heresy prosecutions, and the death penalty to preserve religious unity and eradicate dissent.[111] England was strongly affected by the toleration controversy, which reached its height in a flood of publications and argument in the revolutionary decades of 1640–60.[112] During these twenty years both the English monarchy and Anglican Church, governed by royally appointed bishops, were overthrown. Between 1649 and 1660 England existed as a republic in which there ceased to be a state church and compulsory church attendance, while a number of new denominations and sects established themselves permanently in Britain, notably Presbyterians, Congregationalists or Independents, Baptists, and Quakers. After the revolution's failure in 1660, which resulted in the restoration of kingship in the person of Charles II and the reinstatement of bishops and the ecclesiastical monopoly of the Anglican Church, toleration remained a burning issue in England down almost to the end of the seventeenth century, owing to the government's revival of the regime of persecution of both dissident Protestants and Catholics.

Hobbes would have been fully aware of the toleration controversy, needless to say, and a few scholars have even wished to depict him as a supporter of religious toleration.[113] It is difficult to see him in this light, however, when we think of his advocacy of a national church and the Hobbesian sovereign's extensive power over church and religion, which would appear to be as little compatible with an enduring toleration of religious differences or the existence of religious freedom as it was with political liberty. Several of Hobbes's ideas respecting religion nevertheless attest to his opposition to religious persecution and reflect a broad strain of humanity and liberalism in his perspective on religious diversity.

Among the most important features of his religious thinking in a liberal direction was his skeptical critique and deconstruction of the belief in heresy, a subject on which his attitude was affected by his personal experience. The Christian idea of heresy is traceable back to the New Testament and became one of the foundation stones of the justification of persecution that emerged in the early centuries of the Christian church.[114] A heretic was a Christian condemned by ecclesiastical authority for obstinately persisting in a false religious belief contrary to the orthodox Christian faith despite correction and admonition. A heretic who refused to recant would be excommunicated and handed over to the secular authorities for punishment, which could include imprisonment and death. Hobbes first mentions heresy in *Leviathan*. There he states that the difference in men's passions causes them to give different names to the same thing, so that those who approve a private opinion call it an opinion, while those who dislike it call it heresy, "yet heresy signifies no more than a private opinion, but has only a greater tincture of choler."[115] Claiming that the sovereign is the sole judge of heresy, he defines it as "a private opinion, obstinately maintained, contrary to the opinion which the public person [i.e., the sovereign] has commanded to be taught."[116] While these formulations retain the notion of heresy, they also diminish and relativize it by reducing its meaning to a private opinion without any inherent stigma, thus corresponding to the original sense of the Greek term *haeresis*, meaning an opinion.

In his Latin version of *Leviathan*, published in 1668, Hobbes added an appendix containing a notable chapter on heresy in the form of a dialogue in which he explained that the word came from the Greek *haeresis* and referred to the doctrine of any sect or a philosophical opinion. He further pointed out that truth and error were irrelevant to the definition of heresy, which merely denoted an opinion. His discussion includes a sketch of the history of heresy in the Christian church up to and after the Council of Nicaea in the fourth century CE, which affirmed the orthodox doctrine of the Trinity as three persons in one substance. Hobbes maintained in his historical account that there was no longer a law of heresy in England. Deploring heresy prosecutions, he called it inequitable "that a man whose faith is chosen at his own peril . . . should be punished on the ground that his faith is erroneous, especially by those whom another's error does not harm. To err, to be deceived, to have wrong opinions [*male sentire*] . . . is not by its nature a crime." He applied Jesus's parable of the tares (Matt. 13.24–30), one of the classic New Testament texts frequently cited in the debate over tolerance, to prove that "a Christian man is prohibited from punishing a heretic with a civil penalty." Condemning the burning of heretics, he pointed out that "no one is accepted by Christ who has been compelled to him by fear of death."[117]

Hobbes may have been the first English thinker to investigate the history and origins of the idea of heresy in a skeptical light and thereby to diminish its significance. Since it was no more than an opinion, its sole importance in his political theory was that the sovereign possessed the authority to decide what was heresy. During the 1660s Hobbes also wrote a short tract entitled *An Historical Narration concerning Heresie, and the Punishment Thereof* and discussed the subject in several other works as well.[118] He had a personal motive for his concern with heresy, since he was sometimes called a heretic and, fearing the possibility of prosecution, consistently contended that no basis for such a proceeding existed in English law. In 1666, *Leviathan* was named in the House of Commons as a profane and atheistic book.[119] In 1669 Daniel Scargill, a young academic disciple of Hobbes at Cambridge University who was accused of Hobbism, was compelled to make a public recantation of certain Hobbesian doctrines.[120] In 1683, as this chapter has already noted, a decree of Oxford University condemned several of Hobbes's books and ordered them to be publicly burned. The philosopher therefore had strong reasons to oppose the idea of heresy and strip it of the terrors of its religious meaning.

A marked strain of religious liberalism in Hobbes is likewise evident in the fact that in his consideration of religion and the Christian faith from a political angle, he was not concerned with the individual's private thoughts but only with publicly stated opinions and doctrinal disputes that might be dangerous to the peace of the commonwealth.[121] He distinguished obedience to the religious ordinances of the state, that is, external conformity, from religious belief and maintained that no one could be forced to believe, since "men's belief and interior cogitations are not subject to . . . commands, but only to the operation of God, ordinary or extraordinary."[122] In *Behemoth*, he declared that "a state can constrain obedience, but convince no error, nor alter the minds of them that believe they have the better reason. Suppression of doctrine does but unite and exasperate, that is, increase both the malice and power of them that have already believed them."[123] It is clear from such statements that Hobbes strongly disapproved of any inquisition into conscience or private religious beliefs and attempts to punish them. In declaring that the work of Christian ministers was to make men believe and have faith in Christ, he pointed out that faith did not depend on compulsion or command but on the certainty or probability of arguments, and that ministers accordingly had no power to punish anyone for not believing or contradicting what they said.[124] He also sought to establish a wide latitude for Christians to avoid persecution, and incurred great disapproval for maintaining that a Christian should seem to obey even a sovereign's command to disbelieve or to verbally disavow Christ. Envisaging such a situation, he noted that a command to disbelieve was of no effect because faith, being a gift of God, could not be commanded. Moreover, disavowal of Christ in words was merely "an external thing," and a Christian who had the faith of Christ firmly in his heart possessed the liberty to follow the biblical example of Naaman the Syrian, a convert to the God of Israel, who was nevertheless permitted by the prophet Elisha to accompany his king in bowing to a pagan idol (2 Kings 5.17–19).[125] Hobbes scholars have apparently not realized that his use of the precedent of Naaman in this case did not originate with him but, as I have shown elsewhere, was a well-known argument cited by many previous authors and biblical commentators to justify religious dissimulation in order to escape persecution.[126] Moreover, when Hobbes spoke of the necessity of a single public church and a uniform worship in the commonwealth, he seems at the same time to have allowed for the possibility of worship in private, which he called "in secret free," that Christians might practice without offending.[127] Basing himself on his theory of the sovereign as authorized representative of the commonwealth, he also stressed that "whatsoever a subject was compelled to do in obedience to his sovereign, and doth it not in order to his own mind, but in order to the laws of his country, that action is not his but his sovereign's." In other words, Hobbes made a strict distinction between the mind's inner state of belief and the exterior actions performed in compliance with a legitimate command, which could be at variance with each other. Hence, commenting on Jesus's saying, "Whosoever denieth me before men, I will deny him before my Father which is in heaven" (Matt. 10:33), he declared that if this denial by a subject was due to the command of the sovereign, the responsibility did not lie in the subject but in the sovereign.[128]

As I noted in the previous chapter, Hobbes affirmed that faith and obedience were the only things necessary for salvation or entrance to the kingdom of heaven. "All that is necessary to salvation," as he put it *Leviathan*, "is contained in two virtues: faith in Christ, and obedience to laws." Concerning obedience, he stated that it expressed itself in the endeavor to obey God, who accepted the will for the deed, and was the same as charity, love, and righteousness. He further explained that the laws of God to which obedience was required were identical with the laws of nature, the principal one being the obligation to abide by agreements, especially in heeding "the commandment to obey our civil sovereigns, which we constituted over us by mutual pact with one another."[129] Analyzing the nature of faith, he went on to declare that according to Scripture, the only article of faith necessary for salvation was that Jesus was the Christ and Messiah whom God had sent to rule over and redeem the world by bringing to human beings the eternal life that was lost to them by the sin of Adam.[130] Among the scriptural proofs for this proposition he cited statements that called the faith necessary for salvation an "easy" doctrine, for if "an inward assent of the mind," he pointed out, to all the doctrines concerning the Christian faith "(whereof the greatest part are disputed)," were necessary for salvation, "there would be nothing in the world so hard as to be a Christian."[131]

In *The Elements of Law* Hobbes called the points of faith necessary to salvation "fundamental" and all other points "a superstruction."[132] This sufficiently indicates the importance of the difference between the two. We should not underestimate the significance of Hobbes's claim that belief in Jesus as the Christ and Messiah was all the faith Christians needed to attain salvation. It constituted a liberal theological position that relegated doctrinal disputes about other issues of belief to a secondary importance. It simplified the Christian religion to its essentials in a single fundamental article of belief. It also possessed an irenic character conducive to concord between Christians, because it centered on a fundamental conviction nearly all believers could accept despite other doctrines on which they might disagree. Hobbes was not the first thinker to hold that salvation through Christ as Messiah and savior was the *unum necessarium* or core of the Christian faith.[133] This was indeed one of the basic Protestant doctrines and related to Martin Luther's original Reformation teaching of justification by faith alone. But with Luther and other Protestant theologians this doctrine came accompanied by others like the Trinity and infant baptism that together defined orthodoxy. Among the exponents of toleration who preceded Hobbes in his view of the faith needed for salvation was the humanist and theologian Sebastian Castellio (d. 1563), the greatest champion of religious liberty and freedom of conscience in the sixteenth century, who also wished to simplify the Christian religion to this one essential doctrine in the hope of reducing theological disputes and promoting harmony among Christians.[134]

The most striking manifestation of Hobbes's affinity with religious liberalism, tolerance, and pluralism was the comments he made in the penultimate chapter of *Leviathan* in favor of ecclesiastical autonomy and freedom of worship. By the time he wrote this treatise there was no longer a state church in England. The Anglican Church and the institution of episcopacy had been legally abolished, and the Presbyterians who had tried thereafter to establish a compulsory national church were also defeated. What took their place in the 1650s under the English republic and the ascendancy of Oliver Cromwell were large numbers of Protestant churches of different denominations, especially Presbyterians, Congregationalists, also called Independents, and Baptists, all of them voluntary bodies whose members were free to meet and worship as they wished. The government largely relaxed its control of religion while retaining an oversight of the ministry and churches to make sure they maintained peaceable relations with one another and avoided inciting sedition through their preaching. Even Anglicans and Catholics were allowed some liberty in these years to meet for private worship.

One might suppose that when Hobbes reflected at the end of *Leviathan* on some of these recent developments he would have considered them manifestations of a deplorable religious anarchy that had been permitted to arise. Instead, he described them as a "dissolving of knots," meaning a granting of liberty, and observed that "we are reduced to the Independency of the primitive Christians, to follow Paul, or Cephas, or Apollos, every man as he liketh best. Which, if it be without contention, and without measuring the doctrine of Christ by our affection to the person of his minister ... is perhaps the best." This was an extraordinary admission to come from a thinker who had insisted in the same work on the necessity of the sovereign's rule of religion, the churches, and the ministry. He offered two grounds for this surprising new judgment. The first was that there ought to be no power over human consciences but the Bible itself, working faith in everyone. The second was that everyone ought to use their own reason in religion instead of following the reason of other men, which was little better, he said, "than to venture [one's] salvation."[135] He combined these sentiments with an expression of the need for intellectual freedom. Referring to the ministers of religion, he declared that they ought not to be displeased with the loss of their ancient authority. since they knew better than anyone that "power is preserved by the same virtues by which it is acquired (that is to say, by wisdom, humility, clearness of doctrine, and sincerity of conversation), not by suppression of the natural sciences and of the morality of natural reason, nor by obscure language, nor by arrogating to themselves more knowledge than they make appear, nor by pious frauds."[136]

A recent book on Hobbes has gone so far as to argue that he actually supported the changes the English revolution and republic had effected in religion, admired the leadership of Cromwell, the foremost man in the faction of the political Independents, and genuinely sympathized with the principle of congregationalism or independency, according to which each individual church should be independent and self-governing.[137] These are questionable claims, but in any case, however, the man who expressed the views on religion that I have just cited above could not have been simply an advocate of untrammeled authoritarian government.

Conclusion

Hobbes's posthumous legacy in the late seventeenth century and the eighteenth century was a complex one. His work was widely known and read not only in Britain but also in France, Germany, the Netherlands, and other parts of Europe. In England his most important successor as a philosopher of natural law was Locke, who put the concept to revolutionary use in his *Two Treatises of Government* (1689) but never developed his theory of natural law as a moral system to the same extent that Hobbes did. In various countries Hobbes's religious skepticism and unorthodoxy, his rationalism, materialism, and determinism, and his bold departures in biblical interpretation influenced readers, who included deists and opponents of institutional religion, to perceive him as a freethinker, anti-Christian, and a major force for intellectual and scientific progress against ecclesiastical obscurantism, superstition, and religious authority. In this way he became one of the inceptive thinkers of the early Enlightenment in Europe.[138] On the other hand, there were numerous philosophical critics, such as Cumberland, Cudworth, and Clarke, who paid little regard to his emphasis on the virtues and on the obligations of the sovereign to its subjects under natural law and attacked his philosophy as fundamentally atheistic and hence a danger to the Christian religion and morality. The philosopher Leibnitz (d. 1716), an admirer of Hobbes but a Christian Platonist and metaphysician, probably had him in mind when he referred to certain philosophers who mistakenly held that that justice and goodness were arbitrary because they were a product of will, instead of recognizing that they belonged, like numbers and proportion, to the eternal and necessary truths about the nature of things. Leibnitz also observed that like the sophist Thrasymachus in Plato's *Republic*, Hobbes exalted power, maintaining that God had a right to do everything because of his omnipotence, thus failing to distinguish between right and fact, since what one can do and should do are two different things.[139] In the domain of natural law, Hobbes was a dominant figure. On the continent, the foremost natural law theorist with an international reputation in succession to Grotius in the later seventeenth century and beyond was the German Samuel Pufendorf.

Pufendorf strove to create a system of natural law independent of theology, though not of God, based, in spite of human self-centeredness, on sociability as the strongest motive and need of human nature. Although he sought to distance himself from Hobbes because of the latter's notorious reputation for irreligion, he reproduced a number of Hobbes's ideas and probably owed more to him than to any other modern philosopher of natural law.[140]

In *Leviathan's* dedication, dated April 1651 from Paris, Hobbes claimed that he had sought to pursue a path between "those that contend on one side for too great Liberty, and on the other side for too much authority," adding that it was hard to pass between the two without being wounded. Most readers would probably have no doubt that he leaned much more to authority than to liberty and would point in particular to his disparaging and generally unsatisfactory treatment of political liberty. From the standpoint of our own time and its twentieth-century history, his refusal, rooted in the logic of his doctrine of sovereignty, to recognize any right of resistance to government or the state, however abusive and oppressive it might be, would have to be seen as a serious deficiency in his moral and political theory.

Nevertheless, as I hope this essay has shown, his psychological naturalism, natural law precepts, and affirmation of a right of nature inherent in human beings are evidence of the humanity and ethical character of his moral philosophy. His greatness in this domain lies in his effort to explain that human beings can and must create their moral world themselves in accord with the needs of their own human nature and the instruction of reason founded on objective principles of rightness. In the political sphere, Hobbes's absolute sovereign and the obedience it requires from subjects do not entail or justify a lawless despotism or dictatorship. On the contrary, the sovereign power as he envisages it is not to rule arbitrarily but in accord with the law it promulgates. It is morally obligated by the law of nature to govern equitably, and its supreme aim as a ruler and legislator should be the safety and happiness of its subjects. Hobbes was a philosopher of secular mind and broad humanity, a natural law theorist who believed in justice and equity as moral norms obliging both the sovereign and its subjects, an analyst of religion who questioned the existence of heresy and was opposed to religious persecution and inquisition of conscience, and a political thinker whose highest aim was to teach men to regard and cherish the peace of the commonwealth and the goods of civilization it made possible as an inestimable benefit to human beings in their life in this world.

NOTES

CHAPTER 1
Some Basic Hobbesian Concepts

1. For the reader's convenience, I note that there are a number of biographies of Hobbes. Among those in English are Miriam Reik, *The Golden Lands of Thomas Hobbes* (Detroit, MI: Wayne State University Press, 1977), and the most recent one, by the philosopher and well-known Hobbes scholar A. P. Martinich, *Hobbes: A Biography* (Cambridge: Cambridge University Press, 1993). Noel Malcolm provides an up-to-date review of Hobbes's life and career in "A Summary Biography of Hobbes," in idem, *Aspects of Hobbes* (Oxford: Clarendon Press, 2002).
2. Otto Gierke, *Natural Law and the Theory of Society, 1500 to 1800* (Boston: Beacon Press, 1960), p. 61; this work is an English translation of a part of vol. 4 of Gierke's *Das deutsche Genossenschaftsrecht*, published in 1913; Carl J. Friedrich, *The Age of the Baroque, 1610–1660* (New York: Harper, 1952), p. 27.
3. Among recent accounts of Hobbes as a natural law theorist, see, e.g., Knud Haakonssen, *Natural Law and Moral Philosophy: From Grotius to the Scottish Enlightenment* (Cambridge: Cambridge University Press, 1996), a helpful survey that is disappointing, however, in its mistaken assumption that Hobbes was a follower of the Dutch jurist Hugo Grotius. The intellectual relationship between Hobbes and Grotius is discussed later in this chapter and the next. J. B. Schneewind includes comments on and selections from Hobbes in his useful collection of texts, *Moral Philosophy from Montaigne to Kant*, 2 vols. (Cambridge: Cambridge University Press, 1990), vol. 1, and rightly calls Hobbes (vol. 1, p. 112) "an indispensable central figure in the history of ethics."
4. Michael Oakeshott, "The Moral Life in the Writings of Thomas Hobbes" (1962), *Rationalism in Politics and Other Essays*, new exp. ed. (Indianapolis: Liberty Press, 1991), pp. 312, 323, and n., 332.
5. David Gauthier, "Hobbes: The Law of Nature," *Pacific Philosophical Quarterly* 82, no. 2 (2001): 258–84, reprinted in *Hobbes on Law*, ed. Claire Finkelstein (Aldershot, UK: Ashgate, 2005). This useful anthology reprints twenty-six essays of recent vintage dealing with Hobbes's legal philosophy.
6. A. P. Martinich, *The Two Gods of Leviathan* (Cambridge: Cambridge University Press, 1992).
7. On the subject of legal positivism and its origins, see H.L.A. Hart, "Legal Positivism," in *The Encyclopedia of Philosophy*, ed. Paul Edwards, 8 vols. (New York: Macmillan and Free Press, 1967); *The Concept of Law* (Oxford: Clarendon Press, 1986), pp. 181–89; "Positivism and the Separation of Law and Morals," in *Essays in Jurisprudence and Philosophy* (Oxford: Clarendon Press, 1983); and "John Austin," in *International Encyclopedia of the Social Sciences*, 17 vols. (New York: Mac-

millan and Free Press, 1968); on the contribution of Bentham, see also Jeremy Waldron, *"Nonsense Upon Stilts?"* (London: Methuen, 1987), chap. 3. Noted twentieth-century legal positivists such as Hart and Hans Kelsen reject the imperative theory of law, which defines it as the command of the sovereign, but continue to maintain that the concept of law does not entail any necessary connection with morals. On the meaning and different interpretations of legal positivism, see the papers collected in *The Autonomy of Law: Essays on Legal Positivism*, ed. Robert P. George (Oxford: Clarendon Press, 1996), and in *Natural Law Theory*, ed. Robert P. George (Oxford: Clarendon Press, 1992).

8 M. M. Goldsmith, "Hobbes on Law," in *The Cambridge Companion to Hobbes*, ed. Tom Sorell (Cambridge: Cambridge University Press, 1996), reprinted in Finkelstein, *Hobbes on Law*, pp. 3–4; Gregory Kavka, *Hobbesian Moral and Political Theory* (Princeton, NJ: Princeton University Press, 1986), p. 249; Jean Hampton, *Hobbes and the Social Contract Tradition* (Cambridge: Cambridge University Press, 1986), p. 107; S. A. Lloyd, *Ideals as Interests in Hobbes's Leviathan* (Cambridge: Cambridge University Press, 1992), p. 15.

9 Gauthier, "Hobbes: The Law of Nature," p. 16; he expresses the same position in "Thomas Hobbes and the Contractarian Theory of Law," *Canadian Journal of Philosophy*, Suppl., 16 (1990): 5–34, reprinted in Finkelstein, *Hobbes on Law*, p. 80. The essays reprinted in ibid. by Mark C. Murphy, "Was Hobbes a Legal Positivist?" originally published in *Ethics* 105 (1995): 846–73, and David Dyzenhaus, "Hobbes and the Legitimacy of Law," originally published in *Law and Philosophy* 20 (2001): 461–98, both argue that Hobbes was not a legal positivist. In "Thomas Hobbes and the Contractarian Theory of Law," Gauthier notes the fact that Hobbes offers "a subversive reinterpretation of the traditional conception of natural right and natural law" (p. 75), but goes seriously astray when he asserts (p. 81) that Hobbesian natural law does not provide an independent standard against which to judge the civil law. On Hobbes and legal positivism, see also James Bernard Murphy, *The Philosophy of Positive Law* (New Haven, CT: Yale University Press, 2005), chap. 3, which gives a critical account of Hobbes's views.

10 Norberto Bobbio, *Thomas Hobbes and the Natural Law Tradition* (Chicago: University of Chicago Press, 1993), pp. 147, 148. The original Italian edition was published as *Thomas Hobbes* (Turin: Einaudi, 1989).

11 Thomas Hobbes, *De Corpore*, 1655, Epistle Dedicatory, EW, vol. 1, pp. viii–ix.

12 DC, Epistle Dedicatory, p. 27; L, A Review and Conclusion, 13.

13 L, chap. 43.24; Hobbes makes this remark in connection with the interpretation of Scripture.

14 Oakeshott, "The Moral Life," p. 332.

15 Arthur O. Lovejoy and George Boas, *Primitivism and Related Ideas in Antiquity* (New York: Octagon, 1973; first published 1935); the quotations are taken from pp. 11–14, "Nature as a Norm," and chap. 3, "Genesis of the Conception of 'Nature' as a Norm." The appendix surveys various meanings of "nature," including twenty-six meanings in classical and medieval writings relating to its normative use in politics and religion. For some works on the history of the concept of

natural law, see Gisela Striker, "Origins of the Concept of Natural Law," in *Boston Area Colloquium in Ancient Philosophy* (1987), vol. 2, pp. 79–94; Leo Strauss, "Natural Law," in *International Encyclopedia of the Social Sciences*; R. W. Carlyle and A. J. Carlyle, *A History of Medieval Political Theory in the West*, 3rd ed., 6 vols. (Edinburgh: Blackwood, 1930–36); Heinrich A. Rommen, *The Natural Law: A Study in Legal and Social History and Philosophy*, rev. ed. (Indianapolis: Liberty Fund, 1998; first published 1947); A. P. d'Entrèves, *Natural Law: An Introduction to Legal Philosophy*, 2nd ed. (New Brunswick, NJ: Transaction Publishers, 1994), with a useful introduction by Cary Nederman; Paul E. Sigmund, *Natural Law in Political Thought* (Cambridge, MA: Winthrop Publishers, 1971), which contains selections from a number of texts with historical commentary. James Bryce's essay, "The Law of Nature," in *Studies in History and Jurisprudence*, 2 vols. (New York: Oxford University Press, 1901), vol. 2, includes some historical comments on the idea of nature in relationship to law.

16 Aristotle, *Nicomachean Ethics*, 1134b–35a, bk. 5, chap. 7; *Politics*, 1252–53, bk. 1, chap. 2.

17 See the article "Stoicism," in *Oxford Classical Dictionary*, 3rd ed., ed. Simon Hornblower and Antony Spawforth (New York: Oxford University Press, 1996), and E. V. Arnold, *Roman Stoicism* (London: Routledge, 1958; first published 1911). The collection of essays *Topics in Stoic Philosophy*, ed. Katerina Ierodiakonou (Oxford: Clarendon Press, 1999), contains an excellent bibliography and valuable discussions of Stoicism; see in particular Brad Inwood, "Rules and Reasoning in Stoic Ethics," and David Sedley, "The Stoic-Platonist Debate on *kathekonta*." Despite its age, the account of Stoicism by Wilhelm Windelband, *A History of Philosophy*, 2nd ed. (New York: Macmillan, 1905), pt. 2, chap. 1, remains illuminating.

18 The continued pertinence of Cicero in natural law thinking is illustrated by Hadley Arkes, "That 'Nature Herself Has Placed in Our Ears A Power of Judging': Some Reflections on the 'Naturalism' of Cicero," in George, *Natural Law Theory*.

19 Cicero, *De Re Publica (On the Commonwealth)*, 3.22. Save for some passages, this work was lost for centuries until the rediscovery of considerable fragments of it in 1820. Its definition of natural law was preserved in the *Divine Institutions* by the Christian apologist Lactantius of the later third century and became very widely known.

20 These opinions, cited in *Digest*, 1, "On Justice and Law," were those respectively of the jurists Ulpian, Gaius, and Paulus; the texts are reproduced in Sigmund, pp. 32–34; on the Roman lawyers' theory of the law of nature, see Carlyle and Carlyle, *A History of Medieval Political Theory*, vol. 1, chap. 3.

21 See Carlyle and Carlyle, *A History of Medieval Political Theory*, vol. 1, chap. 9, on the church fathers and natural law.

22 These passages in *Decretum*, 1, are cited by D. E. Luscombe, "Natural Morality and Natural Law," in *The Cambridge History of Later Medieval Philosophy*, ed. Norman Kretzmann, Anthony Kenney, and Jan Pinborg (Cambridge: Cambridge University Press, 1996), p. 707.

23 See Luscombe's survey of medieval philosophers of natural law in ibid., and Brian Tierney, *The Idea of Natural Rights: Studies on Natural Rights, Natural Law and Church Law 1150–1625* (Atlanta: Scholars Press, 1997), passim.

24 On voluntarism and intellectualism (sometimes called realism) in medieval moral philosophy and the theory of natural law, see Anton-Hermann Chroust, "Hugo Grotius and the Scholastic Natural Law Tradition," *New Scholasticism* 17, no. 2 (1943): 101–33, reprinted in *Grotius*, ed. John Dunn and Ian Harris, 2 vols. (Cheltenham, UK: Elgar Reference Collection, 1997), vol. 1; J. B. Korolec, "Free Will and Free Choice," in Kretzmann, Kenney, and Pinborg, *The Cambridge History of Later Medieval Philosophy*, pp. 636–38; Luscombe, "Natural Morality and Natural Law," pp. 713–15; Francis Oakley, *The Political Thought of Pierre d'Ailly: The Voluntarist Tradition* (New Haven, CT: Yale University Press, 1964), and *Natural Law, Laws of Nature and Natural Rights* (New York: Continuum International Publishers, 2005), chap. 3; J. B. Schneewind, *The Invention of Autonomy: A History of Modern Moral Philosophy* (Cambridge: Cambridge University Press, 1998), pt. 1 and pp. 8–9.

25 A. S. McGrade observes of William of Ockham, for example, that his appeals to natural law "clearly accepted the concept of objective value" common to the scholastic tradition, and that he integrated the principle of ethical objectivity or rationality with his voluntarism; *The Political Thought of William of Ockham* (Cambridge: Cambridge University Press, 1974), p. 190. See also Tierney's account (*The Idea of Natural Rights*, pp. 98–100) of the combination in Ockham's moral philosophy of voluntarism with rationalism and right reason.

26 Rommen, *The Natural Law*, pp. 51–53, deplores the development of voluntarism in the medieval theory of natural law and sees it as the progenitor of modern positivism.

27 On Catholic casuistry and natural law, see Albert E. Jonsen and Stephen Toulmin, *The Abuse of Casuistry: A History of Moral Reasoning* (Berkeley and Los Angeles: University of California Press, 1988), chap. 6; Jill Kraye surveys fifteenth- and sixteenth-century moral philosophy in "Moral Philosophy," in *The Cambridge History of Renaissance Philosophy*, chap. 7, and cites Melanchthon's statement on p. 323; Mordechai Feingold brings out the importance of Aristotle and discusses the teaching of moral philosophy at Oxford University in the late sixteenth and the seventeenth century in *The History of the University of Oxford*, vol. 4, ed. Nicholas Tyacke (Oxford: Clarendon Press, 1997), chaps. 5–6, passim; for the Protestant reformers and the doctrine of natural law, see Stephen J. Grabill, *Rediscovering the Natural Law in Reformed Theological Ethics* (Grand Rapids, MI: Eerdmans, 2006); on Neostoicism, see Richard Tuck, *Philosophy and Government 1572–1651* (Cambridge: Cambridge University Press, 1993), chap. 2.

28 Gierke, *Natural Law*, p. 235 n. 32.

29 See Haakonssen, *Natural Law and Moral Philosophy*, chap. 1, and T. J. Hochstrasser, *Natural Law Theories in the Early Enlightenment* (Cambridge: Cambridge University Press, 2000).

30 This is the title of Koyré's well-known book on the scientific revolution; Alexander Koyré, *From the Closed World to the Infinite Universe* (New York: Harper Torchbooks, 1958).
31 John McDowell, "Two Sorts of Naturalism," in *Virtues and Reasons: Philippa Foot and Moral Theory*, ed. Rosalind Hursthouse, Gavin Lawrence, and Warren Quinn (Oxford: Clarendon Press, 1995), p. 156.
32 G. H. Sabine, *A History of Political Theory*, 3rd ed. (New York: Holt, Rinehart, and Winston, 1964), p. 460.
33 Commenting on the revolutionary conflicts of the later sixteenth and seventeenth centuries, Gierke noted (*Natural Law*, pp. 37, 231 n. 13) that "the champions of popular sovereignty . . . availed themselves of the weapons of Natural Law," and mentions a number of writers as examples; see also Quentin Skinner, *The Foundations of Modern Political Thought*, 2 vols. (Cambridge: Cambridge University Press, 1978), vol. 2, chap. 9, and Jonathan Scott, *Commonwealth Principles: Republican Writing of the English Revolution* (Cambridge: Cambridge University Press, 2004), passim. This subject is further discussed in chap. 2.
34 DC, Preface to the Reader, pp. 30–31.
35 DC, chap. 14.4.
36 DC, chap. 3.31, 32; L, chap. 15.40.
37 EL, p. xvii; pt. 1, chap. 15.1, p. 57; DC, Epistle Dedicatory, pp. 25–26; L, chap. 26.21.
38 *Thomas Hobbes: Three Discourses. A Critical Modern Edition of Newly Identified Work of the Young Hobbes*, ed. Noel B. Reynolds and Arlene W. Saxonhouse (Chicago: University of Chicago Press, 1994), pts. 1, 4.
39 Andrew Huxley, "The *Aphorismi* and *A Discourse of Laws*: Bacon, Cavendish, and Hobbes 1615–1620," *The Historical Journal* 47, no. 2 (2004): 399–412. This work by Bacon, *Aphorismi*, was discussed and translated by Mark Neustadt in "The Making of the Instauration: Science, Politics, and Law in the Career of Francis Bacon," Ph.D. diss., Johns Hopkins University, 1987. It has also been discussed in my *Francis Bacon* (Princeton, NJ: Princeton University Press, 1998), pp. 151, 198–99.
40 *Digest*, 1.1.1, 9; see A. P. D'Entrèves, *Natural Law*, new ed. (New Brunswick, NJ: Transaction Publishers, 1994), p. 29, and the discussion and citations in Carlyle and Carlyle, *A History of Medieval Political Theory*, vol. 1, chap. 3, on the Roman lawyers' theory of the law of nature.
41 See his comment on Aristotle's philosophy in L, 46.11, which is part of a chapter entitled "Of Darkness from Vain Philosophy and Fabulous Traditions," a critical survey of ancient and medieval scholastic philosophy.
42 The Hardwick library catalogue is Chatsworth MS E1 A and is included in an annotated list of the Hobbes manuscripts at Chatsworth, home of the Duke of Devonshire, compiled by Noel Malcolm and printed in his *Aspects of Hobbes* (Oxford: Clarendon Press, 2002), p. 143. Richard A. Talaska has published the entire catalogue in his posthumous *The Hardwick Library and Hobbes's Early*

Intellectual Development (Bowling Green, OH: Philosophy Documentation Center, 2004). His introduction includes an analysis of the catalogue's contents, which he considers vital evidence of Hobbes's intellectual development. Unfortunately, he is not able to show which of these books Hobbes read. As he points out, however, many of the catalogue's titles reflect Hobbes's interests and were probably purchased for him and at his suggestion.

43 Among the works listed in the Hardwick library catalogue is Melchior Goldast's *Monarchia Sancti Romani Imperii* (1611–14), a three-volume collection of political tracts that includes writings by William of Ockham and Marsilio of Padua.

44 L, chap. 8.27.

45 L, chaps. 42, 44, passim.

46 EL, pt. 2, chap. 8.7, p. 137.

47 In her essay "Hobbes and the Beginnings of Modern Political Thought," in Reynolds and Saxonhouse, *Thomas Hobbes: Three Discourses*, Arlene Saxonhouse argues for and considerably exaggerates the points of intellectual contact between Hobbes and Machiavelli based on the attribution to Hobbes of the first discourse, "A Discourse upon the Beginning of Tacitus."

48 Robinson A. Grover, "The Legal Origins of Thomas Hobbes's Doctrine of Contract," *Journal of the History of Philosophy* 18 (1980): 177–94, reprinted in Finkelstein, *Hobbes on Law*, suggests that Hobbes learned a lot about law from the books in the Hardwick library (which he calls the Chatsworth collection), and that one of the sources of his discussion of contracts and the law of nature was St. German's famous work, which is listed in Hobbes's catalogue as no. 687 in Talaska's edition. Grover points to a number of resemblances between statements in St. German's book and statements by Hobbes, but is unaware that some of the former's observations on the law of nature in Question Two of the First Dialogue, such as the identification of the law of nature with the law of reason and on the right of self-defense, were commonplaces of the natural law tradition. Among the main sources on which the English lawyer relied for his knowledge of natural law were Aquinas and Jean Gerson; see Christopher St. German, *Dialogue Between a Doctor of Divinity and a Student of the Laws of England*, ed. T.F.T. Plucknett and J. L. Barton, *Selden Society*, vol. 91 (1974), introduction, pp. xxiii–xxv.

49 Samuel Pufendorf, *On the Law of Nature and Nations* (1672), preface, in *The Political Writings of Samuel Pufendorf*, ed. Craig L. Carr (New York: Oxford University Press, 1994), pp. 95–96; idem, *Specimen Controversiarum circa Jus Naturale* (1678) (*Example of Controversies Concerning Natural Law*), p. 1, cited in Richard Tuck, "The 'Modern' Theory of Natural Law," in *The Languages of Political Theory in Early Modern Europe*, ed. Anthony Pagden (Cambridge: Cambridge University Press, 1987), p. 103. I am reasonably sure that Pufendorf's praise of Grotius for accurately distinguishing natural from positive law is based on Grotius's own claim to have done this, which he states in the Prolegomena to his work; see Hugo Grotius, *The Law of War and Peace*, The Classics of International Law, Latin text and English translation based on the Amsterdam Latin edition of 1646, 2 vols. (Oxford: Clarendon Press, 1925), vol. 2, Prolegomena, 30.

50 Barbeyrac's survey, *An Historical and Critical Account of the Science of Morality*, was included in his French translation of Pufendorf's treatise in 1706. I have used the English version printed as the prefatory discourse in Basil Kennet's English translation of the fifth edition of Pufendorf's treatise; Samuel Pufendorf, *The Law of Nature and Nations: Political Writings* (London, 1749); the passages cited are on pp. 23, 66, 67, 70, and 71. For Barbeyrac's importance in the dissemination and discussion of natural law ideas in the early Enlightenment, see Tuck, "The 'Modern' Theory of Natural Law," p. 107, and Haakonssen, *Natural Law and Moral Philosophy*, pp. 58–59. For other historical accounts than Barbeyrac's of natural law and moral philosophy written in the later seventeenth and eighteenth centuries, see Hochstrasser, *Natural Law Theories in the Early Enlightenment*, passim. The earliest of these seems to have been the first chapter of Pufendorf's *Specimen Controversiarum* (1678), on which see Hochstrasser, pp. 65–71, who calls it "the first history of morality."
51 Barbeyrac, *An Historical and Critical Account of the Science of Morality*, p. 67.
52 Ibid., pp. 67–68.
53 Pufendorf, *The Law of Nature and Nations*, p. 96; *Specimen Controversiarum*, pp. 11–12, cited in Malcolm, "Hobbes and the European Republic of Letters," in *Aspects of Hobbes*, p. 525.
54 Grotius, *The Law of War and Peace*, vol. 2, Dedication, p. 4; Prolegomena, 1–3, 28.
55 Tuck, "The 'Modern' Theory of Natural Law," p. 104.
56 Sabine, chap. 21, "The Modernized Theory of Natural Law;" see also Ernest Barker's introductory essay to his edition of Gierke, *Natural Law*, pp. xli–xlii; Frederick A. Olafson, "Thomas Hobbes and the Modern Theory of Natural Law," *Journal of the History of Philosophy* 4, no. 1 (1966): 15–30; the discussion by Alfred Dufour, *Droits de l'homme, droit naturel et histoire* (Paris: PUF, 1991), pt. 1; the editor's introduction to Pufendorf's *On the Duty of Man and Citizen According to Natural Law*, ed. James Tully (Cambridge: Cambridge University Press, 1991), pp. xvi–xxi; Hochstrasser, *Natural Law Theories in the Early Enlightenment*, pp. 4–7 et passim; and Tuck, "The 'Modern' Theory of Natural Law." Michael P. Zuckert, *Natural Rights and the New Republicanism* (Princeton, NJ: Princeton University Press, 1994), chap. 5 et passim, includes a discussion of Grotius in relation to Hobbes and claims for him a strong influence on English Whig political thought in the later seventeenth century.
57 Rommen, *The Natural Law*, chap. 3; d'Entrèves, *Natural Law*, pp. 53–56; see also Chroust, "Hugo Grotius," pp. 354–55, 364, who stresses the influence of scholasticism and in particular of Suárez on Grotius's theory of natural law.
58 Haakonssen, *Natural Law and Moral Philosophy*, p. 15.
59 Tierney, *The Idea of Natural Rights*, chap. 13, p. 319.
60 Grotius, *The Law of War and Peace*, Prolegomena, 11.
61 For the sources of Grotius's statement and the literature on the subject, see Zagorin, "Hobbes without Grotius," pp. 28–30, and Tierney, *The Idea of Natural Rights*, pp. 319–20; see also the pointed comments of John Finnis, *Natural Law and Natural Rights* (Oxford: Clarendon Press, 2004), pp. 43–44, 54 n.

62 Quoted from Gierke's *Johannes Althusius und die Entwicklung der naturrechtlichen Theorien* in F. W. Maitland's translation of Otto Gierke, *Political Theories of the Middle Ages* (Cambridge: Cambridge University Press, 1913), p. 174 n.
63 For Suárez's reflections on whether natural law might be licit even if there were no God, see *On Laws and God the Lawgiver: Selections from Three Works*, 2 vols., Classics of International Law (Oxford: Clarendon Press, 1994), vol. 2, bk. 2, chap. 6.3, pp.189–90. Bernd Ludwig, *Die Wiederentdeckung des epikureischen Naturrechts* (Frankfurt am Main: Klostermann, 1998), p. 430 and n. 75, emphasizes the direct link between Grotius, Suárez, and Spanish neoscholastic natural law.
64 Grotius, *The Law of War and Peace*, vol. 2, bk. 1, chap. 1.10.1, pp. 38–39.
65 Ibid., bk. 1, chap. 1.10.5, p. 40.
66 Suárez, *On Laws and God the Lawgiver*, vol. 2, bk. 1, chap. 5.16, 24; bk. 2, chap. 5.5–6, pp. 67, 72, 180–81.
67 On the discussion of method in early modern philosophy and Grotius's view of method, see Zagorin, *Francis Bacon*, pp. 51–57, and "Hobbes without Grotius," pp. 22–23.
68 Richard Tuck, "Grotius and Selden," in *The Cambridge History of Political Thought 1450–1700*, ed. J. H. Burns (Cambridge: Cambridge University Press, 1991), p. 518, and *Philosophy and Government*, p. 171.
69 Grotius, *The Law of War and Peace*, Prolegomena, 58.
70 Ibid., bk. 2, chap. 23.1, p. 557.
71 Barbeyrac, *An Historical and Critical Account of the Science of Morality*, pp. 67, 70.
72 Grotius, *The Law of War and Peace*, Prolegomena, 56; see also the discussion of Grotius's method by Alfred Dufour, "L'influence de la méthodologie des sciences physiques et mathématiques sur les fondateurs de l'école du droit naturel moderne (Grotius, Hobbes, Pufendorf)," *Grotiana*, n.s., 1 (1980): 33–52, reprinted in *Grotius*, vol. 2.
73 B. P. Vermeulen and G. A. Van Der Waal, "Grotius, Aquinas, and Hobbes: Grotian Natural Law between *Lex Aeterna* and Natural Rights," *Grotiana*, n.s., 16–17 (1995–96): 70–71, 73, correctly point out that Grotius is in many respects in harmony with scholastic doctrine and that God's independent ontological existence underlies his rationalist philosophy of natural law.
74 Grotius's *De Iure Praedae* or *The Law of Prize*, is available in English translation together with a copy of the original manuscript, 2 vols., Classics of International Law (Oxford: Clarendon Press, 1950), vol. 1. It has been discussed by a number of scholars in recent years, in particular by Richard Tuck, *Philosophy and Government*, pp. 169–79, which includes a number of questionable statements. The latest study is by Martine Julia Van Ittersum, *Profit and Principle: Hugo Grotius, Natural Rights Theories and the Rise of Dutch Power in the East Indies (1595–1615)* (Leiden: Brill, 2006), which also looks at Grotius's career in relation to this treatise. I have discussed the *Commentary* briefly in "Hobbes without Grotius," pp. 21–23, but do not deal with it in the present work because Grotius's contemporaries never saw it and Hobbes could not have read it.

75 There is no adequate biography of Grotius in English or any other language. W.S.M. Knight, *The Life and Work of Hugo Grotius* (London: Sweet and Maxwell, 1925), is a well-known account. For Hobbes's letter of 1636 that reports he was reading Selden's *Mare Clausum*, see *The Correspondence of Thomas Hobbes*, ed. Noel Malcolm, 2 vols. (Oxford: Clarendon Press, 1994), vol. 1, p. 32, and for Selden's reference to Grotius's *The Law of War and Peace*, see Zagorin, "Hobbes without Grotius," pp. 25–26.
76 George Croom Robertson, *Hobbes* (Philadelphia, 1886), p. 143.
77 Grotius, *The Law of War and Peace*, vol. 2, Prolegomena, 40.
78 L, A Review and Conclusion, 15.
79 Grotius, *The Law of War and Peace*, vol. 2, bk. 1, 12.1, p. 42.
80 EL, pt. 1, chap. 15, p. 57; cf. the similar refutation of this view in DC, chap. 2.1.
81 See *The Human Rights Reader*, rev. ed., ed. Walter Laqueur and Barry Rubin (New York: New American Library, 1989), which contains a large selection of documents illustrating the concepts of historical, individual, natural, and human rights, including the American Declaration of Independence, the French Declaration of the Rights of Man and the Citizen, and the United Nations' Universal Declaration of Human Rights, as well as a number of philosophical writings on the subject of rights.
82 Discussions of rights and human rights by leading contemporary philosophers and analysts are available in various collections of essays containing ample bibliographical references and enable the reader to form an idea of the current state of the subject; see, e.g., *Political Theory and the Rights of Man*, ed. D. D. Raphael (London: Macmillan, 1967); *Rights*, ed. David Lyon (Belmont, CA: Wadsworth, 1979); *Human Rights*, ed. J. Roland Pennock and John W. Chapman (New York: New York University Press, 1981); and *Theories of Rights*, ed. Jeremy Waldron (New York: Oxford University Press, 1990). See also the classic analysis of the different meanings of rights by Wesley Hohfeld, *Fundamental Legal Conceptions* (New Haven, CT: Yale University Press, 1978; first published 1919); S. Benn, "Rights," in Edwards, *Encyclopedia of Philosophy*, vol. 7; Louis Henkin, *The Rights of Man Today* (Boulder, CO: Westview Press, 1978); *Philosophical Foundations of Human Rights* (Paris: UNESCO, 1986), by a variety of authors; Loren Lomasky, *Persons, Rights, and the Moral Community* (New York: Oxford University Press, 1987); Norberto Bobbio, *The Age of Rights* (Cambridge: Polity Press, 1996); Jack Mahony, *The Challenge of Human Rights* (Oxford: Blackwell, 2007); Michael J. Perry, *Toward a Theory of Human Rights* (Cambridge: Cambridge University Press, 2007); and Alan Dershowitz, *Rights from Wrongs* (New York: Basic Books, 2007).
83 Quoted in Waldron, *Theories of Rights*, Introduction, p. 4.
84 H.L.A. Hart, "Are There Any Natural Rights?" reprinted in Waldron, *Theories of Rights*.
85 Janet L. Nelson, "England and the Continent in the Ninth Century: III. Rights and Rituals," *Transactions of the Royal Historical Society*, 6th ser., 24 (2004), indicates some meanings of right in the ninth century in the primary sense

of what is right or just and in a secondary sense as a justifiable legal or moral claim.
86 Fred D. Miller, Jr., *Nature, Justice, and Rights in Aristotle's Politics* (Oxford: Clarendon Press, 1995), has argued interestingly but, I think, unconvincingly that Aristotle held a conception of natural rights based on the notion of natural justice. I do not believe this idea was present either in Aristotle or in classical Greek political theory. Philip Mitsis has attempted to show that natural rights originated in ancient Stoicism; see his "The Stoic Origin of Natural Rights," in Ierodiakonou, *Topics in Stoic Philosophy*.
87 The main meaning of *ius* in Roman law is that which is good and equitable or always just and fair. Beside this objective sense, *ius* could also refer to subjective rights; see *Digest*, 1.10.1. It has been noted that when *ius* signified a legal right, it was almost synonymous with the terms *facultas* and *potestas*—that is, a faculty or power; see Adolph Berger, *Encyclopedic Dictionary of Roman Law* (Philadelphia: American Philosophical Society, 1953), s.v. "*facultas*." The Roman jurist Florentinus defined *libertas* or freedom as "a natural faculty [*naturalis facultas*] of doing that which is free to anyone to do unless prohibited by force or law;" *Digest*, 1.5.4, quoted by P. A. Brunt, "*Libertas* in the Republic," in *The Fall of the Republic and Related Essays* (Oxford: Clarendon Press, 1988), p. 290.
88 See the statements by Ulpian and Florentinus quoted in Carlyle and Carlyle, *A History of Medieval Political Theory*, vol. 1, p. 76, from *Digest*, 1.1.4; 1.5.4.
89 See Richard Tuck, *Natural Rights Theories* (Cambridge: Cambridge University Press, 1981), a pioneer work that contains some questionable claims and statements; Brian Tierney, "The Origins of Natural Rights Language: Texts and Contexts, 1150–1250," in *History of Political Thought* 10, no. 4 (1989): 615–46, and *The Idea of Natural Rights*, which offer an excellent account and some corrections; see also A. S. McGrade, "Rights, Natural Rights, and the Philosophy of Law," in Kretzmann, Kenney, and Pinborg, *The Cambridge History of Later Medieval Philosophy*, chap. 39; Oakley, *Natural Law, Laws of Nature, Natural Rights*, chap. 4; and Annabel Brett, *Liberty, Right and Nature: Individual Rights in Later Scholastic Thought* (Cambridge: Cambridge University Press, 1997), which highlights the importance of the sixteenth-century Spanish jurist Fernando Vázquez in the formation of the conception of an absolute natural right to liberty. In the older literature, the chapters in Carlyle and Carlyle, *A History of Medieval Political Theory*, vol. 2, pts. 1–2, remain helpful.
90 Tierney, *The Idea of Natural Rights*, pp. 185, 210; on William of Ockham and natural rights, see also McGrade, *The Political Thought of William of Ockham*, chap. 4.
91 Suárez, *On Laws and God the Lawgiver*, bk. 1, chap.2.5, p. 30; cf. bk. 2, chap.17.2, pp. 325–26, where the author notes that *ius* is an ambiguous term that can mean either a law or a moral right to something.
92 Tierney, "The Origins of Natural Rights Language," p. 619.
93 On Aquinas's interchangeable use of *lex* and *ius* and their relationship to justice, see Thomas Aquinas, *Summa Theologiae*, IIa–IIae, qu. 57, art. 1. In *Aquinas: Political Writings*, ed. R. W. Dyson (Cambridge: Cambridge University Press, 2002),

p. 158 and n.2, the editor comments that "the subtleties of meaning" in Aquinas's various uses of *ius, lex,* and *iustum* "sometimes defy translation." Aquinas conceived of right almost entirely in the objective sense of rightness or justice rather than as a subjective right pertaining to individuals.

94 Suárez, *On Laws and God the Lawgiver,* bk. 1, chap. 2.1,6, 9, pp. 28–29, 31–32, 33.

95 In my essay of 2000, "Hobbes without Grotius," pp. 18–19, I referred to a number of scholars, including Tuck, Haakonssen, and others, who have promulgated the misconception of Grotius as a significant and original theorist of natural rights who had a considerable influence on Hobbes. Since then, Annabel Brett's essay, "Natural Right and Civil Community: The Civil Philosophy of Hugo Grotius," *The Historical Journal* 45, no. 1 (2002): 31–51, does not, despite its title, shed much light on the Grotian theory of natural rights. Martine Julia Van Ittersum's *Profit and Principle* speaks frequently of Grotius as a major theorist of natural rights but offers no analysis of his work to justify this claim. Leon Ingber's discussion of Grotius's treatment of rights makes clear the absence in his work of any concept of natural rights; "The Tradition of Grotius and Human Rights," in *Reason in Law,* 3 vols., ed. Carla Forelli and Enrico Pattaro (Milan: Dott. A. Giuffre Editore, 1987). Pauline C. Westerman's *The Disintegration of Natural Law Theory* (Leiden: Brill, 1998), chap. 5, on Grotius's shift from natural law to natural rights, says little to confirm her view of his status as a natural law theorist. Arthur P. Monahan's discussion of Grotius's thought in *The Circle of Rights Expands* (Montreal: McGill-Queen's University Press, 2007), pp. 57–78, is largely dependent on Tuck and fails to show that Grotius had a well-developed conception of natural rights.

96 Grotius, *The Law of War and Peace,* bk. 1, chap. 1.4–5, pp. 35–36.

97 Ibid., p. 35 n.3.

98 See above, n. 88.

99 Peter Haggenmacher, "Droits subjectifs et système juridique chez Grotius," in *Politique, droit et théologie chez Bodin, Grotius et Hobbes,* ed. Y. C. Zarka (Paris: Éditions Kimé, 1997).

100 Ibid., p. 119 et passim.

101 One of the reasons for the misconception that Grotius was a major theorist of rights and natural rights in *The Law of War and Peace* is the mistranslation in the English versions of his treatise of the Latin term *ius* as a right in many instances where its correct meaning is that of law. While the first English translation of the work in 1659 bore the title *The Law of War and Peace,* most subsequent English translations titled it *The Rights of War and Peace,* a clear misunderstanding, since Grotius's work is largely concerned with law, not rights. In their discussions of Grotius, both Tuck and Haakonssen for unexplained reasons used the English translation of 1738, which often produces confusion by mistakenly translating *ius* as right instead of law; see the reprint of this edition, *The Rights of War and Peace,* ed. Richard Tuck, 3 vols. (Indianapolis: Liberty Fund, 2005). The disparities between this version and the more accurate translation published in 1925 in the Classics of International Law series, on which I draw in this book, are very noticeable. In the 1738 version, the title of the first chapter of book 1 (vol. 1, p. 133)

is given as "What War Is, What Right Is," although the latter term is incorrect and should be "Law," as in the 1925 translation. When the same chapter in the 1738 translation comes to the definition of the law of nature, it uses the phrase "The Law of Nature" in the margin, but then goes on to present a definition of "natural right" (ibid., p. 150). Many more errors of this kind could be cited from this translation. I discuss the problem of the mistranslation of the word *ius* in Grotius's *Law of War and Peace* in "Hobbes without Grotius," pp. 31–33.
102 Grotius, *The Law of War and Peace*, bk. 1, chap. 4.7.2–3, p. 149.
103 Ibid., bk. 1, chap. 3.8.1–2, pp. 103–4.
104 Ibid., bk. 2, chap. 22.11, p. 551.
105 L, chaps. 14.3; 26.44.
106 DC, chap. 14.3.
107 EL, pt. 1, chap. 14.6, p. 55; DC, chap. 1.7.
108 L, chap. 26.44.
109 DC, chaps. 2.10; 14.3.
110 John Locke, *Two Treatises of Government*, ed. Peter Laslett, 2nd ed. (Cambridge: Cambridge University Press, 1967), *Second Treatise*, 57, pp. 323–24.
111 L, chap. 30.21. Quentin Skinner has noticed the similarity between Locke and Hobbes on this point in his essay, "Thomas Hobbes and the Proper Signification of Liberty," *Transactions of the Royal Historical Society*, 5th ser., 40 (1990): 135.
112 DC, chap. 1.7.
113 EL, pt. 1, chap. 14.6, p. 55.
114 Leo Strauss, *Natural Right and History* (Chicago: University of Chicago Press, 1953).
115 Ibid., introduction and pp. 166–202; the quotations are on pp. 169 and 182. Strauss admired Hobbes, whom he praised for the quality of his writing, "his never failing humanity, and his marvelous clarity and force," but did himself no credit by adding that "he was deservedly punished for his recklessness, especially by his countrymen" (p. 166). Although some of his critics accused him of atheism, heresy, and irreligion, Hobbes was never legally or otherwise punished for any offense.

CHAPTER 2
Enter the Law of Nature

1 Thomas Hobbes, *The History of the Grecian War by Thucydides*, EW, vol. 8, p. viii.
2 EL, pt. 1, chap. 2.10, p. 6.
3 L, chap. 46.15. For Hobbes's earlier development as a philosopher, see Frithiof Brandt, *Thomas Hobbes's Mechanical Conception of Nature* (Copenhagen: Leven and Munksgard, 1928), and the biographical accounts in Malcolm, *Aspects of Hobbes*, pp. 9–14, and Martinich, *Hobbes: A Biography*, chap. 4.
4 L, chap. 34.2. Hobbes's argument here relates to his general claim in this chapter that spirits and angels are not immaterial substance but very subtle bodies. In

L, chaps. 4–5, he insists that science requires rigorous definitions of names and consistent adherence to them. Incorporeal substance is touched on also in his discussion of the misuse of language and senseless speech in L, pt. 4, "The Kingdom of Darkness," which includes chapters on darkness from vain philosophy.

5 This tripartite division of philosophy is briefly described by Hobbes in DC, Preface to the Reader, p. 35, and is later discussed in *De Corpore* (1655), EW, vol. 1, pt. 1.
6 DC, Epistle Dedicatory, pp. 25–26.
7 L, chap. 4.12.
8 On Hobbes's conception of science, see Brandt, *Thomas Hobbes's Mechanical Conception of Nature*; the critical account by Tom Sorell, "The Science in Hobbes's Politics," in *Perspectives on Thomas Hobbes*, ed. G. A. Rogers and Alan Ryan (Oxford: Clarendon Press, 1988), and idem, "Hobbes's Scheme of the Sciences," in Sorell, *The Cambridge Companion to Hobbes*; Yves Charles Zarka, "First Philosophy and the Foundations of Knowledge," in ibid.; Douglas Jesseph, "Hobbes and the Method of Natural Science," in ibid.; and Malcolm, "Hobbes's Science of Politics and His Theory of Science," in *Aspects of Hobbes*. In propounding the idea of politics and moral philosophy as sciences, Hobbes seems to articulate two notions of science, one modeled on geometry and aimed at the establishment of universal necessary truths and the other based on the analysis of the properties of bodies and the demonstration of the causes of their generation.
9 EL, Epistle Dedicatory, p. xvii.
10 Grotius, *The Law of War and Peace*, vol. 2, Prolegomena, 5–6.
11 Hobbes stated at the beginning of EL (pt. 1, chap. 1.1, p. 1) that "the true and perspicuous explication of the elements of laws, natural and politic," depended upon "the knowledge of what is human nature, what is a body politic, and what it is we call a law." Of his three major works of political theory, EL and L begin with an account of man and human nature; DC omits this preliminary discussion and opens with a chapter on man in the state of nature that includes numerous observations on human nature necessary to Hobbes's argument.
12 See Michael Frede, "On the Stoic Conception of the Good," in Ierodiakonou, *Topics in Stoic Philosophy*, who comments (p. 71) that the Stoics believed that "nature has constructed human beings in such a way that, if nothing went wrong, we would in the course of our natural development become virtuous."
13 DC, chap. 1.2.
14 Ibid.
15 EL, pt. 1, chap. 7.3, p. 22; DC, chap. 1.2. Hobbes took no account of *akrasia*, or weakness of will, a subject much discussed by present-day moral philosophers, or of the fact that weakness of the will could lead individuals to desire things they knew were not good.
16 EL, pt. 1, chap. 14.6, p. 54.
17 Thomas Hobbes, *On Man* (1658) in *Man and Citizen*, ed. Bernard Gert (Indianapolis: Hackett, 1991), chap. 11.6; DC, chap. 3.12; for the term "reproach" in the English translation of DC, Hobbes's original Latin version uses *contumeliam*, which is better translated as slander or insult.

18 Hobbes, *On Man,* chap. 11.6.
19 EL, Epistle Dedicatory, p. xvii.
20 L, chap. 11.1.
21 L, chap. 6.58.
22 DC, Preface to the Reader, p. 33.
23 L, chap. 13.10. Hobbes expresses this point even more strongly in L, chap. 27.1, when he denies that the pleasure one may take in imagining the death of another man or the possession of his goods or wife is a sin unless there is also an intention to carry out such thoughts. He adds strikingly that

>   to be pleased in the fiction of that which would please a man if it were real is a passion so adherent to the nature both of man and every other living creature, as to make it sin were to make sin of being a man. The consideration of this has made me think them too severe, both to themselves and others, that maintain that the first motions of the mind (though checked with the fear of God) be sins.

24 Hobbes does speak, however, of Adam's sin in eating of the tree of knowledge, for which he and his posterity were punished by the loss of eternal life; L, chap. 38.2.
25 EL, pt. 1, chap. 16.4, p. 64.
26 EL, Dedicatory Epistle, p. xvii.
27 It should be noted that Aristotle's *Rhetoric* includes an analysis of the passions and that Hobbes held this work in the highest regard despite his general disparagement of Aristotle's philosophy. In the 1630s he made a Latin translation and an English paraphrase of the *Rhetoric*, which subsequently influenced his discussion of the passions in EL; see Quentin Skinner, *Reason and Rhetoric in the Philosophy of Hobbes* (Cambridge: Cambridge University Press, 1996), p. 38.
28 EL, pt. 1, chap. 9.1–2, pp. 28–29.
29 L, chap. 6.14, 15, 19, 20, 22, 26, 27.
30 EL, pt. 1, chap. 9.21, pp. 36–37.
31 L, chap. 11.2.
32 L, chap. 10.1.
33 L, chap. 13.1.
34 For the idea of natural human equality in Stoicism, Cicero, Seneca, and the New Testament, see the discussion and texts cited in R. W. Carlyle and A. J. Carlyle, *A History of Medieval Political Theory,* vol. 1, chaps. 1, 2, 7, 10.
35 William James, *Pragmatism* (Philadelphia: Hackett, 1981; first published 1907), Lecture I.
36 EL, p. xviii.
37 For a historical sketch of this idea, see the article by George Klosko, "The State of Nature," in *The New Dictionary of the History of Ideas*, ed. Maryanne C. Horowitz, 6 vols. (Detroit, MI: Charles Scribner, 2005), vol. 5. J. W. Gough, *The Social Contract*, 2nd ed. (Westport, CT: Greenwood Press, 1978), contains numerous references to the notion of philosophers and political theorists from the Greeks

onward of a primitive natural condition of individual freedom and independence as a background to the concept of a social or political contract as the origin of civil society and the state.
38 See Carlyle and Carlyle, *A History of Medieval Political Theory*, vol. 1, pp. 23–26.
39 Gratian, *Decretum*, the dictum in Distinctio 7, c. 1, cited by Tierney, *The Idea of Natural Rights*, p. 145, whose account I have followed. Tierney, ibid., chap. 6, deals with medieval conceptions of the state of nature and the origin of property.
40 Quentin Skinner notes its use by Molina, however, who spoke of the "*status naturae*"; Skinner, *The Foundations of Modern Political Thought*, vol. 2, p. 155.
41 Ibid., pp. 154–61.
42 Richard Hooker, *The Laws of Ecclesiastical Polity* (1593), in *Works*, ed. John Keble, 2 vols. (New York, 1873), vol. 1, bk. 1, chap. 10.1.4.
43 Suárez, *On Laws and God the Lawgiver*, vol. 2, bk. 3, chap. 1.2–3, pp. 363–64.
44 Johannes Althusius, *Politica* (1614 ed. abridged), ed. Frederick S. Carney (Indianapolis: Liberty Fund, 1995), chap. 1, pp. 23, 24.
45 Grotius, *The Law of War and Peace*, vol. 2, Prolegomena, 16.
46 Ibid., bk. 2, chap. 2.2.1, pp. 186–87.
47 Ibid., bk. 1, chap. 1.14.1, p. 44.
48 Ibid., bk. 1, chap. 4.7.2–3, p. 149.
49 François Tricaud, "Hobbes's Conception of the State of Nature from 1640 to 1651: Evolution and Ambiguities," in Rogers and Ryan, *Perspectives on Thomas Hobbes*, p. 114.
50 EL, pt. 1, chap. 14.12, p. 56; L, chap. 13.11.
51 DC, chap. 8.1.
52 EL, pt. 1, chap. 14.3–5, p. 54; DC, chap. 1.6.
53 DC, chap. 3.31.
54 L, chap. 13.3–4.
55 L, chap. 13.6–7.
56 See George Klosko and Daryl Rice, "Thucydides and Hobbes's State of Nature," *History of Political Thought* 6, no. 3 (1985): 405–9.
57 EL, pt. 1, chap. 14.13, p. 56; cf. the discussion in DC, chap. 1.13–14.
58 DC, chap. 1.13.
59 L, chap. 13.8.
60 L, chap. 13.9.
61 L, chap. 13.11–12.
62 EL, pt. 1, chap. 14.6, p. 55; cf. the passage in DC, chap. 1.7, which I have quoted in the previous chapter: "It is therefore neither absurd nor reprehensible; neither against the dictates of true reason for a man to use all his endeavours to preserve and defend his Body and the Members thereof from death and sorrowes; but that which is not contrary to right reason, that all men account to be done justly and with right."
63 EL, pt. 1, chap. 14.6, 13, pp. 55, 56.
64 L, chap. 13.13.

65 DC, chap. 10.
66 EL, pt. 1, chap. 14.10, p. 55.
67 DC, chap. 1.11.
68 DC, chap. 1.12.
69 L, chap. 13.13–14.
70 EL, pt. 1, chap. 15.1, pp. 57–58.
71 L, chap. 14.3; DC, chap. 2.1.
72 L, chap. 14.4.
73 Bernd Ludwig's *Die Wiederentdeckung der epikureischen Naturrechts* advances the view that Hobbes's theory of natural law underwent a significant change in *Leviathan* from what it had been in *The Elements of Law* and *De Cive*. His argument on behalf of this thesis is unsupported by the evidence and wholly unconvincing, as is his claim, set forth in chap. 9, that Hobbes became an Epicurean; see also Karl Schuhmann's review of Ludwig's work in *Archiv für Geschichte der Philosophie* 83, no. 1 (2001): 100–103.
74 EL, pt. 1, chap. 17.9, p. 71.
75 L, chap. 14.5.
76 L, chap. 14.7–33; cf. EL, pt. 1, chap. 15.3–18, pp. 58–62; DC, chap. 2.3–23.
77 L, chap. 15.1.
78 L, chap. 15.21. In formulating this law of nature, Hobbes explicitly repudiates the famous Aristotelian doctrine that men are born unequal by nature and states that "the inequality that now is has been introduced by the laws civil."
79 L, chap. 15.34–35.
80 L, chap. 15.16, 17, 19–23.
81 L, chap. 15.10.
82 L, chap. 15.36–37, 39.
83 On the contractual tradition of political theory, see Otto Gierke, *The Development of Political Theory* (New York: Norton, 1939), chap. 2, and idem, *Natural Law*, pt. 3, sec. 14, chap. 4, both valuable discussions with rich documentation which note among other things Hobbes's unique position in this tradition; see also Gough, *The Social Contract*, chaps. 5–8. The contractual tradition has been revived in our time by the influential treatise of John Rawls, *A Theory of Justice* (Cambridge, MA: Harvard University Press, 1971).
84 L, chap. 14.18.
85 Among the Hobbes scholars who have discussed this problem are David Gauthier, *The Logic of Leviathan* (Oxford: Clarendon Press, 1969), and "Hobbes's Social Contract," in Rogers and Ryan, *Perspectives on Thomas Hobbes*; Kavka, *Hobbesian Moral and Political Theory*; and Hampton, *Hobbes and the Social Contract Tradition*.
86 L, chap. 13.14.
87 L, chaps. 17.15; 18.1; A Review and Conclusion, 8.
88 L. chap. 17.1.
89 L, chap. 15.38, 40.

90 See above, chap. 1, in which Gratian is quoted; for Aquinas's statement, see Thomas Aquinas, *Summa Theologiae*, Ia–IIae, qu. 94, art. 4. In pointing out that whatever belongs to natural law is contained in the law and the Gospel, Aquinas cites the words of Gratian referring to the natural law command that everyone should do to others as he would be done by. Curley's editorial comment (L, p. 80 n.) that Hobbes's identification of the fundamental law of nature with the Golden Rule may seem "a bold act of appropriation" is misguided, since this identification was a commonplace in the Christian natural law tradition.

91 On the concept of right reason and its history, see Robert Hoopes, *Right Reason in the English Renaissance* (Cambridge, MA: Harvard University Press, 1962), and Herschel Baker, *The Wars of Truth* (Cambridge, MA: Harvard University Press, 1952), chap. 3 et passim.

92 Cicero, *De Legibus*, 1.6.18; *Disputationes Tusculanae*, 4.15.34; Seneca, *Epistulae Morales*, 66.33; the latter two passages are quoted in Hoopes, *Right Reason*, p. 35.

93 Aquinas, Ia–IIae, qu. 95, art. 2.

94 Hooker, *The Laws of Ecclesiastical Polity*, bk. 1, chap. 7.4.

95 DC, chap. 1.7.

96 J.W.N. Watkins, *Hobbes's System of Ideas* (London: Hutchinson, 1965), pp. 84–85.

97 See, e.g., Strauss, *Natural Right and History*, chap. 5; M. M. Goldsmith, *Hobbes's Science of Politics* (New York: Columbia University Press, 1966); Gauthier, *The Logic of Leviathan*; Kavka, *Hobbesian Moral and Political Theory*; Hampton, *Hobbes and the Social Contract Tradition*; Johann P. Sommerville, *Thomas Hobbes: Political Ideas in Historical Context* (New York: St. Martin's Press, 1992).

98 Beyond the remarks that immediately follow, the relationship between the self and others in Hobbes's moral philosophy is discussed more fully below in chap. 4.

99 See the discussion of Hobbes's ethics in Hampton, *Hobbes and the Social Contract Tradition*, pp. 27–57, who regards him as an ethical relativist or subjectivist. She surveys the views of a number of scholars who deny that he had a moral philosophy or ethical system because of the primacy he assigned to individual self-interest and self-preservation in his theory of natural law. Critics of this kind argue that his theory was not a moral but a prudential doctrine that had no place for moral obligation. It has been wrongly suggested that by attempting to make moral philosophy an objective science grounded in self-preservation, Hobbes emptied the laws of nature "of any specifically moral as opposed to self-interested content"; Sommerville, *Thomas Hobbes*, p. 79. If this view were correct, Hobbes would have had to be a very self-deceived thinker, since he never doubted that the law of nature was a moral law because of its relationship to peace, conscience, and the virtues. He frequently calls it a "moral law;" see, e.g., DC, chap. 4.1, and L, chap. 26.41. On this entire subject, see the further discussion below, chap. 4.

100 DC, chap. 2.1.

101 See Luscombe, "Natural Morality and Natural Law."

102 DC, chap. 13.4; L, chap. 13.9, 14.

103 Aquinas, Ia–IIae, qu. 94, art. 2.

104 Suárez, *On Laws and God the Lawgiver*, vol. 2, bk. 2, chap. 6. 5; chap. 7.7, pp. 191, 212.
105 Grotius, *The Law of War and Peace*, vol. 2, Prolegomena, 39; bk. 1, chap. 10.10, pp. 38–39. Richard Tuck has attempted to show that Grotius preceded Hobbes in arguing that self-preservation and self-interest were the basis of natural law; see "The 'Modern' Theory of Natural Law"; "Grotius and Selden," in Burns, *The Cambridge History of Political Thought 1450–1700*, pp. 506–7, 516; *Philosophy and Government*, pp. 172–74. I do not believe that Grotius's *Law of War and Peace* contains any support for this claim. Grotius founded his concept of natural law on the social nature of human beings, not on individual self-interest and the desire for self-preservation, as is evident in his remarks in Prolegomena, 6–7; see also the critical comments on Tuck's view by Tierney, *The Idea of Natural Rights*, pp. 322–23, and by Sommerville, *Thomas Hobbes*, pp. 168–70, n. 7.
106 L, chap. 15.41; see also EL, pt. 1, chap. 17.12, p. 72; DC, chap. 3.33. Hobbes also touched on the status of natural law in his reply to Bishop Bramhall's attack on *Leviathan*, in which he says that before they were delivered in the word of God, the laws of nature were not properly laws and were known to men only as theorems of their natural reason tending to peace; Thomas Hobbes, *An Answer to a Book Published by Dr. Bramhall . . . Called "The Catching of the Leviathan"* (1682), EW, vol. 4, pp. 284–85.
107 Hobbes may perhaps have had a predecessor in Marsilio of Padua (d. 1342), author of *Defensor Pacis*, in his conception of natural law as not truly law. Marsilio was an advocate of state sovereignty and something of a legal positivist for whom the law of nature became law only insofar as it is a law of the state; see the remarks and passages cited by Alan Gewirth, *Marsilius of Padua: The Defender of Peace*, 2 vols. (New York: Columbia University Press, 1956), vol. 1, *Marsilius of Padua and Medieval Political Philosophy*, pp. 149, 151.
108 Aquinas, Ia–IIae, qu. 95, art. 2.
109 Hooker, *The Laws of Ecclesiastical Polity*, bk. 1, chap. 10.5.
110 Suárez, *On Laws and God the Lawgiver*, vol. 2, bk. 1, chap. 3.9, 11; chap. 5; bk. 2, chap. 5.5, pp. 42, 44, 58–72, 181; cf. the discussion of Suárez's concept of natural law and obligation by Finnis, *Natural Law and Natural Rights*, passim, and M.W.F. Stone, "The Scope and Limits of Moral Deliberation: *Recta Ratio*, Natural Law, and Conscience in Francisco Suárez," in *Imagination in the Later Middle Ages and Early Modern Times*, ed. Lodi Nauta and Detlev Patzold (Louvain: Pesters, 2004).
111 A. E. Taylor, "The Ethical Doctrine of Hobbes," first published in 1938 and reprinted in Brown, *Hobbes Studies*; Howard Warrender, *The Political Philosophy of Hobbes: His Theory of Obligation* (Oxford: Clarendon Press, 1957). Taylor wrote (p. 50) that "a certain kind of theism is absolutely necessary to make [Hobbes's] theory work." The role Taylor and Warrender assigned to God as the imperative source of obligation of the Hobbesian law of nature also enabled them to argue that Hobbes's moral philosophy was not a prudential system of precepts based on human self-interest but a deontology founded on genuine moral values and oughts.

112 Willis B. Glover, "God and Thomas Hobbes," in Brown, *Hobbes Studies*, pp. 160–61.
113 Frederick A. Olafson, "Thomas Hobbes and the Modern Theory of Natural Law," *Journal of the History of Philosophy* 4, no. 1 (1966): 15–30. Note also the essay by G.A.J. Rogers, "La religion et la loi naturelle selon Hobbes, *Les lois de la nature et la loi morale*," in *Politique, droit et théologie chez Bodin, Grotius et Hobbes*, ed. Y. C. Zarka (Paris: Éditions Kimé, 1997), which concludes (p. 281) that the laws of nature in Hobbes are both scientific theorems conducive to human conservation and commandments of God.
114 Martinich, *The Two Gods of Leviathan*, pp. 100–101, chap. 4.
115 Ibid., pp. 104–10, 135; for Hobbes's distinction between right and law as the difference between liberty and obligation, see L, chap. 14.3.
116 In a recent essay on the controversy between the religious and secularist interpretations of Hobbes, Greg Forster discusses the views of a number of scholars and in particular the differences between Martinich and Edwin Curley's secularist interpretation, see "Divine Law and Human Law in Hobbes's *Leviathan*," *History of Political Thought* 24, no. 2 (2003): 189–217. Forster admires but dissents from Martinich's account and maintains that Hobbes was an irreligious, insincere Christian who deliberately deceived his readers and pretended to believe that the obligation of natural law derived from God's command. Despite this conclusion, I have not been persuaded by Forster's arguments and must observe that, like Martinich, he takes little notice in his essay of Hobbes's account of the relationship between natural and civil law.
117 This is spelled out at greatest length in DC, chap. 4, which quotes many scriptural passages as divine confirmation of the laws of nature.
118 Hobbes says in L, chap. 26.37, that natural laws "have been laws from all eternity, and are called not only natural but also moral laws, consisting in the moral virtues."
119 Note Glover's formulation (p. 160) that for "all who believe in God's governance of the world ... this belief is sufficient to transform the laws of nature ... into the commands of God." Karl Schuhmann has similarly and correctly pointed out that the laws of nature are not laws except for those who believe in God; see his "La notion de loi chez Hobbes," in Karl Schuhmann, *Selected Papers on Renaissance Philosophy and Thomas Hobbes* (Dordrecht: Kluwer Academic Publishers, 2004), pp. 187–88.
120 See L, chap. 31.2. Hobbes, some of whose critics wrongly accused him of being an atheist, touches on atheism in several of his works. In DC, chap. 14.19, for example, he speaks of those who either deny that there is a God or that God governs the world, and asserts that God's existence can be known by natural reason, but that most people lack the natural capacity to achieve this knowledge. He also distinguishes in DC, chap. 16.1, between superstition and atheism, the first consisting of fear of invisible things without right reason, the second of an opinion of right reason without the fear. In L, chap. 31.2, he comments that atheists are not subjects of God's kingdom but enemies of God. See on this subject R. Woodfield,

"Hobbes on the Law of Nature and the Atheist," *Renaissance and Modern Studies* 15 (1971): 134–43.

121 I believe that this was the case despite the importance that Quentin Skinner's *Reason and Rhetoric in the Philosophy of Hobbes* has attributed to Hobbes's use of rhetorical devices in *Leviathan*.
122 L, chap. 17.2.
123 L, chap. 17.13.
124 L, chap. 26.8.
125 L, chap. 26.2–3.
126 L, chap. 26.8.
127 Hobbes here makes the important comment consistent with his general viewpoint that it is the sovereign power that makes the law of nature law, otherwise it would be "a great error to call the laws of nature unwritten law (whereof we see so many large volumes published, and in them so many contradictions of one another, and of themselves)"; L, chap. 26.22.
128 L, chap. 26.8, 21, 37, 38. Hobbes also distinguishes between human and divine positive law, the latter being God's commands that are not from eternity nor addressed universally to all men, but only to certain persons; L, chap. 26.39–49. On the origin, meaning, and understanding of the concept of positive law in legal philosophy, see James B. Murphy's valuable work, *The Philosophy of Positive Law*.
129 Grotius, *The Law of War and Peace*, vol. 2, Prolegomena.16, 41; bk. 1, chap. 1.14, p. 44.
130 Ibid., bk. 2, chap. 2.5, p. 192.
131 Aquinas, Ia–IIae, qu. 90, art. 4; qu. 91, art. 3; qu. 95, art. 2.
132 Ibid., qu. 91, art. 3.
133 Ibid., qu. 95, art. 2. On Aquinas's view of the relationship between natural and positive law and the derivation of the latter from the former, see Finnis, *Natural Law and Natural Rights*, p. 28 and chap. 10.7, and Murphy, *The Philosophy of Positive Law*, chap. 2. In chap. 3 of ibid., Murphy discusses Hobbes's conception of positive law, in which he finds various inconsistencies.
134 DC, chap. 14.10, marginal annotation.
135 L, chap. 14.4; chap. 26.4.
136 L, chap. 29.6.
137 Hobbes argues in L, chap.5.3, that although arithmetic is a certain and infallible art, unpracticed persons and even experts may nevertheless err in their sums; and similarly, while "reason itself is always right reason," neither the reason of one man or that of of any number of men can be known for certain to be right reason. Hence "when there is a controversy . . . the parties must by their own accord set up for right reason the reason of some arbitrator or judge to whose sentence they will both stand, or their controversy must either come to blows or be undecided, for want of a right reason constituted by nature."; see also EL, pt. 2, chap. 10.8, p.150, and DC, chap.2. 1, where Hobbes observes that in civil government, the reason of the sovereign and civil law is to be received by every subject as right reason, and that without civil government, "no man can know right rea-

son from false, but by comparing it with his owne." These comments seem to signify quite a relativization of right reason in order to assure the supremacy of the sovereign's reason.
138 S. A. Lloyd, "Hobbes's Self-Effacing Natural Law Theory," *Pacific Philosophical Quarterly* 82, no. 3 (2001): 285–308, reprinted in Finkelstein, *Hobbes on Law*.
139 See above, chap. 1.
140 Tierney, *The Idea of Natural Rights*, pp. 340–41.
141 L, chap. 14.18.
142 EL, pt. 1, chaps. 15, 19; pt. 2, chap. 1, pp. 58–62, 77–92; DC, chaps. 2–3.
143 See Quentin Skinner's discussion of Hobbes's use of this concept in "Hobbes on Persons, Authors and Representatives," in Springborg, *The Cambridge Companion to Hobbes's Leviathan*.
144 L, chap. 16.13.
145 L, chap. 17.13.
146 L, chap. 17.13.
147 L, Introduction, 1.
148 There has been considerable discussion of the symbolism, meaning, and intellectual and artistic background of *Leviathan*'s title page; among others, see Keith Brown, "The Artist of the Leviathan Title Page," *British Library Journal* 4 (1978): 24–36; M. M. Goldsmith, "Hobbes's Ambiguous Politics," *History of Political Thought* 11, no. 4 (1990): 639–73; Noel Malcolm, "The Title Page of *Leviathan*, Seen in Curious Perspective," in *Aspects of Hobbes*; Horst Bredekamp, "Thomas Hobbes's Visual Strategies," in Springborg, *The Cambridge Companion to Hobbes's Leviathan*; Johan Tralau, "Leviathan, the Beast of the Myth: Medusa, Dionysos, and the Riddle of Hobbes's Sovereign Monster," in ibid. Quentin Skinner discusses the symbolism of the title page in *Hobbes and Republican Liberty* (Cambridge: Cambridge University Press, 2008), pp. 185–96. Carl Schmitt, the well-known German legal and political philosopher (d. 1985), a Hobbes scholar, supporter of authoritarian government, and Nazi sympathizer, dealt with the subject in his *The Leviathan in the State Theory of Thomas Hobbes*, original German ed. 1938 (Westport, CT: Greenwood Press, 1996), esp. chaps. 1–2.
149 L, chap. 17.13–14.
150 L, chaps. 18–20.
151 L, chap. 20.11.
152 Grotius, *The Law of War and Peace*, vol. 2, bk. 1, chap. 3.7, p. 102.
153 L, chap. 20.3.
154 L, chaps. 18.4–18; 20.3.
155 L, chap. 18.20.
156 L, chap. 14.8, 29–30. Both Richard Tuck and Deborah Baumgold, who follows Tuck's view, have created confusion for readers by mistakenly arguing that in EL, in contrast to DC and L, Hobbes was unclear regarding the retention of rights and held that subjects did not retain their right of self-defense but were obliged to surrender it to the sovereign; see Tuck, *Natural Rights Theory*, pp. 120–22, and Deborah Baumgold, "Subjects and Soldiers: Hobbes on Military

Service," *History of Political Thought* 4, no. 1 (1983): 43–64, reprinted in Finkelstein, *Hobbes on Law*, pp. 443, 444. I believe that all three of Hobbes's political treatises express essentially the same opinion that certain natural rights, including the right to resist in self-defense, are inalienable and cannot be renounced by subjects. In EL, in accord with his psychological naturalism, Hobbes questions whether it is possible to renounce this right, noting that "covenants bind but to the utmost of our endeavour" (pt. 2, chap. 1.8, p. 86). Earlier, he states (ibid., pt. 1, chap. 17.2, p. 69) that there is a necessity for a man to retain his right to some things, including "his own body . . . the right of defending whereof he could not transfer." Among other retained rights he also lists "the use of fire, water, free air, and a place to live in, and to all things necessary for life." I discuss these retained rights further in the next chapter in connection with the liberty of the subject.

157 L, chap. 21.11.
158 L, chap. 21.12–16.
159 L, chap. 21.17.
160 L, chap. 21.15.
161 L, chap. 21.21.
162 L, chap. 20.11. Hobbes finds no incompatibility between conquest, force, and the principle of consent. Given his expansive view of the presupposition of consent in political subjection, he might perhaps be accused of straining the concept of consent beyond plausibility.
163 L, chap. 21.10.
164 DC, chap. 2.16; cf. EL, pt. 1, chap. 15.13, p. 61: "It is a question often moved, whether such covenants oblige, as are extorted from men by fear." For a recent discussion of the subject as a problem in moral philosophy, which includes references to some of the literature, see David Owens, "Duress, Deception, and the Validity of a Promise," *Mind* 116, no. 462 (2007): 293–313.
165 Grotius, *The Law of War and Peace*, vol. 2, bk. 2, chap. 11.7.2, p. 335.
166 L, chap. 21.3. This proposition is contextually related to Hobbes's philosophical denial of the freedom of the will, which will be discussed later in this essay. Briefly put, his position on this subject is that the will is always determined by external causes, but that a person is nevertheless free if he can do what he wills to do; see among other places L, chap. 6.53–54, in which he explains and defends his rejection of free will and its compatibility with voluntary action.
167 L, chap. 21.3; Grotius, *The Law of War and Peace*, bk. 2, chap. 11.7.2, p. 335; Aristotle, *Nicomachean Ethics*, 1110a, bk. 3, chap. 1. Aristotle takes a more nuanced view than Hobbes in attempting to draw the line between voluntary and involuntary actions.
168 L, chap. 14.27.
169 L, chap. 21.3.
170 I have not been able to find the exact source of this often used Latin phrase, which enjoins that covenants should be kept. A probable source is Cicero, *De Officiis* (*On Duties*), 1.7.23, which associates the idea with the Stoics and calls good

faith in abiding by promises and agreements the foundation of justice. Grotius states that "it is a rule of the law of nature to abide by pacts"; Prolegomena, 15.
171 L, chap. 14.27.
172 L, chap. 20.2.
173 DC, chap. 14.2.
174 An example he cites (L, chap. 14.27) is being forced to redeem oneself from a thief by promising him money, which one is obliged to pay until the promise is discharged by the civil law. Most people, I think, would hold that no one is obliged by a promise to pay money to a thief, a kidnapper, or a blackmailer.
175 DC, chap. 2.16; cf. EL, pt. 1, chap. 15.13, p. 61.
176 L, chap. 14.31. In his treatment of crimes, Hobbes stated that fear "is the only thing (when there is appearance of profit or pleasure by breaking the laws) that makes men keep them." L, chap. 2.19.
177 Gierke, *The Development of Political Theory*, pp. 155–58, and see also pt. 2, chaps. 2–3, on the doctrines of the state contract and popular sovereignty; J. N. Figgis, *Studies of Political Thought from Gerson to Grotius 1414–1625*, 2nd ed. (Cambridge: Cambridge University Press, 1931; first published 1907), p. 127, and chap. 5 on the Monarchomachs.
178 The *Vindiciae contra Tyrannos* is listed as no. 1219 in Richard A. Talaska's edition of the Hardwick library catalogue that Hobbes compiled; see Talaska, *The Hardwick Library and Hobbes's Early Intellectual Development*. No. 317 of the "Libri Theologici" in this catalogue is headed "Monarcho-Machia" and lists an antimonarchomach work by John Barclay against the revolutionary theory of George Buchanan.
179 See *Vindiciae contra Tyrannos* in *Constitutionalism and Resistance in the Sixteenth Century*, ed. Julian H. Franklin (New York: Pegasus, 1969), the Third Question, pp. 158 ff; the quotation is on p. 181. The author of this anonymously published Latin Huguenot work in defense of the right of rebellion on both religious and juridical-political grounds was probably, as the editor suggests (pp. 138–39), the French Protestant writer Philippe du Plessis-Mornay.
180 Henry Parker, *Observations upon Some of His Majesties Late Answers and Expresses*, 1642, quoted in Margaret Judson, *The Crisis of the Constitution* (New Brunswick, NJ: Rutgers University Press, 1949), p. 416.
181 Richard Overton, *An Arrow against Tyrants*, 1646, in *The Levellers in the English Revolution*, ed. G. E. Aylmer (Ithaca, NY: Cornell University Press, 1975), p. 69.
182 John Milton, *The Tenure of Kings and Magistrates*, 1649, in Milton, *Prose Selections*, 2nd ed., ed. Merritt Y. Hughes (New York: Odyssey Press, 1947), pp. 277, 280.
183 Suárez, *On Laws and God the Lawgiver*, bk. 3, chap. 4.2, 8, pp. 384, 388.
184 EL, pt. 2, chap. 8.2–6, pp. 133–38; DC, chap. 12.3, 4, 7; L, chaps. 21.9; 29.9–10.
185 EL, pt. 2, chaps. 2.11; 8.9, pp. 97–98, 138; DC, chaps. 6.1; 12.8.
186 EL, pt. 1, chap. 19.9–10, p. 81; DC, chap. 5.9–10.
187 See Skinner, *Hobbes and Republican Liberty*, pp. 159–61, which includes the quotation from Parker's *Observations*.
188 EL, pt. 2, chap. 1.15–16, p. 89.

189 L, chaps. 18.16; 29.16. The theory of mixed monarchy and government was quite widely entertained in England and elsewhere during the sixteenth and seventeenth centuries; see the account of the sources and exponents of this theory in Zera S. Fink, *The Classical Republicans* (Evanston, IL: Northwestern University Press, 1945), and Michael Mendle, *Dangerous Positions* (Tuscaloosa: University of Alabama Press, 1985).

190 L, chap. 19.2.

191 L, chap. 20.19.

CHAPTER 3
The Sovereign and the Law of Nature

1 L, chaps. 36.20; 20.16–18, includes some of the scriptural justifications of sovereignty, a subject dealt with at length in the third part of L.

2 L, chap. 31.1.

3 In his discussion in EL of the emergence of the body politic and the attributes and purpose of sovereignty, Hobbes says that he is speaking of the sort of political union and government instituted for the perpetual benefit and defense of those who make it, "which therefore men desire should last for ever"; EL, pt. 2, chap. 1, p. 85. In DC, chap. 6.19, he compares the sovereign power's relation to the polity to the human soul's relation to the body.

4 See Walter Ullmann, *Principles of Government and Politics in the Middle Ages*, 2nd ed. (London: Methuen, 1986), p. 72. Ullmann says that the "idea of the pope's unfettered freedom to legislate was nothing else but legislative sovereignty," and, with some exaggeration, that "although the term sovereign was not applied to the medieval pope, there can be little doubt that the notion of sovereignty was perfectly clearly grasped."

5 Bodin defines sovereignty in bk. 1, chap. 8, of his treatise, which I have used in the English translation of 1606 by Richard Knolles, *The Six Bookes of a Commonweale*, ed. Kenneth D. McRae (Cambridge, MA: Harvard University Press, 1962). The treatment of this subject is continued in the remainder of bk. 1, and the types of state and kinds of monarchy are dealt with in bk. 2. For discussions of Bodin's idea of sovereignty, see Gierke, *The Development of Political Theory*; Skinner, *The Foundations of Modern Political Thought*, vol. 2, pp. 286–303, which includes an analysis of the limits Bodin placed on absolute sovereign power; the account by Julian Franklin, "Sovereignty and the Mixed Constitution: Bodin and His Critics," in Burns, *The Cambridge History of Political Thought 1450–1700*, chap. 10; and Richard Bonney, "Bodin and the Development of the French Monarchy," *Transactions of the Royal Historical Society*, 5th ser., 40 (1990).

6 EL, pt. 2, chap. 8, p. 137; the Hardwick library catalogue, nos. 546, 547, and 1280, list French, Latin, and English editions of Bodin's treatise; see Talaska, *The Hardwick Library and Hobbes's Early Intellectual Development*.

7 L, chap. 18.6.

8 L, chap. 22.5.
9 L, 20.18.
10 DC, chap. 6.18.
11 L, chap. 26.10–11, 21.
12 L, chap. 26.7.
13 L, chap. 26.11. Hobbes also expressed his criticism of Coke and the common lawyers' view of law in *A Dialogue Between a Philosopher and a Student of the Common Laws of England* (1681), ed. Alan Cromartie (Oxford: Clarendon Press, 2005). For Coke's conception of the artificial reason of the law and the supremacy of the common law, see John Underwood Lewis, "Sir Edward Coke (1552–1634): His Theory of 'Artificial Reason' as a Context for Modern Basic Legal Theory," and Charles M. Gray, "Further Reflections on 'Artificial Reason,'" both in *Law, Liberty, and Parliament*, ed. Allen D. Boyer (Indianapolis: Liberty Fund, 2004).
14 L, chap. 18.10.
15 DC, chap. 6.16.
16 EL, pt. 2, chap. 1.14, pp. 88–89; DC, chap. 12.7; L, chaps. 18.10; 24.7.
17 Seneca, *De Beneficiis*, 7.4, quoted in C. H. McIlwain, *The Growth of Political Thought in the West* (New York: Macmillan, 1932), p. 394.
18 L, chap. 18.9.
19 See the discussion of *Areopagitica* in Perez Zagorin, *Milton, Aristocrat and Rebel* (Woodbridge, Suffolk, UK: D. S. Brewer, 1992), pp. 49–59.
20 Erastianism was a label that took its name from the Swiss Protestant physician and theologian Thomas Erastus (d. 1583), who maintained that the authority of the civil power must extend to the control of the church and its imposition of spiritual censures and penalties such as ex-communication. Erastianism was a major issue in the religious debates of England's mid-century revolution. Hobbes, who was always an Erastian, though he did not use the term, expressed this position most fully in *Leviathan*.
21 L, chap. 39.5.
22 L, chap. 42.67–70.
23 L, chap. 33.1.
24 L, chaps. 31.1; 33.24.
25 L, chap. 43.3, 5, 11.
26 L, chap. 21.21.
27 L, chap. 29.23.
28 The Act for Subscribing the Engagement is printed in *The Stuart Constitution*, ed. J. P. Kenyon, 2nd ed. (Cambridge: Cambridge University Press, 1986), pp. 307–8.
29 The present writer, I believe, was the first historian to discuss some of the contemporary works in the Engagement controversy and to point out Hobbes's influence on them; see Perez Zagorin, *A History of Political Thought in the English Revolution*, 2nd ed. (Bristol, UK: Thoemmes Press, 1997; first published 1954), chap. 5. There is now a large literature on this subject; see, among others, John M. Wallace, *Destiny His Choice: The Loyalism of Andrew Marvell* (Cambridge: Cambridge University Press, 1968); chap. 1; Quentin Skinner, "Conquest and Consent: Thomas

Hobbes and the Engagement Controversy," in *The Interregnum: The Quest for Settlement 1649–1660*, ed. G. E. Aylmer (London: Macmillan, 1972); Sommerville, *Thomas Hobbes*, chap. 3; and Kinch Hoekstra, "The De Facto Turn in Hobbes's Political Philosophy," in *Leviathan after 350 Years* (Oxford: Clarendon Press, 2004). The study by Jeffrey R. Collins, *The Allegiance of Thomas Hobbes* (Oxford: Oxford University Press, 2005), advances the interesting thesis that *Leviathan* signalizes Hobbes's shift of allegiance to the new Cromwellian regime and in particular to its religious settlement of an Erastian character that did away with all coercive power on the part of the churches and clergy. Most of the scholars who have touched on the Engagement controversy have mistakenly supposed that the Engagement was an oath, as does Quentin Skinner, "Thomas Hobbes on the Proper Signification of Liberty," 142 n. It was not an oath, however, which calls on the presence of God as a witness to a promise, but simply a promise. As Hobbes pointed out, the moral obligation of a promise was not lessened because it was not accompanied by an oath; L, chap. 14. 33. It should be noted that the Engagement's wording contained only the promise of future obedience to the Commonwealth and made no reference to approval of the past actions that brought the new regime to power.

30 L, A Review and Conclusion, 6–8.
31 L, A Review and Conclusion, 17.
32 Thomas Hobbes, *Six Lessons to the Professors of the Mathematics*, 1656, EW, vol. 7, p. 336.
33 The most recent accounts of the seventeenth-century reception of *Leviathan* and Hobbes's philosophical and religious ideas are Jon Parkin's essay, "The Reception of Hobbes's *Leviathan*," in Springborg, *The Cambridge Companion to Hobbes's Leviathan*, and the same writer's comprehensive study *Taming the Leviathan* (Cambridge: Cambridge University Press, 2007).
34 Edward Hyde, Earl of Clarendon, *A Brief View and Survey of the Dangerous and Pernicious Errors in Church and State, in Mr. Hobbes's Book, Entitled Leviathan* (1676), quoted in Perez Zagorin, "Clarendon against *Leviathan*," in Springborg, *The Cambridge Companion to Hobbes's Leviathan*, p. 466.
35 Quoted in Hoekstra, *The De Facto Turn in Hobbes's Political Philosophy*, p. 33, from a letter written by Saye in 1657.
36 DC, chap. 1.7.
37 DC, chap. 13.4; L, chap. 13.9, 14.
38 Skinner, "Thomas Hobbes on the Proper Signification of Liberty"; see Hobbes's reference to the subject's "harmlesse liberty, which supreme Commanders are bound to preserve . . . by the Lawes of nature"; DC, chap. 13.15. A similar expression occurs in the Latin 1668 edition of *Leviathan*, quoted by the editor in L, chap. 30, 21 n.: "the end of laws is not to restrain people from a harmless liberty."
39 Skinner, "Thomas Hobbes on the Proper Signification of Liberty," is mistaken, I think, in stating (pp. 126–28) that Hobbes was not an exponent of a pure negative theory of liberty.
40 Isaiah Berlin, *Two Concepts of Liberty* (Oxford: Clarendon, Press, 1958), reprinted with some changes in the same author's *Four Essays on Liberty* (Oxford: Oxford

University Press, 1969), p. 7. Berlin refers to Hobbes in *Two Concepts* on p. 8 n. For the convenience of the reader, it is worth paraphrasing the definitions of the theories of negative and positive liberty given by Matthew H. Kramer, a rigorous advocate of the theory of negative liberty, in *The Quality of Freedom* (Oxford: Oxford University Press, 2003), pp. 2–3, 92–104. According to the negative theory, a person is free to X (where X represents the performance of some action) if and only if it is possible for him to X, or alternatively, if and only if he is not prevented from X-ing. The positive theory holds that a person is free if he is in a state that exercises certain faculties, or reaches certain decisions, or attains certain objectives, or follows certain procedures.

41 Skinner, *Hobbes and Republican Liberty*.

42 Skinner gives a historical account of the republican theory of liberty in *Hobbes and Republican Liberty*, preface et passim, and in a previous work, *Liberty before Liberalism* (Cambridge: Cambridge University Press, 1998), as well as in various essays. He has acknowledged in these books and elsewhere his indebtedness to the writings of the contemporary republican political theorist Philip Pettit. I have discussed Pettit and the current republican theory in a review essay, "Republicanisms," *British Journal for the History of Philosophy* 11, no. 6 (2003): 701–14. The republican theory includes a number of claims and is also intended as a critique of liberalism, but in this discussion of Hobbes, I deal only with the part of it on which Skinner concentrates in *Hobbes and Republican Liberty*. For a thorough critique of Skinner's views, see Kramer, *The Quality of Freedom*, chap. 2. The critical treatment of the republicanism of Skinner and several other authors by Alan Patten, "The Republican Critique of Liberalism," *British Journal of Political Science* 26, no. 1 (1996): 28–36, is not mainly concerned with the republican theory theory of liberty but with its emphasis on communitarianism and the essential importance of citizen participation in government..

43 Skinner, *Hobbes and Republican Liberty*, p. x.

44 Ibid., p. xiv.

45 James Harrington, *The Prerogative of Popular Government*, 1658, quoted in Zagorin, *A History of Political Thought in the English Revolution*, p. 134; see the accounts of English republicanism in the mid-seventeenth century by Jonathan Scott, "Classical Republicanism in Seventeenth-Century England and The Netherlands," and Blair Worden, "Republicanism, Regicide and Republic: The English Experience," in *Republicanism*, ed. Martin Van Gelderen and Quentin Skinner, 2 vols. (Cambridge: Cambridge University Press, 2002), vol. 1. Recent scholars have used the term "republicanism" quite loosely and expansively and have much exaggerated the presence of republicanism in England before the mid-seventeenth-century.

46 Thomas Hobbes, *De Corpore*, EW, vol. 1, p. viii.

47 See L, chap. 6.1–2; this chapter's title explains that it deals with "the interiour beginnings of voluntary motions, commonly called the passions."

48 The centrality of motion in Hobbes's natural philosophy dated back to the 1630s and appears in various chapters in *De Corpore*, as well as in numerous allusions in his political writings, which also contain statements concerning the will. In

Leviathan he defines the will or act of willing as the last appetite or aversion in deliberation immediately adhering to the action. He calls a voluntary act one that proceeds from the will; L, chap. 6.53. Frithiof Brandt, *Thomas Hobbes's Mechanical Conception of Nature* (Copenhagen: Leven and Munksgaard, 1928), discusses the significance of motion in Hobbes's philosophy. Cees Leijenhorst, *The Mechanization of Aristotelianism* (Leiden: Brill, 2002), chap. 5, contains a genetic account of Hobbes's theory of causality, motion, and necessity. Jurgen Overhoff deals with Hobbes's idea of the will and its implications in *Hobbes's Theory of the Will* (Lanham, MD: Rowman and Littlefield, 2000).

49 EL, pt. 2, chap. 4.9, p. 105; there is a close resemblance between Hobbes's formulation and Hume's statement in discussing liberty and necessity that "by liberty, then, we can only mean a power of acting or not acting, according to the determination of the will"; David Hume, *An Enquiry Concerning Human Understanding*, ed. L. A. Selby-Bigge, 2nd ed. (Oxford: Clarendon Press, 1951), sec. 8, pt. 1, p. 95.

50 DC, chap. 9.9.

51 DC, chap. 13.15.

52 Thomas Hobbes, *Of Liberty and Necessity*, 1654, EW, vol. 4, pp. 274, 275–76. Skinner, *Hobbes and Republican Liberty*, pp. 130–31, gives an account of the context of this discussion of liberty and necessity, which took place in Paris at the behest of the marquess of Newcastle, Hobbes's friend and a patron to whom he dedicated *The Elements of Law*. On Hobbes's view of the freedom of the will and his controversy on the subject with Bishop Bramhall, see also Nicholas D. Jackson, *Hobbes, Bramhall, and the Politics of Liberty and Necessity* (Cambridge: Cambridge University Press, 2007), and *Hobbes and Bramhall on Liberty and Necessity*, ed. Vere Chappell (Cambridge: Cambridge University Press, 1999).

53 Skinner, *Hobbes and Republican Liberty*, pp. xvi, 129.

54 L, chap. 21.1, 2, 4. Kramer, *The Quality of Freedom*, pp. 33–41, emphasizes that the theory of negative liberty must be desire-independent. He criticizes Hobbes and others who define liberty as being free to do what one wills or wants for failing to recognize that desires and wishes are irrelevant to freedom. It is the ability to X, not the desire or wish, he argues, that is crucial to a person's freedom, and he notes that it would be wrong to think that the bounds of the potential freedom of individuals are set by their desires. He does not address the fact that if one has the ability to X but never any desire or wish to do it, then this particular liberty means nothing to the person involved, and may not even be thought of as a liberty.

55 Skinner, *Hobbes and Republican Liberty*, pp. 150–52.

56 L, chap. 21.3–5.

57 Skinner, *Hobbes and Republican Liberty*, pp. 163, 165.

58 Kramer, *The Quality of Freedom*, pp. 38–39, notes this point as a criticism of Hobbes's position.

59 L, chap. 21.6.

60 DC, chap. 13.15.

61 L, chap. 21.7.

62 It should be noted that the idea of liberty as one's inheritance and birthright, which Hobbes was attacking here, was not related to the republican theory of liberty but was very much a part of the English conception of liberty as based on law and precedent prescribed in the kingdom's ancestral constitution.
63 L, chap. 21.8-9.
64 EL, pt. 2, chaps. 5.3-8; 8.3, pp. 110-13, 134; DC, chap. 10. 3-19; L, chap. 18.4-9.
65 DC, chap. 10.8.
66 L, chap. 21.10.
67 L, chap. 21.11-17.
68 John Bramhall, *The Catching of Leviathan* (1658), reprinted in *Leviathan: Contemporary Responses to the Political Theory of Thomas Hobbes*, ed. G.A.J. Rogers (Bristol: Thoemmes Press, 1995), p. 145-46; this collection also contains selections from Filmer's, George Lawson's, and Clarendon's critiques of *Leviathan*.
69 Hampton, *Hobbes and the Social Contract Tradition*, pp. 197-205, which includes references to Hobbes's contemporary critics; the quotations are on pp. 202 and 203.
70 See EL, pt. 2, chap.3.3, p. 100; DC, chap. 8.2; L, chap. 20.10.
71 DC, chap. 14.21.
72 Glenn Burgess has discussed the question of Hobbes's treatment of the subject's right of self-defense and related issues in his interesting essay, "On Hobbesian Resistance Theory," *Political Studies* 42, no. 1 (1994): 62-83, which suggests that Hobbes's work harbors a resistance theory. It would be more accurate to say that while Hobbes allows for certain cases in which the subject's resistance is legitimate, he has no theory of resistance, and always holds that the sovereign has the right to suppress any resistance to its government.
73 See Desiderius Erasmus, *The Education of a Christian Prince*, ed. Lisa Jardine (Cambridge: Cambridge University Press, 1997).
74 Among the three discourses of the 1620s that Noel B. Reynolds and Arlene W. Saxonhouse attributed to Hobbes and that I discussed in a previous chapter, one was "A Discourse upon the Beginning of Tacitus"; see Reynolds and Saxonhouse, *Thomas Hobbes: Three Discourses* (Chicago: University of Chicago Press, 1995).
75 DC, chap. 12.12.
76 Noel Malcolm, *Reason of State, Propaganda, and the Thirty Years' War* (Oxford: Clarendon Press, 2007), pp. 109-23. Note Malcolm's comment (p. 118) that while Hobbes's political theory has a number of points of contact with the concept of reason of state ("*ragion di stato*"), "the overall flavour of his work is very different." One might go further and say that in no sense is Hobbes's political philosophy a part of the doctrine of reason of state.
77 L, chap. 30.1. On the duties of the sovereign in governing, see the discussion by Deborah Baumgold in *Hobbes's Political Theory* (Cambridge: Cambridge University Press, 1988), chap. 6, on the art of government. While she does not notice that the sovereign has a moral obligation to govern well in the interests of its people, she brings out very clearly that the necessity of good government, in-

cluding the rule of law, is an integral and significant part of Hobbes's absolutist political theory.
78 L, chap. 30.1–2.
79 L, chap. 25.2–4; in distinguishing in *The Elements of Law*, pt. 2, chap. 8.6, p. 136, and *De Cive*, chap. 14.1, between counsel and command, Hobbes does not mention that a command is directed to the benefit of the commander. The general point he emphasizes is that the reason of a command is the will of the commander, whereas the reason of counsel is the substance of its advice.
80 EL, p. 2, chaps. 5.1; 9.1, pp. 108, 142.
81 L, chap. 30.3–5, 7–14.
82 It is important to realize that insofar as Hobbes's absolute sovereign is the good and effective governor the philosopher wants it to be, it will govern according to law, not by arbitrary power. The Hobbesian political system in this sense is based on the rule of law, and it is the law, fairly administered and enforced by the sovereign, from which subjects derive their security. Hobbes takes care to show that the law must be authoritatively promulgated and made known to subjects, and that it should be clear and certain. He propounds such principles as that all punishments must be the result of legal procedure and that no ex post facto law can make an act a crime; see the discussion of crimes and punishments in L, chaps. 27–28. He emphasizes that "it is a great part of that liberty which is harmlesse to civill government, and necessary for each subject to live happily, that there be no penalties dreaded, but what they may both foresee, and look for." He also states that "it pertains to the harmlesse and necessary liberty of subjects, that every man may without feare, enjoy the rights which are allowed him by the Lawes"; DC, 13.16–17. As is explained later in this chapter, the sovereign, while not bound by the civil law, is morally accountable to the law of nature and equity.
83 L, chap. 30.15–19.
84 See Noel Malcolm, "Hobbes, Sandys, and the Virginia Company," in *Aspects of Hobbes* (Oxford: Clarendon Press, 2002).
85 Keith Thomas, "The Social Origins of Hobbes's Political Thought," in Brown, *Hobbes Studies*, contains an excellent account of the philosopher's social and economic ideas.
86 L, chap. 30.20–22.
87 Hobbes deals at length with crimes and punishments in L, chaps. 27–28; see on this subject Mario A. Cattaneo, "Hobbes's Theory of Punishment," in Brown, *Hobbes Studies*, reprinted in Finkelstein, *Hobbes on Law*, and Dieter Hüning, "Hobbes on the Right to Punish," in Springborg, *The Cambridge Companion to Hobbes's Leviathan*.
88 L, chap. 30.23.
89 L, chap. 30.24–29.
90 EL, pt. 2, chap. 9.2, p. 142; DC, chap. 13.5.
91 EL, pt. 2, chap. 9. 3–4, p. 143.
92 DC, chap. 13.6.

93 L, chap. 26.8; DC, chap. 14.10.
94 L, chap. 24.7: "in what cases the commands of the sovereigns are contrary to equity and the law of nature is to be considered hereafter." The reference is probably to L., chap. 30, on the duties of the sovereign.
95 L, chaps. 21.7; 26.41; 28.22.
96 DC, chap. 7.14.
97 L, chaps. 29.9; 30.1.
98 EL, pt. 2, chap. 9.1; chap. 10.5, pp. 142, 148.
99 DC, chap. 13.2, 8.
100 DC, chap. 7.3; L, chap. 19.2.
101 L, chap. 18.20; see the similar argument in DC, chap. 6.13.
102 Hobbes, *A Dialogue Between a Philosopher and a Student of the Common Laws of England*. This work, which may be unfinished, was first published posthumously in 1681. For Hobbes's view of equity, see the essays by Larry May, "Hobbes on Equity and Justice," and William Mathie, "Justice and Equity: An Inquiry into the Meaning and Role of Equity in the Hobbesian Account of Justice and Politics," in *Hobbes's Science of Natural Justice*, ed. C. Walton and P. Johnson (Dordrecht: Nijhoff, 1987), reprinted in Finkelstein, *Hobbes on Law*.
103 St. German, *Dialogue Between a Doctor of Divinity and a Student of the Laws of England*.
104 Suárez, *On Laws and God the Lawgiver*, vol. 2, bk. 1, chap. 2.9–10; bk. 2, chap. 16, pp. 33–35, 309–25.
105 See, e.g., Grotius, *The Law of War and Peace*, vol. 2, bk. 3, chap. 20.47.1–2, p. 824; in this passage Grotius contrasts law with the fairness of equity in discussing the task of an arbitrator, who exists, he says, so that equity might prevail. Grotius's *De Aequitate*, based on the text in the Amsterdam 1670 edition of *De Iure Belli ac Pacis*, is printed with an English translation in Andrew J. Majeske, *Equity in English Renaissance Literature* (New York: Routledge, 2006), Appendix B; this short treatise offers a clear account of equity in relation to law and legal interpretation and follows Aristotle in defining equity as a virtue of the will "which corrects what is lacking in the law because of its universality"; Majeske, ibid., p. 128.
106 Aristotle, *Nicomachean Ethics*, 1137b–38a, bk. 5, chap. 10. Aristotle also discusses equity in his *Rhetoric*, 1374a24–b23, bk. 1, chap. 13, where he says, among other things, that equity makes up for the defects in a written code of laws and requires thinking less about what the legislator said than what he meant.
107 EL, pt. 1, chap. 17.2, 14–15.
108 DC, chaps. 3.15, 31; 4.12; 13.10–11. It is worth pointing out that among Hobbes's predecessors, Suárez had noted that "natural equity" was identical with "natural justice" and had quoted instances of this concept in the Roman law's *Digest*. From these citations he inferred that "equity is not an emendation of legal justice [*ius*], but rather the source or rule thereof"; Suarez, *On Laws and God the Lawgiver*, bk. 1, chap. 2.9, p. 34.
109 L, chaps. 15.26; 24.7; 30.15; chap. 15.24 lists equity as a law of nature.

110 L, chap. 26.26, 28, 37.
111 This work by Hobbes was criticized by the lawyer and judge Sir Matthew Hale (d. 1676) in his *Reflections on Mr. Hobbes's Dialogue of the Law*, written in the later seventeenth century and published by Sir William Holdsworth, *A History of English Law*, 7th ed., 14 vols. (London: Methuen, 1957), vol. 5. A champion of the common law, Hale was a pious Christian, a great judge, and a great lawyer and legal scholar. His critique of Hobbes is discussed with references to the literature in Harold J. Berman, "The Origins of Historical Jurisprudence: Coke, Selden, Hale," *Yale Law Journal* (1994), pp. 1651–738, and Alan Cromartie, *Sir Matthew Hale 1609–1676* (Cambridge: Cambridge University Press, 1995), chap. 7.
112 *Dialogue*, pp. 29–30, 65–66, 68.
113 May, p. 242.
114 L, chap. 24.7.
115 L, chap. 31.40.
116 See Perez Zagorin, *Rebels and Rulers, 1500–1660*, 2. vols. (Cambridge: Cambridge University Press, 1982).
117 DC, Preface, pp. 30–31, 35–36; this preface was published in 1651 with the English translation of DC.
118 DC, Preface, pp. 31–32.
119 H.L.A. Hart, *The Concept of Law* (Oxford: Clarendon Press, 1986), p. 193.

CHAPTER 4
Hobbes, the Moral Philosopher

1 For the seventeenth-century reception in England of Hobbes's philosophical and religious ideas, see Parkin, *Taming the Leviathan*. Paul Russell, *The Riddle of Hume's Treatise: Skepticism, Naturalism, and Irreligion* (Oxford: Oxford University Press, 2008), brings out some of the connections between Hobbes and Hume's *Treatise of Human Nature* and shows the extent to which Hobbes was considered by many eighteenth-century British thinkers to be an atheistic philosopher.
2 Richard Cumberland, *A Philosophical Inquiry into the Laws of Nature* (*De Legibus Naturae*), ed. Jon Parkin (Indianapolis: Liberty Fund, 2005; first published 1672, first English translation 1727), pp. 612, 753. Parkin discusses (pp. 272–82) Cumberland's critique and attempted refutation of Hobbes's view of the law of nature.
3 John Locke, *Questions concerning the Law of Nature*, ed. Robert Horwitz (Ithaca, NY: Cornell University Press, 1990), question VIII, p. 203. This work, which dates from the 1660s, has been published in an earlier edition as *John Locke: Essays on the Law of Nature*, ed. Wolfgang von Leyden (Oxford: Clarendon Press, 1954).
4 Parkin, *Taming the Leviathan*, pp. 371–75.
5 Joel Kupperman, "Classical and Sour Forms of Virtue," in *Morality and Self-Interest*, ed. Paul Bloomfield (Oxford: Oxford University Press, 2008), p. 280.

6 Gauthier, *The Logic of Leviathan*, p. 98, cited by Hampton, *Hobbes and the Social Contract Tradition*, p. 56.
7 Thomas Nagel, "Hobbes's Concept of Obligation," *Philosophical Review* 68, no. 1 (1959): 74, quoted in Lloyd, *Ideals as Interests in Hobbes's Leviathan*, p. 325, n. 9.
8 Lloyd, *Ideals as Interests in Hobbes's Leviathan*, p. 12.
9 See in particular R. E. Ewin, *Virtues and Rights* (Boulder, CO: Westview Press, 1991), and David Boonin-Vail, *Thomas Hobbes and the Science of Moral Virtue* (Cambridge: Cambridge University Press, 1994).
10 EL, pt. 1, chap. 14.6, p.54; DC, chap. 1.13; L, chap. 6.7.
11 Plato, *Protagoras*, 358d. A friendly critic has commented that the mention here of Socrates is unhelpful because of the latter's belief that being just is always in one's interest and his doctrine of the soul, which held that to do wrong is the worst thing that can happen to a person.
12 Hobbes in Gert, *Man and Citizen*, pp. 47, 48. This edition contains a portion of the English texts of *De Homine* and *De Cive*.
13 EL, pt. 1, chap. 7.3, p. 22; L, chap. 6.7. As I pointed out in an earlier chapter, Hobbes's proposition that whatever men desire they call good can't be universally true, because all human beings know that some of their desires are contrary to their good.
14 As John Rawls has commented, "Every interest is an interest of a self (agent), but not every interest is in benefits to the self that has it. Indeed, rational agents may have all kinds of affections for persons and attachments to communities and places, including love of country and nature; and they may select and order their ends in various ways." John Rawls, *Political Liberalism* (New York: Columbia University Press, 1996), p. 51.
15 See Gert's discussion of tautological and psychological egoism in Hobbes in the introduction to *Man and Citizen*, pp. 5–10. Gert points out (p. 5) that psychological egoism "rests upon [the] claim that men *never* act in order to benefit others or because they believe a certain course of action to be morally right." It is obvious enough that Hobbes never subscribed to this view. See also Boonin-Vail's comments on this entire question with references to the literature, *Thomas Hobbes and the Science of Moral Virtue*, pp. 42–47, which find that despite some of his formulations, Hobbes was not a psychological egoist and did not maintain that people are exclusively concerned with their own welfare and incapable of acting with regard for others. Stephen Finn deals with psychological and tautological egoism in Hobbes in *Hobbes: A Guide for the Perplexed* (London: Continuum, 2007), pp. 51–56. He defines tautological egoism (p. 51) as the "logically true claim that people desire the object of their desire," and observes indications of both tautological and psychological egoism in Hobbes.
16 L, p. 1. The dedication is addressed to Francis Godolphin, the brother of the deceased Sidney Godolphin, to honor the latter. It should be noticed that "generous," the term Hobbes used, referred to a quality or virtue that had very definite class and aristocratic overtones in his time, being derived from the Latin *genero-*

sus, which meant well-born or noble. See also Hobbes's praise of Sidney Godolphin in L, Review and Conclusion, 4.

17 See the selections from Joseph Butler, *Fifteen Sermons*, 1726, and *Dissertation on the Nature of Virtue*, 1736, in *British Moralists 1650–1800*, ed. D. D. Raphael, 2 vols. (Oxford: Clarendon Press, 1969), vol. 2. Ralph Wedgwood's careful account of Butler's moral philosophy, "Butler on Virtue, Self-Interest, and Human Nature," in Bloomfield, *Morality and Self-Interest*, concludes that his arguments for the harmony of virtue and self-interest are "pure wishful thinking" and "implausible" (pp. 203–204).

18 W. D. Falk, "Morality, Self, and Others," in Bloomfield, *Morality and Self-Interest*, p. 234.

19 L, Review and Conclusion, 13.

20 L, Introduction, p. 4: "To describe the nature of this artificial man, I will consider first, the matter thereof, and the artificer, both which is man."

21 Grotius, *The Law of War and Peace*, vol. 2, Prolegomena, 16.

22 L, Review and Conclusion, 4

23 DC, 3.5; cf. the parallel passage in L, chap. 15.9.

24 See above, chap. 2.

25 In a well-known but now dated article of 1938, A. E. Taylor sought to show that Hobbes's ethical theory, if considered apart from his psychological egoism, was a strict deontology analogous to that of Kant; Taylor, "The Ethical Doctrine of Hobbes." The differences between Hobbes and Kant are far greater, however, than any similarity. Taylor also argued that the obligatory character of Hobbes's laws of nature was due to the fact that they were commands of God. A similar view was advanced by Howard Warrender in *The Political Philosophy of Hobbes*. I have shown in chap. 2 that this opinion is mistaken.

26 The recent work by Howard Williams, *Kant's Critique of Hobbes* (Cardiff: University of Wales Press, 2003), contains an interesting discussion and comparison of Kant and Hobbes that brings out clearly points of agreement and disagreement between the two. Williams states (p. 9) that in political philosophy, "Kant always treats Hobbes's thinking as of the first importance." Kant's most important comments on Hobbes's occur in his essay of 1793, "On the Common Saying: 'This May Be Correct in Theory, But It Does Not Apply in Practice,'" pt. 2, reprinted in *Kant's Political Writings*, ed. Hans Reiss, 2nd ed. (Cambridge: Cambridge University Press, 2006).

27 Immanuel Kant, *Idea of a Universal History from a Cosmopolitan Point of View* (1784), in *Kant on History*, ed. Lewis White Beck (Indianapolis: Bobbs-Merrill, 1985), pp. 17–18.

28 Kant's main work in moral philosophy is his *Groundwork of the Metaphysics of Morals*, in which he sought to establish the supreme principles of morality. Williams notes (pp. 106–7) that the perspective of Kant's moral imperative that we should always treat other persons as ends, not as means, was that "every human individual is of equal worth," and he quotes Kant as calling this rule "a principle of humanity."

29 L, chap. 14.4–5.
30 L, chap. 15.35.
31 L, chap. 15.36.
32 L, chap. 15.40.
33 L, chap. 15.17, 18, 19, 20, 34.
34 Because "every man is presumed to do all things in order to his own benefit," the sixteenth law of nature prohibits a man from being a judge or arbitrator in his own cause; L, 15.31.
35 DC, chap. 5.4.
36 L, chap. 19.4.
37 L, chap. 30.20.
38 L, chap. 30.1.
39 I owe this formulation to my friend Professor George Klosko of the Department of Political Science of the University of Virginia, who has written extensively on the subject of political obligation.
40 L, chap.14. 7.
41 L, chap. 14. 7; cf. DC, chap. 8.3: "all obligation derives from Contract."
42 DC, chap. 15.7; L, chap. 31.5.
43 L, chap. 21.10.
44 See the discussion of legal duty and obligation by H.L.A. Hart, *Essays on Bentham* (Oxford: Clarendon Press, 1982), chap. 6. Hart notes (pp. 127, 128) the frequent use of "obligation" in reference to both law and morals and points out that some writers hold that there is a common element in legal and moral obligation and that the former in some sense presupposes the latter. This, I believe, accords with Hobbes's view.
45 DC, chap. 14.9.
46 L, chap. 26.3, 8; in DC, chap. 14.2, Hobbes also makes a distinction, as I have noticed previously, between being obliged and being tied. Thus contracts oblige, and a person ought to perform because he has promised, while the law ties the person who is obliged, that is, "it compels him to make good his promise, for fear of the punishment appointed by the Law."
47 L, chap. 15.1–2.
48 DC, chap. 14.10.
49 On *pacta sunt servanda* as an obligation of the law of nature, see above, chap. 2.
50 Watkins, *Hobbes's System of Ideas*, pp. 76–77, 83, 84, 87; Watkins states (p. 84) that "Hobbes wanted to reduce morality to rational self-interest."
51 Philip Pettit, *Made With Words: Hobbes on Language, Mind, and Politics* (Princeton, NJ: Princeton University Press, 2008), p. 165, n.5.
52 Taylor, "The Ethical Doctrine of Hobbes."
53 Stuart M. Brown, Jr., "The Taylor Thesis: Some Objections," in Brown, *Hobbes Studies*.
54 C. B. Macpherson, *The Political Theory of Possessive Individualism* (Oxford: Clarendon Press, 1962), pp. 72–74; Gauthier, *The Logic of Leviathan*, pp. 91, 98, quoted in Boonin-Vail, *Thomas Hobbes and the Science of Moral Virtue*, p. 62.

55 Lloyd, *Ideals as Interests in Hobbes's Leviathan*, p. 14.
56 Falk, "Morality, Self, and Others," pp. 230, 232.
57 H. A. Prichard, "Does Moral Philosophy Rest Upon A Mistake?" (1912), reprinted in idem, *Moral Obligation* (Oxford: Oxford University Press, 1968); see the discussion of Prichard's essay and moral philosophy by David Schmidtz, "Because It's Right," in Bloomfield, *Morality and Self-Interest*, and W. D. Hudson's excellent *Modern Moral Philosophy* (Garden City, NJ: Doubleday, 1970), pp. 89–92.
58 Aristotle, *Nicomachean Ethics*, 1140a 25–27, bk. 6, chap. 5.
59 Aquinas, *Summa Theologiae*, Ia–IIae, qu. 57, art. 4.
60 L, chaps. 3.7.10; 5.21; 8.11; 46.2.
61 Thomas Hobbes, *Behemoth,* ed. Ferdinand Tönnies and Stephen Holmes (Chicago: University of Chicago Press, 1990), p. 44. Hobbes wrote this work in the 1660s.
62 Further on in L, Hobbes includes among the false principles that breed crime the opinion that "justice is but a vain word," but he does not discuss or attempt to refute it; L, chap. 27.10.
63 L, chap. 15.4–5.
64 It is not quite clear to me whether Hobbes is referring to the state of nature when he uses the example of the keeping of covenants in a condition of war. If he is, this may be his only mention of the possibility of confederacies or alliances in that condition.
65 L, chap. 15. 5.
66 Unlike the just man, the fool's will "is not framed by justice, but by the apparent benefit of what he is to do"; L, chap. 15.10.
67 Hobbes's answer to the fool has been discussed by a number of scholars, among others Gregory S. Kavka, "Right Reason and Natural Law in Hobbes's Ethics," *The Monist* 66, no. 1 (1983): 120–33, reprinted in Finkelstein, *Hobbes on Law*; Hampton, *Hobbes and the Social Contract Tradition*, pp. 55–56, 64–66; Boonin-Vail, *Thomas Hobbes and the Science of Moral Virtue*, pp. 147–50; and Kinch Hoekstra, "Hobbes and the Foole," *Political Theory* 25, no. 5 (1997): 620–54, who offers a lengthy examination of the subject with references to the recent literature.
68 L, chap. 15.6–9.
69 Quoted from Philippa Foot, "Moral Beliefs," *Proceedings of the Aristotelian Society* 59 (1958–59): 103–4, in Hudson, *Modern Moral Philosophy*, pp. 272–73.
70 L, chaps. 14.7; 23.6.
71 David Hume, *A Treatise of Human Nature*, ed. David Fate Norton and Mary J. Norton (Oxford: Oxford University Press, 2003), bk. 3, pt. 1, sec. 1, p. 302.
72 The literature relating to the problem of is and ought and facts and values is very large and controversial. On the interpretation of Hume's comment and the issue of facts and values, see Jonathan Harrison, *Hume's Moral Epistemology* (Oxford: Clarendon Press, 1976); idem, "Ethical Naturalism," in Edwards, *Encyclopedia of Philosophy*, vol. 3; and Hudson, *Modern Moral Philosophy*, chap. 6. John Finnis deals with Hume's statement in relation to the law of nature in *Natural Law and Natural Rights*, pp. 36–42. He denies (p. 37) that the gap between is and

ought justifies Hume's conclusion that distinctions between vice and virtue are not perceived by reason. Leo Strauss attacked the distinction between facts and values, to which he attributed a major role in the decline of classical natural law (which he usually and misleadingly calls natural right). His critique of this distinction contains no reference to Hume or the question of is and ought, and makes the German sociologist Max Weber (d. 1920) and his aspiration toward a value-free social science the main object of his criticism. Straus was convinced that the bifurcation of facts and values led to the prohibition of value judgments in social science and therefore to nihilism; see his *Natural Right and History*, chap. 2.

73 See the discussion of natural law and legal positivism in chap. 1.
74 Lloyd L. Weinreb, *Natural Law and Justice* (Cambridge, MA: Harvard University Press, 1987), p. 3.
75 Rommen, *The Natural Law*, pp. 85, 141–43, and chap. 8.
76 Finnis, *Natural Law and Natural Rights*, chap. 2
77 Finnis's work is discussed in Neil Maccormick's appreciative essay, "Natural Law and the Separation of Law and Morals," in George, *Natural Law Theory*, p. 105. George defends it against a number of criticisms in his essay, "Natural Law and Human Nature," in ibid. Weinreb discusses it in chap. 4, entitled "Natural Law without Nature."
78 See Hobbes's discussion of metaphysics in L, chap. 46.14–15, which defines it as '"first philosophy" consisting of the definition of the most universal terms that pertain to the nature and generation of bodies. This chapter in L is mainly a critique of "vain philosophy" as exemplified in the metaphysics and ethics of Aristotle and the "supernatural philosophy" of scholasticism.
79 Hume, *Treatise*, 1.4.7, p. 177.
80 See above, chap. 1
81 For these quotations and references to Cudworth's *A Treatise Concerning Eternal and Immutable Morality* (1st ed. 1731), see Perez Zagorin, "Cudworth and Hobbes on Is and Ought," in *Philosophy, Science, and Religion in England 1640–1700*, ed. Richard Kroll, Richard Ashcraft, and Perez Zagorin (Cambridge: Cambridge University Press, 1992), pp. 130–31. Selections from Cudworth's *Treatise* and its criticisms of Hobbes are printed in Raphael, *British Moralists*, vol. 1, and in Schneewind, *Moral Philosophy from Montaigne to Kant*, vol. 1.
82 Samuel Clarke, *A Discourse of Natural Religion* (1706), in Raphael, *British Moralists*, vol. 1; see pp. 194–95, 212–13, 217–24. Selections from this work are also printed in Schneewind, Moral Philosophy from Montaigne to Kant, vol. 1. Both Cudworth's and Clarke's critique of Hobbes presuppose, as Clarke states (Raphael, *British Moralists*, vol. 1, p. 212) that the law of nature is an "eternal rule of equity" and "right reason" that "was founded in the nature of things and did not begin to be law when first written and enacted by men, "but is of the same original with the eternal reasons or proportions of things, and the perfections and attributes of God himself." Finnis (*Natural Law and Natural Rights*, pp. 38–42) criticizes Clarke's moral philosophy and notes that Hume's remarks on is and

ought were directed at him. Russell's recent book on Hume devotes a good deal of attention to both Clarke and Cudworth.

83 R. S. Peters, *Hobbes* (Harmondsworth: Penguin, 1956), p. 170; Watkins, *Hobbes's System of Ideas*, p. 76, which also cites the work by Peters.

84 Macpherson, *The Political Theory of Possessive Individualism*, pp. 13–15, 76–77, 81–87. The position he states is not easily intelligible: "I shall argue that in any sense short of strict logical entailment it is possible to deduce obligation from fact; that senses short of entailment are so important as to make it humanly necessary to attempt such a deduction; that the deduction is possible, even in these senses, only when the social facts contain a significant equality of men; that Hobbes grasped this; and that his attempt to deduce obligation from fact was therefore valid in principle" (pp. 81–82). Macpherson had not noticed the equality of men was a principle long associated with the natural law tradition.

85 Zagorin, "Cudworth and Hobbes on Is and Ought."

86 See, e.g., DC, Epistle Dedicatory, pp. 25–27.

87 DC, Epistle Dedicatory, p. 27; L, Review and Conclusion, 13.

88 DC, Preface to the Reader, p. 36.

89 L, chap. 14.4.

90 DC, chap. 1.7.

91 Noel Malcolm has given a somewhat analogous account of Hobbes's proceeding. He observes that to show that men can all agree on the need to pass from a state of conflict to a state of peace, Hobbes argues that it is possible to abstract a set of universal rules of human action from the contingent facts of conflicting individual desires. Malcolm goes on to explain that of all these desires, Hobbes gives priority to the desire to avoid death, and from this general truth draws a system of optimum means toward the avoidance of death. These means are the laws of nature, which provide a set of rules of actions that all men must find valid if they reason correctly; Noel Malcolm, "Hobbes and Spinoza," in *Aspects of Hobbes*, pp. 31–32.

92 On Hobbes's religion and beliefs, see the discussion by Sommerville, *Thomas Hobbes*, chaps. 5–6, and Patricia Springborg, "Hobbes on Religion," in Sorell, *The Cambridge Companion to Hobbes*.

93 L, chap. 11.25; see also Hobbes's objections to the Third Meditation in Descartes, *Meditations on First Philosophy*, 1641, in which he argues that we have no image or idea of God in our mind but know there must be an eternal first cause from which the thought of such a being ultimately derives, and to this eternal something we give the name God; René Descartes, *Philosophical Essays and Correspondence*, ed. Roger Ariew (Hackett: Indianapolis, 2000), pp. 171–72. Among the best accounts of Hobbes's view of God are Glover, "God and Thomas Hobbes," and Arrigo Pacchi, "Hobbes and the Problem of God," in Rogers and Ryan, *Perspectives on Thomas Hobbes*.

94 L, chap. 3.12.

95 L, chap. 31.4, 5, 7.

96 L, chap. 6.36.

97 L, chap. 32.2–3.
98 L, chap. 12.11.
99 L, chaps. 33; 42.3; on Hobbes's negative view of Moses's authorship of the Pentateuch and its historical context in earlier biblical scholarship, see Noel Malcolm, "Hobbes, Ezra, and the Bible: The History of a Subversive Idea," in *Aspects of Hobbes*.
100 L, chap. 12.
101 L, chap. 8.26.
102 L, Dedication, p. 2.
103 Quoted from Edward Hyde, Earl of Clarendon, *A Brief View and Survey of the Dangerous and Pernicious Errors in Church and State, in Mr Hobbes's Book, Entitled Leviathan*, 1676, in Perez Zagorin, "Clarendon against *Leviathan*," in Springborg, *The Cambridge Companion to Hobbes's Leviathan*, p. 473.
104 L, chap. 31.1.
105 L, chap. 43.1.
106 *The Correspondence of Thomas Hobbes*, vol. 1, p. 140.
107 *Behemoth*, ed. Tönnies and Holmes, pp. 89, 95.
108 L, chaps. 26.40; 31.7.
109 L, chap. 31.24.
110 L, chap. 21.37; see Jeremy Waldron, "Hobbes on Public Worship," in *Toleration and Its Limits*, ed. Melissa S. Williams and Jeremy Waldron, Nomos 48 (New York: New York University Press, 2008).
111 On the Christian theory of persecution, see Perez Zagorin, *How the Idea of Religious Toleration Came to the West* (Princeton, NJ: Princeton University Press, 2003), chap. 2.
112 Ibid., chap. 6.
113 See the balanced account by Edwin Curley, "Hobbes and the Cause of Religious Toleration," in Springborg, *The Cambridge Companion to Hobbes's Leviathan*, which refers to previous writings on this subject.
114 See the discussion of the origin of the concept of heresy in Zagorin, *How the Idea of Religious Toleration Came to the West*, chap. 2.
115 L, chap. 11.19.
116 L, chap. 42.130.
117 The chapter on heresy from the 1668 Latin translation of *Leviathan* is printed in L, Appendix, chap. 2; the quotations are on pp. 527 and 536–37. On the importance of the parable of the tares in the toleration controversy, see Zagorin, *How the Idea of Religious Toleration Came to the West*, pp. 28–29 et passim; on the appendix to the Latin *Leviathan*, see George Wright, "The 1668 Appendix and Hobbes's Theological Project," in Springborg, *The Cambridge Companion to Hobbes's Leviathan*.
118 Hobbes's *An Historical Narration Concerning Heresie, and the Punishment Thereof* was published posthumously in 1680. He dealt with heresy also in *A Dialogue Between a Philosopher and a Student of the Common Laws of England*, pp. 91–103.

119 See the details of this attack on Hobbes in England's Parliament in Tuck, "Hobbes and Locke on Toleration," pp. 157–58.
120 On the Scargill affair, see Parkin, *Taming the Leviathan*, pp. 244–52.
121 Alan Ryan touches on this subject in his essay, "Hobbes, Toleration, and the Inner Life," in *The Nature of Political Theory*, ed. David Miller and Larry Siedentop (Oxford: Clarendon Press, 1983).
122 L, chap. 26.41.
123 *Behemoth*, ed. Tönnies and Holmes, p. 62.
124 L, chaps. 42.9; 46.37.
125 L, chap. 42.11–12.
126 On the precedent of Naaman, see Perez Zagorin, *Ways of Lying: Dissimulation, Persecution, and Conformity in Early Modern Europe* (Cambridge, MA: Harvard University Press, 1990), pp. 32–34 et passim.
127 L, chap. 31.12.
128 L, chap. 42.11.
129 L, chap. 43.3–5.
130 L, chap. 43.11–13.
131 L, chap. 43.14.
132 EL, pt. 2, chap. 6.5, p. 116; Hobbes uses the term "superstructure" in the same sense in L, chap. 42.25.
133 The concept of limiting the Christian faith to a few necessary fundamentals was entertained by William Chillingworth, author of *The Religion of Protestants* (1638), and several others who belonged to the Tew Circle, the group of friends from Oxford University and elsewhere who for a few years in the 1630s gathered at Lord Falkland's house at Great Tew in Oxfordshire for discussions of religion and philosophy. The Tew Circle was associated with a certain degree of rationalism, skepticism, and latitudinarianism in religion and disapproved the persecution of heterodox beliefs; see the comments by Sommerville, *Thomas Hobbes*, pp. 146–49. Hobbes's claim that belief in Jesus as the Christ was the only article of faith required for salvation was a much more radical position.
134 On Castellio, see Zagorin, *How the Idea of Religious Toleration Came to the West*, chap. 4.
135 L, chap. 47.20.
136 L, chap. 47.20.
137 Collins, *The Allegiance of Thomas Hobbes*, chaps. 4–6.
138 See Malcolm, "Hobbes and the European Republic of Letters." In recent years Jonathan I. Israel has argued in his important book, *Radical Enlightenment* (Oxford: Oxford University Press, 2001), and other writings that the Dutch Jewish philosopher Spinoza (d. 1677) was the central figure and source of greatest influence in the spread of ideas of secularism, irreligion, republicanism, pantheism, equality, freedom of thought, and so forth, that constituted the most radical side of the European Enlightenment. Malcolm (pp. 535–37) has criticized Israel's view for its underestimation and negative view of Hobbes's importance in this connection. He argues that Hobbes was perhaps both a more significant influence

than Spinoza on the radical Enlightenment and also "a rich and multifarious influence on mainstream thinking throughout this period."

139 A great many-sided thinker and also a theorist of natural law, Leibnitz made various references to Hobbes. In two letters he wrote him in the 1670s that may never have been delivered, he said he had read most of Hobbes's works and had "profited from few other works of our age as much as I have from yours," and also offered some high praise of *De Cive*; *The Correspondence of Thomas Hobbes*, vol. 2, pp. 716, 733. Leibnitz's criticisms of Hobbes are taken from his "Meditations on the Common Concept of Justice," printed in his *Political Writings*, 2nd ed., ed. Patrick Riley (Cambridge: Cambridge University Press, 1988), pp. 45–47.

140 In the area of natural law, Pufendorf's main works were *The Elements of Universal Jurisprudence* (1660), *On the Law of Nature and Nations* (1672), and *On the Duty of Man and Citizen According to Natural Law* (1673), all written in Latin. A reader will note numerous formulations of his that show the influence of Hobbes. Hochstrasser, *Natural Law Theories in the Early Enlightenment*, chap. 2, and Craig Carr in his introduction to *The Political Writings of Samuel Pufendorf* discuss the relationship between the thought of Pufendorf and of Hobbes. Fiammetta Palladini, *Samuel Pufendorf, Discepolo di Hobbes* (Bologna: Il Mulino, 1990), regards Pufendorf as Hobbes's disciple.

INDEX

absolutism, 1, 2, 53–54, 58, 70, 95. *See also* government
Adam, Fall of, 37
Althusius, Johannes, 37
altruism, 34, 86, 100, 102
Ambrose, St., 7
American Declaration of Independence, 21
analytical philosophy, 31
Anglican Church, 120, 121, 126
Aquinas, Thomas: and civil law, 53; and Grotius, 19; Hobbes's knowledge of, 14; and intellectualism, 9; and legal positivism, 50; and natural law, 8, 10, 49, 53, 113–14; on prudence, 108–9; and reason, 47; and rights, 24; and sovereignty, 64
aristocracy, 65, 66, 67
Aristotle: and democracy, 85; and equality, 35; and equity, 92, 93; and good, 101; and Grotius, 19; Hobbes's critique of, 14, 30, 32, 81; and natural rights, 138n86; and nature, 6; *Nicomachean Ethics*, 6, 9, 61, 93; and passion, 142n27; *Politics*, 1, 6, 32, 82; on prudence, 108; and scholastic philosophers, 8
artificial body/person, 31, 56, 57, 64, 66, 69–70, 103, 116–17
atheism, 16, 51, 118, 147n120
Athens, 30, 39
Augustine, St., 7
Austin, John, 3
authorization, 56, 64, 95

Bacon, Francis, 11, 13, 15, 18, 97
Barbeyrac, Jean, 15–16, 19
Bayle, Pierre, 16
Bellarmine, Robert, 15, 121
benevolence, 34, 36, 43, 48, 115
Bentham, Jeremy, 3, 12, 22
Berlin, Isaiah, 76
Bible: and conscience, 126; fool in, 110; and Golden Rule, 43, 47, 105; Leviathan in, 57; and natural law, 8, 51; and political analysis, 119–20; and reason, 118; and religious toleration, 124; sanction of, 120; and sovereign, 66, 69; and treatment of others, 105
Biel, Gabriel, 17
Bodin, Jean, 15, 67–68
body. *See* corporealism
Boyle, Robert, 11
Bramhall, John, 79, 83
Brown, Stuart M., Jr., 108
Butler, Joseph, 102

Castellio, Sebastian, 125
Catholic papacy, 15, 24, 67, 120, 121
Catholics/Catholicism, 9, 117, 120, 121, 126
censorship, 71
Charles I, 12, 59, 63, 72, 74, 77, 120
Charles II, 73, 74, 121
Christian church, 71–72, 120, 121, 122
Christian thought: and equality, 35; and equity, 92; and facts and values, 113; and faith, 125; and Hobbes's belief, 118; and natural law, 7, 8, 11, 47, 48, 51, 52; and persecution, 121; and politics, 123; primitive, 126. *See also* religion; religious faith
Cicero, 7, 35, 46, 47, 81, 92
civilization, 36, 40, 48, 75, 97
civil society: and consent, 46, 56; emergence of, 37, 38; and Grotius, 25; and human nature, 103; and liberty of subjects, 81; and natural law, 43, 114; and passions, 33; and self-preservation and self-interest, 16; and social contract, 45
Clarke, Samuel, 115, 127
clergy, 71, 120
coercion, 56, 61
Coke, Sir Edward, 69, 94
commodious living, 42, 43, 45, 104
common defense, 88
common good, 53, 63, 101, 102, 106, 117

171

commonwealth, 31; by acquisition, 60; Christian, 71, 117, 119–20; and civil vs. natural law, 90; and common good, 106; and covenants, 44, 45; creation of, 52, 75; and danger of private judgment, 54; by force, conquest, and acquisition, 57–58; by institution, 57, 60; and natural law, 42; and natural rights, 54–60; and sovereignty, 1, 46
communist states, 59
competition, 32, 34–35, 39, 99, 100
conscience, 44, 55, 101, 105, 121, 126
consent: to civil society, 46; and commonwealth, 57–58, 60–61; to government, 22–23; and Grotius, 25; and obligation to obey civil law of sovereign, 4; to political association, 37; and political order, 1; of subjects, 90
constitution/constitutionalism, 29, 62, 67, 97. *See also* government
contempt/hatred, expressions of, 44
contract(s): and civil society, 46; and liberty of subjects, 81; and natural rights, 43; and obligation, 106; and origins of sovereignty, 56; and political order, 1; of rulership, 45; and sovereign, 58
contractual tradition, 44–45, 62–63, 65
Copernicanism, 11
Copernicus, Nicolaus, 4, 119
corporation, 64
corporealism, 16, 30, 31, 118. *See also* materialism
Corpus Iuris Civilis, 7
covenant(s): and commonwealth, 56, 57–58, 60–61; and morality, 105; and natural law vs. civil law, 52; and natural rights, 43, 59; and obligation, 61–62, 106, 107–8, 110–11; and performance, 45–46; and political order, 1; and sovereignty, 68
crime, 88–89
Cromwell, Oliver, 73, 74, 89, 126
Cudworth, Ralph, 114–15, 127
Cumberland, Richard, 10, 99, 127

death, 27, 32–33, 34, 38, 42, 47, 75, 84. *See also* self-preservation
Declaration of the Rights of Man and the Citizen, 21

democracy, 30, 65, 66, 67, 81, 82, 85. *See also* government
deontology, 114
Descartes, René, 11, 18
Digest of Justinian, 7, 13
domination, 32, 77, 99
Dominicans, 10
Duns Scotus, 8, 9
duty, 6, 104, 112. *See also* obligation

education, 32
egoism, 86, 102, 108
empiricism, 11
Engagement controversy, 73
English civil war, 12, 59, 65, 72, 77, 109
English common law, 69
English Commonwealth, 73
English revolution, 59
English royalists, 73, 74
Enlightenment writers, 55
enmity, 39, 40
equality: and ability to kill, 35, 39; civil, 22; and equity, 93, 94; before law, 87–88; and morality, 105; and prepolitical conditions, 37; and reciprocity, 43; and right and obligation, 116
equity, 44, 53, 92–95, 105
Erasmus, Desiderius, 85
Erastianism, 71, 120
etiamsi daremus, 17
expediency, 108
experimentalism, 11

facts and values, 113, 114, 115, 117
Falk, W. D., 103, 108
fascism, 59
fear, 36, 39, 40, 61–62, 80
Figgis, J. N., 62
Filmer, Sir Robert, 83
Finnis, John, 114
Foot, Philippa, 111
Forster, Greg, 147n116
freedom/liberty: and Grotius, 25, 26; and law, 26–27; and Levellers, 63; and motion, 78; of movement, 89–90; and natural rights, 21, 22, 24, 28, 29; and obligation, 26, 106; and political association, 38; positive and

negative, 76; and prepolitical conditions, 37; relinquishment of, 46; republican theory of, 76–77, 80; and right, 26; for self-preservation, 27, 55, 75; and state of nature, 38, 82; of subjects, 75–84; of will, 9, 30

Gaius, 13
Galileo, 4, 11, 18, 30, 78, 119
Gauthier, David, 100, 108
geometry, 31, 116, 141n8
Gerson, Jean, 8, 24
Gert, Bernard, 101–2
Gierke, Otto, 62
glory, 34, 39
Glover, Willis, 50
God: and equity, 94; and Grotius, 19; and morality, 9; and natural law, ix, 7, 8, 9, 10, 12, 17–18, 48, 49, 50–51, 52; and natural rights, 22, 23, 24; nature of, 118; obedience to, 72, 106, 119–20, 124–25; and sovereign, 66, 86, 90, 91; and state of nature, 41
Godolphin, Sidney, 102
golden age. See primitivism
government: authoritarian, 29, 64, 65; by consent of governed, 22–23, 63; constitutional, 29; and contract, 44–45; emergence of, 37, 38; and Grotius, 25; and justice, peace, and security, 37; limits on, 55; as product of sociability and mutual needs, 37; and rights, 22; right to establish, 55. See also absolutism; constitution/constitutionalism; democracy; monarchy
Gratian, 47; *Decretum*, 8, 24, 37
gratitude, 43, 105
Greeks, ancient, ix, 5–6, 23, 36
Gregory of Rimini, 17
Grotius, Hugo: and civil law, 53; *De Iure Praedae Commentarius*, 19; on equity, 92; and fear an coercion, 61; *The Law of War and Peace*, 10, 15–19, 20, 24–25, 31–32, 37–38, 49, 58, 61, 92; *Mare Liberum*, 19–20; and natural law, 10, 15–19, 31–32, 37–38, 49, 53, 103, 127; and natural rights, 24–26; and sovereignty, 58

Haggenmacher, Peter, 25
Hampton, Jean, 83–84

happiness, 6, 21, 48, 75, 86, 90, 92, 102, 104, 128
Hardwick Hall library, 14, 15, 68, 85
Harrington, James, 77
Hart, H. L. A., 3, 22, 97
heresy, 121, 122–23
Hobbes, Thomas, 88; *Behemoth*, 109, 120, 123; *De Cive*, 4, 12, 20, 26, 31, 41, 42, 46, 54, 56, 62, 78, 81, 85, 89, 90, 91, 96, 116, 117; *De Corpore*, 78; *De Homine*, 101; *A Dialogue Between a Philosopher and a Student of the Common Laws of England*, 92, 94; "A Discourse of Laws" (attributed), 13; *The Elements of Law*, 12, 14, 15, 20, 30, 31, 33–34, 36, 40, 41, 42, 43, 56, 68, 78, 86, 89, 91, 125; *An Historical Narration concerning Heresie, and the Punishment Thereof*, 123; *Horae Subsecivae* (attributed), 13; letter to Earl of Devonshire, 120; *Leviathan*, 4, 14, 20, 31, 33, 34, 39, 41, 42, 43, 46, 49, 52, 53, 56, 61, 68, 69, 72, 73, 74, 76, 77, 79, 83, 85, 89, 90, 91, 93, 94, 95, 97, 103, 105, 107, 114, 116, 117, 118, 120, 122, 123, 126, 128; translation of Thucydides' *History of the Peloponnesian War*, 14, 30, 39, 85
Hooker, Richard, 10, 15, 37, 47, 50
Huguenots, 12
human beings/human nature, 115; characteristics of, 32–36; and civil duty, 103; as competitive and dominating, 32, 99; as corrupt, 9; highest good for, 33; and morality, 114; motives of, 32, 34; and natural rights, 22, 28; and reality, 30, 31; and reason, 8; refusal to condemn, 104; and self-interest, 101, 104–5; as sociable and inclined to cooperative association, 32; and state of nature, 39
human rights, 21
Hume, David, 12, 112, 114, 116
Hyde, Edward, Earl of Clarendon, 74, 83, 119

imagination, 33, 34
inheritance, 23
intellectualism, 9, 18, 115
is and ought, 112–17
Isidore of Seville, St., 7
ius, 23, 24, 25
ius gentium, 7, 23
ius naturale, 24, 27

James, William, 35, 36
Jesuits, 10
Jesus, 51, 72, 123, 124, 125, 126
Jewish tradition, 10
judgment: and commonwealth, 56; personal, 60, 72, 83–84, 95; private, 72, 87; public vs. private, 54; and sovereign, 58
Julius Caesar, 89
justice: and Aquinas, 50; and civil law, 53; and Cudworth, 115; and *dikaion*, 23; and equity, 93, 94; and human nature, 103; and legal positivism, 3; and *lex* and *ius*, 24; and natural law, 53, 105; and passion, 33; and refusal of sovereign's commands, 59–60, 83; and sovereign's instruction, 87; and state of nature, 41
Justinian, 13

Kant, Immanuel, 10, 104
Kepler, Johannes, 11
kings, 16, 62, 77. *See also* monarchy
Koyré, Alexander, 11

law: and early modern thought, 7, 10; and equity, 93; and fear, 62; and freedom, 26–27; good, 106; good vs. just, 88; governance by, 84; imperative theory of, 3; and injustice vs. iniquity, 94; interpretation of, 69; as it is vs. as it ought to be, 113; language of, 88; medieval, 7–8; and morality, 3, 113; of nations, 13, 16, 23; as natural or positive, 94; obedience to, 46; peace and security from, 48; positive, 10, 15, 22; and reason, 18, 47; reasons for, 84; and rights, 24, 25, 28, 51, 55; Roman, 7, 8, 23, 25; rule of, 87, 96; and sovereign, 3, 86, 91, 106; and state of nature, 41
law, civil: consent to obey, 4; and equity, 94; and liberty of subjects, 80–81; and natural law, 7, 23, 50, 51, 52–54, 90, 92, 114; and obligation, 107; and property, 70; and rights, 26; and sovereign, 3, 58, 61, 62, 64, 68–70, 72, 91; and state of nature, 36, 37, 55
legal positivism, 3–4, 9, 49–51, 54, 95, 113
legislation/legislator, 18, 94
Leibnitz, Gottfried, 11, 127
Levellers, 63, 77

Leviathan, figure of, 57, 66
lex, 24
liberalism, 62
Lloyd, S. A., 3, 54, 100, 108
Locke, John, 10, 15, 26, 55, 99–100, 127
logical positivism, 31
Luther, Martin, 9, 121, 125

Machiavelli, Niccolò, 1, 15, 29, 85
Macpherson, C. B., 108, 115–16
Malcolm, Noel, 85, 166n91
Marsilio of Padua, 14, 146n107
Martinich, A. P., 50–51
materialism, 30, 35, 78, 99, 127. *See also* corporealism
mathematics, 18–19
May, Larry, 94
McDowell, John, 11
McIlwain, C. H., 70
medieval tradition, 17, 47, 55. *See also* scholasticism
Melanchthon, Philipp, 9
Milton, John, 63, 71
Monarchomachs, 62–63
monarchy, 65, 66, 67, 81, 82, 106. *See also* government; kings
morality: certainty in questions of, 19; and covenants, 110; and God, 9; and interest and wants, 47; and law, 3, 113; and legal positivism, 3; and natural law, ix, 5, 6, 44, 47–48, 51, 52–53, 54, 92, 93, 94, 101, 103, 105, 106, 107, 109, 113–14; and natural right, 75; and nature, 12, 22; and obligation, 107, 108; and passions, 33; precepts of as genuine and universal law, 5; and prudence, 109; and reason, 6, 112; and reciprocity, 42; and self-interest, 102–3; and sovereign, 84–98, 128; and state of nature, 40, 41; and virtue, 6; and voluntarism vs. intellectualism, 9
moral philosophy, 2, 9, 12, 31
motion, 78, 79

Nagel, Thomas, 100
natural law, 5–11, 41–54; in ancient philosophy, 5–7; and Aquinas, 8, 49; and Bodin, 67; and civil law, 51, 52–54, 90, 92, 114;

and common consent, 20; as common to humans and living creatures, 13; definition of, ix, 42–43; as deontic, 51; as divine law, 51; and equity, 93, 94; and facts and values, 113; and fall of Adam, 37; and Finnis, 114; and God, 3, 7, 8, 9, 10, 17–18; and good and evil, 49; and Grotius, 16–17, 19, 20; and human good, 114; as immutable and eternal, 46; instrumental value of, 109; and law of nations, 13; and legal positivism, 3–4; legal status of, 49–50; and Locke, 127; and medieval philosophy, 7–8; and morality, ix, 5, 6, 44, 47–48, 51, 52–53, 54, 92, 93, 94, 101, 103, 105, 106, 107, 109, 113–14; and moral philosophy, 2, 12; and natural rights, 24, 28, 55; and obligation, 73, 107; and ought statements and value propositions, 112; and peace, 48–49; and positive law, 10; and protection, 73; and prudence, 109; and reason, 3, 6, 7, 8, 49–50, 51, 105, 114; and reciprocity, 35; and right reason, 7, 114; and science, 31; and self-preservation, 48, 49, 75; and sovereign, 3, 54, 66–98; as unalterable by any human power, 10; as universal, 7, 11

natural law tradition: development of, 5–11; Hobbes's departure from, 11–20, 47–50, 53–54; Hobbes's use of, 46–47; and law, 63

natural rights, 20–29; and the creation of the commonwealth, 54–60; defined, 22; development of concept of, 23–27; and duties vs. rights, 28; and Finnis, 114; and freedom, 29, 55, 79; and Grotius, 17, 19; and liberty of subjects, 82; and moral philosophy, 2; and natural law, 24, 28; and obligation, 107; as prepolitical freedom, 28, 29; proof of existence of, 20–21; recognition of, 21, 22; relinquishment of, 66, 109; as remaining in subject, 59–60; renunciation of, 105; and resistance to rulers, 55; and self-preservation, 27–28, 29, 41, 75; and state of nature, 1, 29, 40; tradition of, 61. *See also* right(s)

nature: as filled with meaning, 11; as intelligent, rational, purposive, and ethical, 5; and morality, 12, 22; and natural rights, 23, 24; and reason, 6, 47; and scientific revolution, 11; teleological conception of, 6, 8. *See also* state of nature

Nazism, 59, 91
necessity, 79
Neostoicism, 9–10
Newton, Sir Isaac, 11
nomos, 6

Oakeshott, Michael, 2–3, 4
oaths, 46
obedience: and conquest, 73–74; duty of, 96; to God, 72, 106, 119–20, 124–25; to law, 46; to sovereign, 12, 46, 72, 79, 119–20, 124, 125, 128; of subject, 79, 90
obligation, 25, 106–12; and commands contrary to end of sovereignty, 83; and consent, 61; defined, 106; and duty, 112; and freedom, 26; moral, legal, and political, 107; and protection, 72–74; as prudential, 108, 109; and reason, 18, 116, 117; and self-interest, 100–101; and superior/legislator, 18; as voluntary act, 107
Olafson, Frederick A., 50
oligarchy, 65
opinion, public, 71
ought, 112–17
Oxford University, 100, 123

Parker, Henry, 63, 64–65
passions, 32, 33, 34, 42, 55
Paul, St., 7
peace: and common good, 106; and commonwealth, 56; and doctrine, 71; as first and fundamental natural law, 46; and Leviathan, 97; means to achieve, 36, 55, 66; and moral virtues, 105; and natural law, 42, 43, 44, 48–49, 104, 105; and obligation, 107; preservation of, 1; and right reason, 47; and self-preservation, 75; and sovereignty, 82
Peters, R. S., 115
Pettit, Philip, 108
Plato, 1, 5, 35, 47, 85, 92, 127
polis, 6
Polybius, 85
popular sovereignty, 62–64
populism, 62, 63, 64, 65
poverty, 87, 88

Presbyterians, 120, 126
Prichard, H. A., 108
primitivism, 5, 36, 37, 38, 40, 97
property: development of private, 37; and Grotius, 25; private, 36, 38, 70; right to, 64; and Romans, 23; and sovereign, 58, 87; and state of nature, 41; and Suárez, 24
prudence, 108–9
psychological naturalism, 83, 102, 104, 128
Pufendorf, Samuel, 10, 15, 16, 19, 127–28
punishment, 44, 88–89

reason: and absolute sovereignty, 87; and common good, 106; and covenants, 110, 111; as divinely ordained and naturally implanted, 11; and Grotius, 19; and human nature, 33; and iniquity, 94; and justice and righteousness, 44; and law, 18; and Melanchthon, 9; and morality, 112; natural endowment of, 35; and natural law, 8, 42, 46, 101, 105, 114; and natural rights, 23, 28, 40, 55; and nature, 6, 47; and obligation, 18, 116, 117; and peace, 42; in religion, 126; and right, 26; and Scripture, 118; and sovereign, 66, 69–70
reason, right *(recta ratio)*: and Aquinas, 50; and natural law, 47, 49, 114; and obligation, 107; and self-preservation, 48, 75, 117; and sovereign, 91
reason of state, 85
reciprocity, 35, 42–43, 105
religion, 71–72, 117–27. *See also* Christian thought
religious faith, 72, 122, 123, 124, 125
religious toleration, 121–27
representation, 56, 57, 64, 68, 95
republicanism, 77, 78, 81
revolution, 29, 63, 64, 95, 96
right(s): to all things, 41, 43, 44; and ancient Greeks, 23; as aptitude, 25; conflation with law, 24, 26; contractual, 25; divestment of, 44; as faculty, 25; and freedom and obligation, 40, 79; as freedom to do or forbear, 26, 55; and law, 28; as moral quality, 25; and objective rightness, 26; and positive law, 22; and power, 41; relinquishment of, 46, 56; of resistance, 12, 29, 55, 60, 62, 63, 64, 76, 83, 128; of self-defense, 22; and state of nature, 41; subjective, 23, 24, 25, 26; surrendered to sovereign, 57, 59. *See also* natural rights
Romans, ancient, 7, 8, 23, 25, 35, 36, 89, 92

Sabine, G. H., 11–12, 17
Sallust, 85
Scargill, Daniel, 123
scholasticism, 8–9, 10, 14, 17, 19, 31, 47, 48, 55, 114, 117
science, 11, 18, 30, 31
security, 39, 46, 48, 52, 55, 56, 66, 86, 87, 104. *See also* self-preservation
Selden, John, 10, 16, 19–20
self-accusation, 59, 82
self-defense, 55, 59, 60, 72
self-incrimination, 59
self-interest, 16, 32, 34, 36, 43, 86, 99, 100–103, 108
self-preservation: and civil society, 16; and commonwealth, 55; and covenants, 110; criticisms of, 99–100; freedom of, 55; as greatest good, 101; and Grotius, 25; and human nature, 32–33; and morality, 105; and natural law, 48, 49, 51; and natural rights, 27–28, 29, 41, 117; and peace, 43; as prerequisite to other goods, 46; and refusal of commands of sovereign, 82, 83; retention of natural right of, 60; and right reason, 47, 117; and state of nature, 40. *See also* death; security
Seneca, 35, 36, 47, 70
sin, 33, 36, 37, 125, 142nn23, 24
Skinner, Quentin, 37, 64, 76, 79, 80
slavery, 23, 25, 35, 76–77, 78, 81, 83; defined, 84
sociability, 43, 48
social contract, 44–45
Socrates, 47, 101
Sophists, 5
sovereign: as absolute ruler and sole lawmaker, 68; as answerable to God, 86; and Christian church, 120, 121, 122; and church and religion, 71–72; coercion by, 55, 56; and common good, 106; and consent, 57–58; and contract, 58; and covenant, 44, 45; duties of, 84–91, 112; and equity, 93–95;

and fear, 62; and God, 90, 91; independent judgment of, 54; and law, 3, 52, 64, 68–70, 88, 91, 106; and Leviathan, 57; and liberty of subjects, 78, 81; limits on, 65, 68; and morality, 84–98, 128; and natural law, 66–98, 114; obedience to, 12, 46, 79, 119–20, 124, 125, 128; peace and security from, 48; and people's good, 86, 90, 106; and people's safety, 86, 87, 106; powers of, 58, 66, 69, 86; and private judgment, 54; and private property, 70; and public expression, 71; and punishment and rewards, 88–89; refusal of commands of, 59–60, 82–83; representation of people's will by, 64, 68; resistance to, 60, 64; rights of, 58, 86–87; rights surrendered to, 57, 59; and rule of religion, churches, and ministry, 126; subjects as enslaved to, 83, 84; will of, 58

sovereignty: absolute, 64, 65; commands contrary to end of, 60, 83; divided, 87; and Grotius, 25; and natural law, 42; origins of, 56; and peace, 46, 82; popular, 25; as rational and moral necessity, 97; and right of resistance, 128; and state, 1; theory of, 66–74

Spinoza, Baruch, 11

state of nature, 36–42; early ideas of, 36–38; freedom in, 82; and Grotius, 17, 25; and human nature, 39; and Leviathan, 97; and natural law, 44; and natural rights, 1, 29, 40; and private judgment, 54; as thought experiment, 38–39; and war, 1, 75. *See also* nature

St. German, Christopher, 15, 92

Stoicism, 6–7, 9, 32, 33, 35, 36, 47, 48

Strauss, Leo, 28–29

Suárez, Francisco, 15; and equity, 92, 159n108; and natural law, 10, 14, 18, 49, 50; and power in community, 64; and rights, 24; and state of nature, 37

subjects: consent of, 90; duties owed by sovereign, 75; good of, 86, 90; liberty of, 75–84; obedience of, 79, 90; private, personal judgment of, 83–84; rights of, 77

superstition, 118, 119

Tacitus, 85
taxes, 59, 70, 88
Taylor, A. E., 50, 108
Thucydides, *History of the Peloponnesian War*, 14, 30, 39, 85
Tierney, Brian, 17, 24, 54–55
Tricaud, François, 38
Tuck, Richard, 16–17, 18
tyranny, 64, 65, 87, 91–92, 96

United Nations, Universal Declaration of Human Rights, 20–21
universities, 87

Vindiciae contra Tyrannos, 63
virtue(s), 34, 35, 47, 101, 105
Voltaire, 118
voluntarism, 8–9, 18, 114

war: civil, 40, 58, 65, 81, 92, 95; escape from, 46; and Grotius, 16, 26; and natural right, 55; and private judgment, 54; refusal of service in, 59, 82; and state of nature, 38, 40, 41–42
Warrender, Howard, 50
Watkins, J. W. N., 47, 108, 109, 115
Weber, Max, 38
will, 46, 56, 78, 79, 80
William of Ockham, 8, 9, 14, 24, 132n25